NEW LABOUR'S COUNTRYSIDE

Rural policy in Britain since 1997

Edited by Michael Woods

This edition published in Great Britain in 2008 by

The Policy Press
University of Bristol
Fourth Floor
Beacon House
Queen's Road
Bristol BS8 1QU
UK

Tel +44 (0)117 331 4054
Fax +44 (0)117 331 4093
e-mail tpp-info@bristol.ac.uk
www.policypress.org.uk

British Library Cataloguing in Publication Data
A catalogue record for this book is available from the British Library.

Library of Congress Cataloging-in-Publication Data
A catalog record for this book has been requested.

ISBN 978 1 86134 932 3 hardcover

Cover design by Robin Hawes.
Front cover: image kindly supplied by Magnum Photos.
Printed and bound in Great Britain by Athenaeum Press, Gateshead.

Contents

List of tables and boxes

Tables

Boxes

Notes on contributors

Nick Gallent is Reader in Housing and Planning in the Bartlett School of Planning at University College London. His research focuses on UK housing policy and, in particular, rural housing and the provision of affordable homes. His publications include *Delivering new homes* (with M. Carmona and S. Carmona, Routledge, 2003), *Housing in the European countryside* (co-edited with M Shucksmith and M Tewdwr-Jones, Routledge, 2003), *Second homes: European perspectives and UK policies* (with A. Mace and M. Tewdwr-Jones, Ashgate, 2005), *Planning on the edge* (with J. Andersson and M. Bianconi, Routledge, 2006), *Decent homes for all* (with M. Tewdwr-Jones, Routledge, 2007) and *Introduction to rural planning* (with M. Juntti, S. Kidd amd D. Shaw, Routledge, 2008).

Graham Gardner is an RCUK Research Fellow at Aberystwyth University, where he previously worked as a Research Associate for the Wales Rural Observatory. His research interests include citizenship, local democracy and community governance, with a particular focus on the implications of contemporary agendas for community empowerment and democratic renewal in rural and urban areas. Major research undertaken over the last five years includes a study of parish and town councils for Defra (with M. Woods), a review of community and town councils for Defra (led by M. Woods and B. Edwards), and, for the Wales Rural Observatory, studies of rural poverty, community regeneration, local capacity building, the changing significance of the public sector, and living and working in rural Wales.

Mark Goodwin is Professor of Human Geography at Exeter University. His research centres on analysis of the structures and processes of sub-national government, and has included work on partnership working in rural regeneration and economic governance and devolution. He has undertaken a review of rural governance for Defra and was a contributor to the *Rural audit* produced by the Rural Group of Labour MPs in 1999.

Alan Greer is Reader in Politics and Public Policy at the University of the West of England. His research interests focus on agricultural policy and politics and he is author of *Agricultural policy in Europe* (Manchester University Press, 2005) and *Rural politics in Northern Ireland* (Avebury, 1996).

Martin Jones is Professor of Human Geography at Aberystwyth University. His research interests include welfare and labour market policy and regional governance, including work on rural employment zones. He has worked as a research associate with the Unemployment Unit and Youth Aid, and has been an advisor to the Education and Employment Select Committee of the House of Commons. His publications include *The nature of the state* (with M. Whitehead and R. Jones, Oxford University Press, 2007), *State/space* (with N. Brenner, R. Jessop and G. MacLeod, Blackwell, 2003) and *New institutional spaces: training and enterprise councils and the remaking of economic governance* (Routledge, 1999).

Paul Milbourne is Professor of Human Geography and Planning in the School of City and Regional Planning at Cardiff University and Director of the Wales Rural Observatory. His research centres on rural housing and homelessness and the geographies of poverty and social exclusion. His publications include *Rural poverty* (Routledge, 2004), *Rural homelessness* (with P. Cloke and R. Widdowfield, The Policy Press, 2002) and *International perspectives on rural homelessness* (co-edited with P. Cloke, Routledge, 2006).

Gavin Parker is Senior Lecturer in Town and Country Planning at Reading University. His research centres on citizenship and the governance of land use, including public access. His publications include *Citizenships, contingency and the countryside* (Routledge, 2002). He is chair of the Community Council for Berkshire.

Mark Shucksmith is Professor of Planning at Newcastle University. He is a commissioner with the Commission of Rural Communities, chair of the Committee of Inquiry on Crofting for the Scottish Government and was a member of the Affordable Rural Housing Commission in 2005–06. His research focuses on rural development, social exclusion in rural areas and rural housing. His publications include *CAP and the regions* (co-edited with K. Thomson and D. Roberts, CABI, 2005), *Young people in rural areas of Europe* (co-edited with B. Jentsch, Ashgate, 2004) and *Housing in the European countryside* (co-edited with N. Gallent and M. Tewdwr-Jones, Routledge, 2003).

Nicola Thompson is Runciman Research Fellow in the Centre for Rural Economy at Newcastle University. Her research focuses on questions of the impact of changes in public policy and the structure of governance on rural localities, including her PhD work on governing National Parks in a devolving UK.

Neil Ward is Dean of the Faculty of Social Sciences at the University of East Anglia and was formerly Professor of Rural and Regional Development and Director of the Centre for Rural Economy at Newcastle University. He has observed the development of New Labour's rural policy at close quarters on a secondment to the Rural Team in the Cabinet Office Performance and Innovation Unit in 1999–2000. His publications include *The differentiated countryside* (with J. Murdoch, P. Lowe and T. Marsden, Routledge, 2003).

Suzie Watkin is a Research Associate in the Institute of Geography and Earth Sciences at Aberystwyth University. Following the completion of a PhD on welfare governance and the 'New Deal' in rural Wales, she has worked on projects on grassroots rural protests and connections between rural people and the land. She has also worked as a Rural Housing and Transport Advisor with the Countryside Agency.

Michael Winter is Professor of Rural Policy and Director of the Centre for Rural Policy Research at Exeter University. He has an extensive record of research on rural and agricultural policy and is author of *Rural politics* (Routledge, 1996). He was a member of the Devon Foot and Mouth Inquiry and of the Burns Inquiry into Hunting with Dogs, and has also served as chair of the South West Rural Affairs Forum, a board member of the Countryside Agency, a commissioner with the Commission for Rural Communities and an advisor to the Campaign to Protect Rural England (CPRE). He was a contributor to the *Rural audit* produced by the Rural Group of Labour MPs in 1999.

Michael Woods is Reader in Human Geography at Aberystwyth University and Co-Director of the Wales Rural Observatory. His research has focused on rural politics and governance, including recent projects on grassroots rural protest and on power, participation and rural community governance for the Economic and Social Research Council, and major studies of town, parish and community councils for Defra and the Welsh Assembly Government. He is author of *Contesting rurality: Politics in the British countryside* (Ashgate, 2005) and *Rural geography* (Sage, 2005), and co-author (with M. Jones and R. Jones) of *An introduction to political geography* (Routledge, 2004).

Richard Yarwood is Reader in Human Geography at the University of Plymouth. He has research interests in rural social geography, including a strong focus on crime and policing in rural areas. He has studied rural policing in the UK, Australia and New Zealand and has published widely on this topic. He is currently co-editing *Constable County? Policing, governance and rurality* (with R. Mawby, Ashgate, 2009).

Part One
Contexts and political strategies

ONE

New Labour's countryside

Michael Woods

Introduction

Shortly before the 1997 general election, Tony Blair and New Labour embarked on a conspicuous effort to woo wavering rural voters. As Blair's biographer, John Rentoul, observed, he "tried to pitch his tent wide enough to take in most of the countryside, being filmed before the election in green wellingtons, not knowing whether to pat a calf, and giving a transparent interview to *Country Life*. 'I wouldn't live in a big city if I could help it [Blair told the magazine]. I would live in the country. I was brought up there, really'" (Rentoul, 2001, p 422). Whatever the veracity of this claim (Rentoul points out that Blair's upbringing was overwhelmingly urban), it indicated the need of New Labour to challenge the Conservatives' dominance of the rural and semi-rural constituencies of 'Middle England' if it was to secure a majority in the House of Commons.

In electoral terms, New Labour's 'big tent' strategy was to prove to be an unprecedented success. Whilst the precise number of rural constituencies gained by Labour in the 1997 election is a matter of some conjecture, depending on the definition of 'rural' used (Ward, 2002; Woods, 2002), the election of Labour MPs for seats such as North Norfolk, Falmouth and Camborne, Forest of Dean, Shrewsbury, and Inverness, Nairn and Lochaber reflected a considerable incursion into the British countryside. Even the most restrictive definitions of rural constituencies suggest that around 15–25 such seats fell to Labour in 1997; the Rural Group of Labour MPs, meanwhile, claimed to have 180 members from rural and semi-rural constituencies (Woods, 2002).

However, New Labour was soon to discover that governing rural Britain was more complicated than selecting the right colour of waterproof boots or learning basic animal husbandry. Not even three months into Blair's administration, Hyde Park was filled with 120,000 demonstrators gathered for a 'Countryside Rally', designed to articulate a range of rural discontentment, but primarily motivated by the perceived threat of a free vote on a ban on hunting promised in Labour's election manifesto. Five months later, falling farm-gate prices and the lingering impact of the export ban on British beef introduced during the BSE crisis of 1996 prompted farmers in North Wales to mount an impromptu blockade of Holyhead Docks (Woods, 2005). The picket was to spark a series of copycat protests around the country and gave birth to a new vein of farmer militancy that was to lead in

3

September 2000 to the national blockade of fuel depots – at the time the most serious challenge to have been presented to the government's authority, forcing Blair to contemplate resignation (Campbell, 2007) (see Table 1.1).

Meanwhile, the government also had to confront rebellions by residents and local authorities in southern England over the prospect of large-scale rural house-building; lobbying over the closure of rural post offices and other services; opposition to its plans for a 'right to roam' granting public access to open countryside; and a tabloid frenzy over rural crime following the conviction of Tony Martin for shooting a burglar at his remote Norfolk farm in April 2000. Even government preparations for its first re-election campaign in early 2001 were disrupted by the deepening crisis of the foot and mouth epidemic, forcing a postponement of polling day.

Confrontation over some of these issues – hunting and the right to roam, for instance – might have been anticipated. Others, notably the foot and mouth

Table 1.1: Key events for British rural politics and policy, 1997–2007

May 1997	General election: Labour elected
27 July 1997	Countryside Rally: 120,000 pro-hunting supporters in Hyde Park
28 Nov 1997	Second Reading of Foster Bill to ban hunting
30 Nov 1997	Farmers blockade Holyhead docks; protests spread to other ports and depots and continue until 27 January 1998
1 March 1998	Countryside March: 250,000 demonstrators march through London
14 June 1998	EU Summit in Cardiff discusses CAP reform, demonstration by 10,000 farmers outside
Sept-Oct 1998	Farmers protest over lamb prices
1 April 1999	Countryside Agency established in England
May 1999	First elections to Scottish Parliament and Welsh Assembly
June 1999	*Rural audit* report published by the Rural Group of Labour MPs
14 Nov 1999	Burns Inquiry on hunting established
December 1999	PIU report *Rural economies* published
18 April 2000	*A manifesto for rural Britain* published by the Rural Group of Labour MPs
25 April 2000	Tony Martin jailed for shooting a burglar at his Norfolk farm
May 2000	*Rural Scotland: a new approach* published
12 June 2000	Burns Inquiry reports
7-14 Sept 2000	Fuel depots and refineries blockaded by farmers and hauliers
November 2000	Rural White Paper for England published
30 Nov 2000	Countryside and Rights of Way Act passed
19 Feb 2001	Foot and mouth disease confirmed at abattoir in Essex

Table 1.1: Key events for British rural politics and policy, 1997–2007
(continued)

7 June 2001	General election: Labour re-elected
June 2001	Department for Environment, Food and Rural Affairs (Defra) created
August 2001	Policy Commission on the Future of Farming and Food established
16 Dec 2001	Countryside Alliance 'March on the Mound' in Edinburgh
29 Jan 2002	Policy Commission on Farming and Food reports
February 2002	Scottish Parliament bans hunting with dogs in Scotland
9-11 Sept 2002	Public hearings on hunting
22 Sept 2002	Liberty and Livelihood March: 408,000 demonstrators in London
November 2002	Haskins' Rural Delivery Review commissioned
23 Feb 2003	Land Reform (Scotland) Act receives royal assent
11 Nov 2003	Haskins' Rural Delivery Review reports
July 2004	Rural Strategy report published
16 Sept 2004	Hunting protesters invade House of Commons chamber
18 Nov 2004	Hunting Act passed
1 April 2005	Social and economic rural development functions transferred from Countryside Agency to regional development agencies
18 Feb 2005	Ban on hunting with hounds in England and Wales comes into force
5 May 2005	General election: Labour re-elected
5 Dec 2005	Barker Review of Housing Supply published
30 March 2006	Natural Environment and Rural Communities Act gets royal assent
17 May 2006	Affordable Rural Housing Commission reports
1 October 2006	Functions of Countryside Agency transferred to Natural England and the Commission for Rural Communities
5 Dec 2006	Barker Review of Land Use Planning published

epidemic, were entirely unpredictable. In both cases, however, the government frequently appeared to struggle to move beyond basic crisis management, to reassert control of the rural political agenda, and to articulate its own policies for the countryside.

In many ways, New Labour in 1997 was distinctly unprepared for the challenges that it would face from the countryside. Its 1997 election manifesto had included just 55 lines on 'life in our countryside'. As well as controversial pledges to "a free vote in Parliament on whether hunting with hounds should be banned by legislation", and "greater freedom for people to explore our open countryside"

(Labour Party, 1997, p 30), the manifesto included policies on opposition to the privatisation of the Post Office and large-scale sales of Forestry Commission land, the reform of the Common Agricultural Policy, linking all schools to 'the information superhighway' and an 'anglers' charter'. Alongside these were broad statements that "Labour recognises the special needs of people who live and work in rural areas", and "We recognise that the countryside is a great natural asset, a part of our heritage which calls for careful stewardship. This must be balanced, however, with the needs of people who live and work in rural areas" (Labour Party, 1997, p 30).

Such homilies, though, were to prove insufficient once New Labour was in government, facing a highly organised and motivated countryside lobby, needing to protect the seats of rural MPs, and with the rhetoric of a 'one nation' philosophy to be adhered to. Thus, from the autumn of 1997 onwards, Labour became engaged in constructing its own distinctive policy vision for the countryside. As the chapters in this volume detail, this process was far from straightforward, revealed tensions between different rhetorical strands in Labour's discourse, and was riddled with internal contradictions. Yet, it arguably represented the most significant attempt to redefine the scope and direction of rural policy – and the political construction of the countryside – for over 50 years.

Although New Labour's rethinking of rural policy may have had a practical political impetus, it was also embedded in and informed by its wider ideological agenda. Commonly characterised as the 'third way', this agenda sought to "combine economic efficiency with social justice, free markets with universal welfare" (Gamble, 2005, p 435). This blending of economic and social concerns was translated into rural policy as an inclination towards market solutions and an uncritical stance towards the interests of corporations active in the rural economy (including supermarkets and large agri-food companies), placed alongside an emphasis on identifying and addressing issues of social exclusion and disadvantage in rural areas. Similarly, the tone and tenor of rural policy became infused with the spirit of key motifs in the third way discourse, notably 'modernisation' and 'one nation politics' (Fairclough, 2000). While 'modernisation' became a mantra driving change in rural policy, as well as justifying challenges to traditional rural interest groups (see Chapter 2 in this volume), the 'one nation' rhetoric was employed to downplay rural–urban distinctions and highlight common problems and solutions.

Moreover, the 'third way' advanced not only new policy objectives for government, but also new ways of delivering governance. In rural policy, as elsewhere, the third way became identified with partnership working, new localism, experiments in deliberative decision-making, and the re-articulation of an active citizenship cast around rights and responsibilities (see also Glendinning et al, 2002; Imrie and Raco, 2003). At the same time, New Labour's periodic enthusiasm for devolution and regionalisation cross-cut its engagement with rural policy, producing new territories for governance with the potential to fragment rural policy approaches.

There is, however, a danger of overstating the novelty and distinctiveness of New Labour's rural policies. In many respects, Labour's approach has been simply an expression of neoliberalism, and as such has both echoed developments in other countries (see Chapter 4 in this volume), and continued a direction of flow in UK rural policy that originated in the Thatcher administration of the 1980s (Cloke, 1992). Indeed, in its description and problematisation of the countryside, and in the mechanisms employed for the delivery of rural policy, New Labour has developed the 'governing through communities' strategy of governmentality that Murdoch (1997) identified in the 1995-6 Rural White Papers produced by John Major's Conservative government.

This chapter seeks to disentangle the complicated provenance of New Labour's rural policy by examining this as a discursive process. It focuses on the 'political construction' of the countryside as an object of governance, including the identification of the key 'problems' to be addressed by rural policy and the establishment of legitimacy for proposed policies – as articulated through policy papers, research reports and political speeches. The discussion demonstrates that this process is both contingent and contested: framed by historical antecedents and wider ideological forces, yet punctuated by events and challenged by political opponents. As such, the chapter sketches out the discursive context for the substantive issues and policy developments examined in more detail by later chapters in this volume.

The political construction of the countryside

"The government of territory", observed Murdoch and Ward (1997), "entails somehow *knowing* that territory; it requires an understanding of what the territory consists of, and what the objectives of government should be" (p 309; emphasis in original). The description, documentation and interpretation of territory hence form part of the practice of governmentality – the means by which society is rendered governable (Foucault, 1991). While all parts of the state are to some degree concerned with territorial governance, and hence with knowing territory, strategies of governmentality in general involve a compartmentalisation of society into different policy fields – health, education, transport, and so on – as manageable units of governance. Rural policy (like urban policy), however, stands apart in being defined in territorial terms, and as such its very existence and scope is dependent on not only the description and interpretation of rural space, but also the construction of the countryside as an object in need of governing. Thus, as Richardson (2000) notes, understanding rural policy and the political processes that produce it, "means focusing on how rural spaces are constructed within the policy process" (p 55).

In comparison with the extensive body of work that now exists charting the social construction of the rural through film, television, literature, art, folk traditions and lay discourses, relatively little attention has been paid to the role of policy in the social construction of the rural – or, as labelled here, the *political construction* of the countryside. This is in spite of the fact that policy discourses are likely to have far greater impact on the everyday lives of people in rural areas, and on rural landscapes, than media representations. Deborah Dixon and Holly Hapke (2003) reinforce this point in their examination of the discursive construction of the US Farm Bill. Noting the relative neglect of agricultural legislation in rural research, they comment:

> Where legislation has been noted, it has usually been presented as a backdrop to current events, effectively providing a context against which the practices of actors, groups, and institutions can be demarcated. And yet, this process of foregrounding – and simultaneous backgrounding – further mythologizes the discursive framing of constructs within legislation: they become 'facts of life,' to be acknowledged and accommodated. We suggest that for rural geographers, the examination of agricultural legislation is crucial, because it has such an extensive impact upon the lives not only of farmers but also of rural residents, migrant workers, consumers, businesses at home and abroad, and a host of other groups. (Dixon and Hapke, 2003, p 143)

While these remarks are addressed at US agricultural legislation, they are just as pertinent if applied to 'rural policy' more broadly and transposed to the United Kingdom. Studies of rural policy in Britain are relatively limited in number (see, for example, Self and Storing, 1962; Grant, 1983; Smith, 1992, 1993; Greer, 1996; Winter, 1996), and as most of these focus on the policy-making process, critical discussions of the discourses of rurality that underpin rural policy are restricted to no more than a handful. The notable exceptions include analyses by Jon Murdoch and colleagues of the 1995 Rural White Paper for England (Murdoch, 1997), the National Farm Survey (Murdoch and Ward, 1997) and preservationist discourses in planning policy (Murdoch and Lowe, 2003); work by John Gray and Tim Richardson on European Union rural policy (Gray, 2000; Richardson, 2000); and Keith Halfacree's scrutiny of representations of the rural in debates around the 1994 Criminal Justice and Public Order Bill (Halfacree, 1996).

These few studies nonetheless indicate that the relationship between policy and the rural as a social or political construction is dialectical. On the one hand, the 'rural' is fixed through policy – government agencies employ definitions of rural areas; 'rural' institutions of governance have authority over delimited territories; and the implementation of rural policies helps to shape the socioeconomic, cultural and environmental characters of the areas concerned. Yet, on the other hand, policy also follows discourses of rurality – the identification of 'rural' problems and the adoption of appropriate solutions and responses depend on the ways in which the rural is defined and described.

The political construction of the countryside is hence both contingent and contested, and both fuels and is informed by wider conflicts within rural society.

Indeed, as Richardson (2000) observes, understanding the latter may first require understanding of the former:

> In analysing the contested nature of rurality, and the effects of power on rural society, there is ... a need to focus specifically on how policy knowledges and rationalities are shaped by power struggles within the policy process as new policy discourses of rurality are structured and institutionalised. (Richardson, 2000, p 54)

From the collection of raw statistical data to the implementation of policies, the political construction of the countryside involves political decisions, dictated by electoral calculations and by ideological principles. At each juncture there are alternatives that could have been selected, and which may be championed by political opponents. The discourses that constitute the political construction of the countryside only get translated into actual policies implemented in reality if the political actors that champion them can achieve sufficient capacity to act.

As such, the political construction of the countryside can be modelled to include at least four stages:

1. Describing the social, economic and environmental characteristics of rural space, through, for example, the production of statistics and maps, and the representation of the rural through photography, prose text and anecdote.
2. Identifying from this description the major problems of rural people and rural areas needing to be addressed by government, thus setting the priorities for rural policy.
3. Establishing the legitimacy of the political actors concerned to propose solutions to rural problems and to intervene in the areas identified.
4. Proposing and implementing a programme of rural policies.

The performance of each of these stages may involve a number of different elements, but all involve the production of documents which form the 'immutable mobiles' (Latour, 1990) by which the process proceeds from one stage to the next. Thus, as Mougenot and Mormont (1988) describe:

> The first form taken by the invention of the rural is of documents, that is, a discourse. But these texts are also actions, positions taken that seek at the same time to make known the rural world, and to identify the rural with the definition that they propose. (Mougenot and Mormont, 1988, p 29)[1]

Documents hence provide the window through which the political construction of the countryside can be observed, and it is on the documents that comprised New Labour's efforts to develop its own distinctive rural policy that this chapter will primarily focus. However, the contingent nature of the political construction of the countryside means that such processes cannot be understood in isolation, and it is therefore first necessary to take a brief historical excursion in order to understand the legacy on which Labour was seeking to build.

Labour and the political construction of rural Britain

The countryside has long occupied an enigmatic position in discourses of British governmentality. Commentators have frequently remarked on the absence of a coherent rural policy in Britain (at least until the publication of the first Rural White Papers in 1995–96), yet this is not to say that rural Britain has not had a presence in policy discourses and strategies of governmentality. The political construction of the countryside as an object of state governance in Britain may be traced to the late 19th and early 20th centuries and the dismantling of the 'estates system' through which the governance of much of rural Britain had been conducted as an effectively private undertaking by large landowners (Woods, 2005). The predominant representation of the countryside mobilised in political discourse at this time was that of a space in crisis: unsettled by social, economic and political change, threatened by depopulation and urbanisation, and therefore in need of government support and action. There were, however, two distinct narratives that conveyed this representation, and which gave rise to different political constructions of the countryside.

In the first, the countryside was conceptualised as primarily a space of resource production, especially agriculture. The agricultural character of the countryside was, however, represented as being under threat from depressed prices, increased costs, competition and a contracting agricultural workforce, as well as from the intrusion of urban and industrial land uses (Howkins, 1991; Winter, 1996). In particular, this discourse, which was promoted by the rapidly strengthening National Farmers' Union (NFU), presented agriculture as an activity undertaken in Britain by small independent farmers, such that support for small farmers was positioned as the key priority for state policy. Moreover, the conflation of the rural and the agricultural was such that agricultural interests were positioned above all others, establishing an agricultural exceptionalism that persisted in rural policy through much of the 20th century, and legitimising the leading position of farmers in shaping and implementing policy at both local and national scales (Moore, 1991; Woods, 2005).

Significantly, this agrarian discourse was co-opted into Conservative Party rhetoric during the 1920s and 1930s. Through a series of speeches and essays, Conservative leaders not only evoked a romanticised bucolic countryside founded on agriculture, but successfully associated this agricultural idyll with British national identity and the settled security of an ordered, organic society that Conservative values sought to defend (Barnes, 1994; Woods, 2005). The political consequences of this strategy were far-reaching. Not only did it help to cement the relationship between the new farming elite and the Conservative Party (Moore, 1991; Woods, 2005) and to embed a Conservative electoral hegemony in rural areas under the mythic guise of the 'apolitical countryside' (Woods, 2005), but it also critically positioned the Labour Party and socialism as among the key threats to the countryside.

The second narrative also evoked a romantic rural idyll, but mobilised a more aesthetic representation in which the countryside was primarily conceptualised as a space of natural beauty threatened by urbanisation, industrialisation and. modernisation. As advanced by the preservationist movement which coalesced around the Council for the Preservation of Rural England (CPRE), formed in 1926, this discourse positioned urban encroachment and unregulated development within rural areas as the key problems faced by the countryside and identified the solution as being the establishment of a national planning system (Matless, 1998; Murdoch and Lowe, 2003; Woods, 2005). Interestingly, the political construction of the countryside in preservationism was notably more radical than that in Baldwinite Conservatism (Matless, 1998; Woods, 2005), and several Labour Party members and supporters were active in the early CPRE. Ramsay MacDonald had clear preservationist sympathies, and it was his Labour government that introduced the first Town and Country Planning Act in 1932 (Woods, 2005).

For the most part, however, Labour's rural policies during the pre-Second World War era were informed by a third political construction of the countryside. This discourse presented the countryside as a space of inequality and oppression, created by the historical dispossession of working people of land, and the continuing 'tyranny' of an agricultural industry characterised by isolated working conditions, low pay and poor quality tied housing (Griffiths, 2007). As the Labour Party embarked on its 'rural campaign' to win rural constituencies, it was this political construction of the countryside that informed policies including national planning for agriculture, increased agricultural wages, the abolition of tied housing and council house provision in rural areas, the development of public libraries, social clubs and community education in rural communities, land value taxation and a flirtation with land nationalisation (Griffiths, 2007). Yet, the failure of Labour during this period to assert this discourse as a serious challenge to the predominant Conservative-agrarian political construction of the countryside reflected several factors.

First, the Labour Party was divided on the appropriate policy solutions to the problems identified. The redistribution of land was core to Labour's rural agenda, but progress was limited by struggles within the party between supporters of land nationalisation and advocates of land value taxation. Both policies were included in Labour Party pamphlets and manifestos during the inter-war period despite being contradictory in many respects (Griffiths, 2007). Second, as Griffiths (2007) also observes, the dystopian message of this political construction was compromised by an affection for the romance of the rural idyll which meant that Labour publications often reproduced imagery of a bucolic countryside and contented rural residents. Third, the legitimacy of the Labour Party in representing the problems of, and proposing solutions for, the countryside was undermined by its continuing failure to mobilise rural workers and achieve rural representation:

> Labour was, it seemed, 'a thing of the town', the 'great town party'. This
> identity was treated by political opponents as indicative of Labour's
> outlook and priorities, rather than of its experience: a town party
> was judged to be in some way not only ill-suited to represent rural
> Britain, but even opposed to its interests. A polarity had been created
> in which a history of near-exclusive involvement with urban working-
> class interests seemed to disqualify Labour from having any present or
> future interest in the countryside. (Griffiths, 2007, p 4)

Labour's rural breakthrough came in 1945. In its landslide election victory the
party won 69 seats on its own list of 203 'rural constituencies', and these same
'rural constituencies' provided just under a quarter of the total national Labour
vote (Griffiths, 2007). As Herbert Morrison noted, Labour now had "a substantial
number of MPs from the rural divisions" (quoted in Griffiths, 2007, p 332), but
Labour in government shied away from the more militant aspects of its pre-war
rural policy, and instead built on the new consensual political construction of the
countryside that had been forged during wartime.

The foundations for the new political construction of the countryside had been
laid by the reports of four inquiries conducted during the Second World War
– the Barlow Report (1940) of the Royal Commission on the Distribution of the
Industrial Population, the Uthwatt Report (1942) of the Expert Committee on
Compensation and Betterment, the Scott Report (1942) of the Committee on
Land Utilisation in Rural Areas, and the Dower Report on National Parks (1945)
– that collectively comprised the first two stages of the political construction of the
countryside (as described in the previous section), describing rural Britain as an
object of governance, identifying the key problems and proposing solutions. The
policy priorities that followed combined elements of all three pre-war discourses:
the maintenance of the countryside as a space of agricultural production, thus
guaranteeing national food supplies; supporting small farmers and helping them
to modernise; regulating agricultural wages and improving working conditions;
controlling urban expansion and regulating land development in rural areas;
protecting nationally significant rural landscapes; and facilitating the use of
rural land for recreation and leisure (Winter, 1996). These priorities were put
into practice through legislation including the 1947 Agriculture Act, the 1947
Agricultural Wages (Regulation) Act, the 1947 Town and Country Planning Act
and the 1949 National Parks and Access to the Countryside Act, introduced by
the Labour government.

As Murdoch (1997) noted, the post-war legislation "contained a degree of
local sensitivity but situated diverse rural areas within a coherent national policy
framework which sanctioned comprehensive state intervention in the rural
domain" (p 113), conforming to a 'managed liberal' mode of governmentality.
This rationality established the legitimate scope of state intervention in the rural
economy and society, but also framed rural policy at the national scale. For example,
national annual farm surveys compiled a single statistical representation of British

agriculture that allowed the agricultural sector to be managed as a national unit (Murdoch and Ward, 1997). It also, however, isolated agriculture from wider issues and legitimised the role of a narrowly focused policy community in controlling agricultural policy (Smith, 1993; Winter, 1996).

The emphasis on *national planning* was perhaps Labour's most significant contribution to rural policy in Britain. Not only was state 'planning' perceived in the 1940s and 1950s as a distinctive characteristic of Labour policy (compared with a Conservative emphasis on 'freedom') (Self and Storing, 1962), but it was Labour who had championed the idea that the governance of the countryside was a national responsibility in which everyone, rural and urban, had a stake, not something to be left to rural residents alone. Indeed, one of Labour's responses to its pre-war rural electoral problem had been to stress the need for the integrated management of rural and urban interests within economic sectors (Griffiths, 2007). In practice, this meant the segmentation of rural governance between different policy areas, each managed independently. As such, the countryside was in effect deconstructed as an object of governance as there was no such thing as 'rural policy', but rather a series of sectoral policies implemented within rural space.

Yet, in spite of the adoption of farmer-friendly policies, Labour failed to shake off the suspicion of rural voters (Self and Storing, 1962). The party lost many of its rural seats in the 1950 and 1951 elections, and where it held on its grasp was gradually weakened by declining agricultural trade union strength and the 'nationalisation of politics' in an age of mass media (Johnson, 1972). The out-migration of the rural working classes, and in-migration of ex-urban middle classes, reinforced the spatialisation of class politics in Britain, with rural areas moving increasingly towards the Conservatives during the 1960s and 1970s (Curtice and Steed, 1982). With dwindling electoral support in the countryside, the Labour Party accordingly lost interest in developing a distinctive rural policy, beyond specific concerns such as hunting pushed by urban issue groups.

Thus, when the challenge to the post-war consensus came, it came from the Right. Thatcherism was in many ways antithetical to the principles underpinning the consensus, but in practice the capacity of the Thatcher government for wide-reaching reform was restricted by the need to juggle the various interests of different factions of rural Conservatism (Cloke, 1992; Woods, 2005). While the more radical fringes of Thatcherism produced new visions of the countryside without farm subsidies (Body, 1982) or planning controls (Mosbacher and Anderson, 1999), mainstream policy shifts were more subtle. Nonetheless, two key changes can be identified. First, the emphasis on national planning was abandoned for a new competition discourse, with deregulation of planning, housing development, industrial development and public services (Cloke, 1992). Second, a 'new marketplace countryside' was imagined, populated by new rural commodities from niche food products to the recreational potential of privatised forests and reservoirs (Cloke, 1992).

The fundamental break, however, came with the publication by the Major government of the Rural White Paper for England in 1995 (DoE, 1995), and its counterparts in Scotland (Scottish Office, 1995) and Wales (Welsh Office, 1996). The Rural White Papers suggested a political construction of the countryside that differed significantly from that embodied in post-war rural policy in several respects. In presenting an integrated approach to rural policies across the social, economic and environmental domains, the papers emphasised both the diversity of interests in the countryside and the interconnection of these activities, recognising the rural as both a lived space and a worked space. They acknowledged the environmental damage caused by productivist agricultural policies, and placed a stronger emphasis on conservation, with a notable influence of the 'rural idyll' (see Hodge, 1996).

Moreover, in constructing the countryside as a patchwork of diverse activities and interests, the English Rural White Paper, in particular, articulated a new governmental rationality of 'governing through communities'. As Murdoch (1997) detailed, this firstly represented the countryside as "consisting of small, tightly knit communities" (p 117), and secondly proposed that these communities should be encouraged to "help themselves", as the most appropriate vehicle for rural governance, thus facilitating the "covert withdrawal of the state as the contours of governmental responsibility are redrawn" (p 117).

Hodge (1996) and others have critiqued the 1995–96 Rural White Papers for failing to engage the difficult questions about radical agricultural policy reform and lacking a chapter drawing out "the inter-relationships between the arenas of rural policy and between rural conditions and wider social, economic and environmental change" (Hodge, 1996, p 336). In this respect, the papers perhaps betrayed their preoccupation with continuing to juggle rural Conservative interests. Yet, in breaking the post-war consensus, the papers started the process that would be picked up by New Labour's political construction of the countryside.

Constructing New Labour's countryside

On 27 July 1997, 88 days after Labour's emphatic election victory, over 120,000 supporters of hunting assembled in Hyde Park for the Countryside Rally. Speaker after speaker reinforced the carefully constructed core message of a countryside of tradition under threat from 'misguided urban political correctness'. Although studiously avoiding overtly party political accusations, the code hidden within these words had a greater historical resonance: Labour was an urban party with little understanding of rural life, and a Labour government represented a threat to the countryside.

At the time, the Blair administration was still enjoying its honeymoon. A MORI poll in the week of the rally put support for Labour at 57%. The Countryside Rally represented a then unprecedented mass public demonstration against a policy that had at least tacit government support. The challenge hit home, not least because it shook Labour's own belief in "Tony Blair's image as a unifying figure attuned as much to the shires as to the cities" (Wintour, 1998, p 19). A senior Labour advisor told *The Observer* shortly before the Countryside March in 1998 that the rural protests were "on their minds pretty much all the time" (Wintour, 1998, p 19). Thus, as Lowe and Ward observed, "In response to the taunt that Labour does not care for rural areas and people, the government was keen both to show itself responsive to rural issues and to formulate a distinctively New Labour agenda for the countryside" (Lowe and Ward, 2001, p 386).

The attempt to reclaim the rural political agenda for Labour involved two entwined processes. One was governmental, initiated with the establishment of a 'rural team' in the Cabinet Office Performance and Innovation Unit. The other was party political, led by the Rural Group of Labour MPs. Formed after the 1997 election, with Peter Bradley, MP for the Wrekin in Shropshire, as chair and David Drew, MP for Stroud in Gloucestershire, as secretary, the group initially claimed up to 180 members, although later reports put membership at just under a hundred. Both processes produced a number of documents, following the stages of the political construction of the countryside detailed earlier (Table 1.2).

The first stage, therefore, involved a re-description of the characteristics of rural Britain. In the governmental strand this took the form of two publications from the Performance and Innovation Unit (PIU) – a research-based report on *Rural economies*, published in December 1999, and a statistical comparison of rural and urban areas of England, published in February 2000. These were supplemented by annual 'State of the Countryside' reports produced by the Countryside Agency from April 2000 onwards. At the same time, the Rural Group of Labour MPs commissioned the *Rural audit*, written by academic experts and covering topics from agriculture and farm incomes, to work and family life, social care and disability and poverty and social exclusion.

The significance of these documents was that they described the countryside not solely through agricultural statistics, or even the quantification of the broader rural economy, but also through a diverse range of social statistics that highlighted traditional Labour concerns such as poverty, welfare and equality. The overarching themes of the new representation, though, were to emphasise the diversity of rural areas, the declining importance of agriculture, the scale of counter-urbanisation, and the existence of both prosperity and poverty in the countryside.

Although the *Rural economies* report acknowledged that the role of agriculture and the distinctiveness of rural landscapes and habitats justified the existence of a 'rural policy', it also noted that "when statistics are aggregated, rural economies appear similar to their urban counterparts in many ways" and that "for both urban and rural economies, policies with a national sweep – whether instituted by the Government or the EU – have a much greater impact on economic health than any specific urban or rural-tailored initiative" (PIU, 1999, p 5). Hence, the key effects of the re-description were to minimise rural–urban differences, while emphasising diversity within the countryside. The political message was that the farming and hunting lobbies represented by the Countryside Alliance spoke for only a minority of people in rural areas, opening the opportunity for Labour to stake the claim to speak for the majority.

Table 1.2: Key documents in the discursive construction of New Labour's countryside

	Governmental	Political
Description of rural areas	PIU report *Rural economies*, December 1999. Cabinet Office report, *Sharing the nation's prosperity*, February 2000. Countryside Agency, first *State of the countryside* report, April 2000.	*Rural audit*, Rural Group of Labour MPs, June 1999.
Problem identification	Rural England: Discussion document, February 1999, and Summary of responses, November 1999. PIU report *Rural economies*, December 1999.	*Rural audit*, Rural Group of Labour MPs, June 1999.
Establishing legitimacy	Speech by Tony Blair, Exeter, February 2000.	Speeches at Labour Party conference, 1999. Labour Rural Conference, 2002.
Proposing policies	*Our countryside: The future*, Rural White Paper, November 2000.	*A manifesto for rural Britain*, Rural Group of Labour MPs, April 2000.

In the second stage of the process, the new description of rural Britain presented in these documents became the basis for identifying the key problems facing rural areas, and the priorities for policy. Labour used this opportunity to challenge the identification by the Countryside Alliance of hunting, farming and the 'right to roam' as the key problem areas for rural Britain, instead shifting the emphasis onto social exclusion, employment, housing, health and the provision of local services. Thus, Peter Bradley, the chair of the Rural Group of Labour MPs, in the foreword to the *Rural audit*, asserted that rural people "care about education and health; they worry about unemployment and crime; they want the best for their families, for their community, for their country" (RGLMP, 1999, p iv). This message was reinforced visually on the cover of the *Rural audit*, which showed a village or small town scene with no agricultural activity in sight, but prominently featuring a bus stop, a general store, a police car and a former school or chapel converted into a community centre.

By identifying social issues such as health, education, poverty and transport as the key priorities for rural policy, Labour not only marginalised issues such as agriculture and hunting, but also began to construct an argument that rural areas face the same problems as urban areas and, most significantly, shifted the terrain of rural political debate onto policy areas in which Labour was traditionally perceived as strong. Accordingly, in the third stage, Labour set out to establish its legitimacy as a government for the countryside, challenging its representation as an 'urban party'. This involved two key elements. First, the scale of Labour rural parliamentary representation was frequently reiterated, for example in the *Rural audit* and in ministerial speeches:

> Labour is the party of the countryside. That assertion is not intended to be provocative. It is, rather, a statement of fact. For in May 1997, some 180 Labour MPs were elected to represent rural or semi-rural constituencies, more than the Conservatives and Liberal Democrats combined. (RGLMP, 1999, p iv)

> The Labour Party has more Members of Parliament representing rural areas than any other party. We were elected by the whole nation – town and country – and we are now governing the whole nation – town and country. (Speech by Agriculture Minister Nick Brown to the Labour Party Conference, September 1999)

Second, Labour emphasised its 'one nation' credentials and aspirations, asserting that rural and urban communities essentially faced the same problems and had the same interests, and suggesting, therefore, that an urban background need not necessarily be a disqualification from governing the countryside. This message was repeated through ministerial speeches, including those made by Nick Brown and Tony Blair:

> When I attend meetings in rural communities, I'm not surprised to find that their aspirations are no different to my constituents in East Newcastle: decent jobs, good schools, a health service that's there when you need it, protection from crime, and an efficient transport system. (Speech by Agriculture Minister Nick Brown to the Labour Party Conference, September 1999)

> Taken as a whole, what's striking is how similar the priorities are of those in the countryside and those living in towns.... I am a one nation politician and this is a one nation Government. (Speech on farming by Tony Blair, Exeter, February 2000)

The final stage in the construction of New Labour's countryside came in the translation of the rhetoric and discursive representation of the rural into actual policy proposals. *A manifesto for rural Britain* was produced by the Rural Group of Labour MPs in April 2000, outlining over 100 policies covering social exclusion, the rural economy, housing, local services, education, health, policing, local government, transport and the environment. Most of these policies were subsequently incorporated into the second Rural White Paper for England, *Our countryside: The future*, published in November 2000.

As with the *Rural audit*, the discursive priorities of the 2000 Rural White Paper were visually conveyed by its cover illustration. Whereas the cover of the 1995 Rural White Paper had signalled an integrated approach to rural policy by combining images of farming, service sector work and leisure and tourism; the cover of the 2000 one further relegated farming to the background (with fields notably devoid of livestock or agricultural activity), whilst foregrounding an urban-looking high street scene and a child in a baseball cap seated on top of a hay pile. New Labour's countryside, it suggested, put people before land and coexisted alongside the urban. These messages were reinforced in the foreword by John Prescott and Nick Brown, which implicitly attacked the discourse mobilised by the Countryside Alliance:

> Above all we believe in a countryside for everyone. We have listened
> to the whole range of needs and concerns expressed by people living
> in the countryside. It is clear that our rural areas have a diverse set of
> problems and interests. This paper addresses the real needs of people
> in the countryside. It is also clear that in the past some rural voices
> have been louder than others. Government must listen to everyone....
> Some people want to drive a wedge between town and country. While
> we recognise what makes our countryside special, we also believe
> that rural and urban areas are interdependent. Our aim is to deliver
> an improved quality of life for everyone in the countryside – as well
> as in cities and towns. (DETR/MAFF, 2000, p 5)

The imprimatur of New Labour was further reflected in the language and content of the White Paper. There was a section on social exclusion, as well as sections on racism, homelessness and childcare. The core New Labour discourse of 'modernisation' (Fairclough, 2000) was evident not only in the rejection of "an outdated picture-postcard version" of the countryside (DETR/MAFF, 2000, p 5), but also in policies to modernise the rural economy and rural governance (see also Chapter 2 in this volume, and Ward and Lowe, 2007). The blurring of urban and rural boundaries made space for a chapter on market towns, while the retreat from Thatcherite individualism was marked by a shift in the targeting of the 'rights and responsibilities' discourse (Fairclough, 2000), from individuals to communities (see Chapter 10 in this volume; also Edwards et al, 2003; Edwards and Woods, 2004).

Yet, beyond the rhetoric, much of the 2000 Rural White Paper was strikingly similar to its Conservative predecessor. Radical ideas that had been floated early in the Labour administration, such as pay-to-enter national parks, taxes on second homes and reforms to planning controls on greenbelt land, found no place, and plans for a Ministry of Rural Affairs had been dropped. Thus, as Lowe and Ward observed, although the 2000 Rural White Paper set new directions for policy, "it is best seen as a work in progress, with quite a lot of loose ends dangling. New principles and initiatives are put forward that could in the medium term have momentous consequences. There are also questions and relationships that are still being worked out" (Lowe and Ward, 2001, p 386).

Deconstructing New Labour's countryside?

One of the prevailing characteristics of New Labour's rural policy has been the apparent disjuncture between the rhetoric of constructing a new policy discourse and the often conservative and sometimes incoherent delivery of policy. The boldness of the representations discussed in the previous section has not – with a few exceptions – generally been matched by radical changes in policy or practice. The reasons for this discrepancy are various. In part, it reflected the political rather than governmental drive behind New Labour's rural policy. The efforts to construct a distinctive New Labour rural policy discourse were not in order to mark a rupture with previous government rural policy, but to counter the alternative representation of rural interests promoted by the Countryside Alliance. As the perceived political threat from the countryside lobby retreated, so rural policy slipped from the centre of government concerns and the political willingness to follow through the more radical aspects of the new vision faded.

At the same time, the development of a coherent New Labour rural policy had been compromised by a lack of coordination between key actors. While the political project of constructing a new policy discourse was driven by the Rural Group of Labour MPs and the Cabinet Office, the extent to which the new thinking penetrated into the departments responsible for actually delivering rural policy may be questioned. In particular, the persistence in the Ministry of Agriculture, Fisheries and Food (MAFF) of both an agriculture-focused discourse of the rural economy and close ties to the NFU was dramatically exposed in the early stages of the 2001 foot and mouth epidemic as MAFF adopted a control strategy that was subsequently condemned for misunderstanding the economic diversity of the contemporary countryside (see Chapter 5 in this volume; also Woods, 2005).

Problems of coordination had also been generated by the current within New Labour policy towards regionalisation and devolution, most notably with respect to the divergent trajectories of rural policy adopted by Labour administrations in London, Cardiff and Edinburgh. Significant responsibilities for rural policy were already devolved to the Scottish Office and Welsh Office prior to political devolution in 1999, as marked by the publication of three separate Rural White Papers in 1995–96. Interestingly, these papers had notably different emphases, with the Welsh paper more wedded than the English to a production-based representation of the countryside and more strongly promoting an enterprise culture, whilst the Scottish paper stressed issues of peripherality. Political devolution in 1999, with the establishment of the Scottish Parliament and National Assembly for Wales, exaggerated these differences as the Labour administrations in Scotland

and Wales sought to overcome their shared handicap of being perceived as an 'urban party' in different ways (see also Chapter 3 in this volume).

In Scotland, the emphasis was placed by the Labour–Liberal Democrat coalition government (with the Liberal Democrats controlling the Rural Affairs ministry) on challenging the identification of the rural with peripherality by asserting the centrality of rural Scotland to the Scottish nation. The Scottish government also symbolically attacked the previous influence of the landowning class in Scottish rural politics in two ways: first by promoting a social inclusion agenda, with the policy document *Rural Scotland: A new approach* identifying low income households, the elderly, and children and young people as the 'key groups in rural areas'; and second by sponsoring radical land reform legislation (see also Keating and Stevenson, 2006).

The Labour administration in Wales, in contrast, struggled to assert any distinctive approach to rural policy. The rural political debate in Wales had been framed by a collapse in farm-gate prices in the winter of 1997–98 and political mobilisation of Welsh farmers in protest. The farming unions had taken advantage of the political vacuum between the devolution referendum in September 1997 and the first elections to the Welsh Assembly in May 1999 to discursively present the crisis in farming as a rural crisis, and the rural crisis as a national crisis. Thus, by the time the Welsh Assembly Government came into being in 1999, rural Wales had already been constructed as a 'space in crisis'. First Secretary Alun Michael repeatedly tried to challenge the assertion that 'Wales is a rural country' and question the emphasis on agriculture, but with little success. In particular, his appointment of Christine Gwyther, a former rural development officer, as Agriculture and Rural Development Secretary backfired when she was targeted by the farming unions for being a vegetarian. Neither the Welsh Labour Party nor the Welsh Assembly Government possessed the resources to adequately construct an alternative representation of rural Wales, and Assembly Members as a whole both accepted and reproduced the discourse promoted by the farming unions. Significantly, no integrated rural policy document has been produced by the Welsh Assembly Government. Instead it published an agricultural policy paper, *Farming for the future*, which reiterated the centrality of agriculture to rural Wales, stating, for example, that "the family farm defines the character of Welsh rural society and its sense of identity" (NAfW, 2001, p 7).

Even in England, tensions have emerged between the development of a New Labour rural policy and the regionalisation agenda. Most notably, the transfer of rural development responsibilities from the Countryside Agency to Regional Development Agencies (RDAs) in 2005, while consistent with the emphasis within the New Labour discourse on the diversity of the countryside and its interdependence with urban areas, effectively dismantled the primary vehicle for articulating a social issues-based rural policy at a national level in England. Moreover, the regionalisation of rural policy has involved, as Ward et al (2003) note, demands for both rural differentiation and regional integration. Different

RDAs have addressed this conundrum differently, and so regional variation in the positioning and delivery of rural policy has increased (see Chapter 3).

A further, and final, factor in the stalled construction of New Labour's countryside has been the way in which it has approached rural policy making. Superficially, at least, Labour has built an inclusive rural policy network, with an emphasis on negotiation and coalition building. This has been partly borne out of the necessity of connecting devolved ministries and regional agencies, but has also included efforts to engage with rural interest groups (including the Countryside Alliance) in bodies such as the Rural Affairs Forum in England. However, in practice, collaborative forums have had only limited influence over actual rural policy making, which has tended to be more technocratic or managerialist in character.

First, Labour has placed considerable emphasis on evidence-based policy making. This has included not only the work of the PIU and of the academic contributors to the *Rural audit*, but also research activities by the Countryside Agency (and later the Commission for Rural Communities), the establishment of the Rural Evidence Research Centre, the development of a new definition of rural areas, and the introduction of 'rural proofing' to test the impact of government policies on rural communities (Woods, 2006). All of these initiatives suggest that rural problems and interests can be objectively measured and analysed and appropriate responses developed.

Second, Labour has repeatedly turned to independent commissions or expert inquiries to advise on the most difficult rural issues. Critically, while the process of evidence-based policy making has engaged academic experts broadly sympathetic with Labour's political objectives, the 'experts' picked for commissions and inquiries have often been 'establishment' figures with connections to farming or rural business. The most notable of these 'experts' have included Sir Ewan Cameron, a Somerset landowner and former president of the Country Landowners Association, who was appointed as chair of the Countryside Agency and first 'Rural Advocate'; Lord Burns, the former Treasury Permanent Secretary, asked to head the commission of inquiry on hunting; Sir Donald Curry, a Northumberland farmer and chair of the Meat and Livestock Commission, picked to lead the Policy Commission on the Future of Farming and Food after the 2001 foot and mouth epidemic; and Kate Barker, a former economist with Ford and the CBI and a member of the Bank of England Monetary Policy Committee, who has produced two reports on rural housing supply.

The most influential 'expert', however, has been Lord Christopher Haskins, a Labour peer and party donor, and chair of Northern Foods and Express Dairies. Appointed as Rural Recovery Coordinator during the foot and mouth crisis, he was subsequently asked to undertake a review of rural policy delivery. His approach to this task reflected his background in the agri-food industry. Tellingly, his report referred not to rural residents or citizens, but to 'customers', with chapter titles including 'Bringing delivery closer to the customer' and 'Making things better for the customer'. As I have commented elsewhere, "in this linguistic detail, Haskins reinvented the governance of the countryside as a business transaction" (Woods, 2006, p 144).

The Haskins Report proposed wide-sweeping reforms to the organisation of rural policy delivery in England, dismantling the Countryside Agency and merging some of its functions with English Nature to create a new environmental 'super-agency', Natural England, while devolving others to the Regional Development Agencies. The Haskins proposals undoubtedly simplified some of the complex structures of rural governance, but they were premised on an understanding of rural policy viewed from an agricultural or land management perspective. As Neil Ward argues in this volume, Haskins showed antipathy towards the wider rural policy agenda (see Chapter 2), and, as such, his report can be positioned as marking the end of hopes that New Labour might have developed a distinctive, progressive rural policy, as tantalisingly hinted in its early discursive rewriting of rural interests.

Overview of this volume

The contributors to this volume map, analyse and critique the complicated topography of New Labour's rural policy since 1997. They follow the policy developments that emerged from the political processes outlined in this chapter, describing their evolution and implementation and examining their impact. The authors also position rural policy reforms in Britain since 1997 within a broader context, drawing on wider analytical frameworks and exploring links to larger-scale political agendas and processes of restructuring.

The book is divided into three parts. The chapters in the first part address the broad themes and features of New Labour's rural policy, developing perspectives flagged in this introductory chapter. Neil Ward, in Chapter 2, examines the implementation of a 'modernisation' agenda in Labour's rural policy, detailing the work of the Cabinet Office PIU in preparing for the 2000 Rural White Paper, before discussing the disruption of the foot and mouth crisis and critiquing what he perceives as the 'eclipse of rural policy' by the Haskins reforms. In Chapter 3, Mark Goodwin focuses on the institutions and structures through which rural policy is devised and delivered, discussing the impact of devolution and the Haskins reforms, and arguing that New Labour has completely transformed the institutional landscape of rural policy. Mark Shucksmith, in Chapter 4, places British rural policy developments in the context of international economic, social and political trends and measures the achievements of New Labour's rural policy against the internationalist aspirations of the party's Commission on Social Justice in 1994, finding the outcome to be uneven.

The second part of the book focuses on the key issues that have defined New Labour's engagement with rural politics – the foot and mouth crisis, hunting, housing development, the 'right to roam' and agricultural policy reform. In Chapter 5, Michael Winter reviews the handling of the 2001 foot and mouth crisis, highlighting the failure of attempts to model the epidemic and its impact and the alienation of rural communities by the government's strategy, and discussing the longer-term implications of the episode. In Chapter 6, Michael Woods traces the prolonged struggle behind the 2004 Hunting Act, arguing that the ban on the hunting of wild mammals with hounds represented not a triumph for New Labour but rather the failure of the New Labour leadership to persuade MPs to back a distinctive 'third way' approach based on compromise and evidence-based policy.

Nick Gallent, in Chapter 7, explores the intransigent politics of rural housing development and the attempts by the Labour government to make progress through the Barker reviews of housing supply and the 'Communities Plan'. Focusing on a case study of the South East of England, Gallent suggests that New Labour is engaged in a struggle for 'hearts and minds' with the necessity of development ranged against environmental concerns, and the outcome still undetermined. In Chapter 8, Gavin Parker discusses the culmination of Labour's historic campaign for a 'right to roam' in the 2000 Countryside and Rights of Way Act, but notes that with the legislation based on complicated managerial provisions, the issue of access is still the subject of debate and conflict. Finally in the section, Alan Greer, in Chapter 9, examines Labour's approach to agricultural policy reform, in particular its engagement with CAP reform and agricultural trade liberalisation, and its response to the challenges of animal disease and risk management. Greer argues that Labour has made substantial progress on major long-term policy objectives, but that these have been overshadowed by failures in policy implementation.

The third part of the book examines the treatment of rural issues within broader policy arenas. Graham Gardner, in Chapter 10, positions initiatives to promote community development, encourage participation and empower community governance as manifestations of a strategy of 'governing through communities' – introduced into rural policy by the Major government but refined and extended by New Labour. Gardner identifies both positive and negative implications of this process, with opportunities for local action created but questions raised about power and exclusion. In Chapter 11, Paul Milbourne examines Labour's approach to poverty and welfare issues in rural areas, highlighting the adoption and implementation of 'third way' policies. Milbourne argues that New Labour's anti-poverty strategies have reduced levels of poverty and social exclusion, but that their specific impact in rural areas is difficult to establish due to a lack of rural differentiation and an absence of appropriate indicators.

In Chapter 12, Richard Yarwood discusses policies for crime and policing in rural areas, identifying three phases during the New Labour government: a period of continuation of existing trends up to 2000, a renewed focus on rural policing problems from 2000 (a response, in part, to the Tony Martin case), and a shift in emphasis from rurality to locality after 2006. Yarwood suggests that debates about rural policing under New Labour have tended to focus not on whether rural areas are being policed, but on what offences, or what aspects of rurality, are being policed. Suzie Watkin and Martin Jones, in Chapter 13, examine the development of Labour's skills and training policies and their implementation in rural areas. Drawing on a case study of the 'New Deal' in rural Wales, they demonstrate the difficulties in delivering a workfare-based national programme in rural labour markets. Lastly, in Chapter 14, Nicola Thompson discusses policy on National Parks and the governance of the rural environment. Noting the establishment under New Labour of two new National Parks in England and the creation of the first National Parks in Scotland, as well as reforms to national park governance, she nonetheless reveals disjunctures between the government's approach to sustainable rural development and the idea of National Parks, and highlights the need to rethink the function of National Parks.

Finally, the concluding chapter, by Michael Woods, returns to the broad sweep of New Labour's rural policy, evaluating its impact and identifying its lasting legacies. It is suggested that while the measurable outcomes for people living and working in the countryside are mixed, New Labour's rural policy has been more successful in achieving its political objectives, and that it has left enduring consequences in its restructuring of the institutions of rural governance, and in prompting the politicisation of the rural population.

Note
[1] Author's translation. Original text: "La première forme que prend l'invention du rural, ce sont des écrits, c'est un discours. Mais ces textes sont aussi des actes, des prises de position qui cherchent à la fois à faire connaître le monde rurale et à faire s'identifier les ruraux à la définition qu'on leur propose."

References

Barnes, A. (1994) 'Ideology and factions', in A. Seldon and S. Ball (eds) *Conservative century*, Oxford: Oxford University Press, pp 315-45.

Body, R. (1982) *Agriculture: The triumph and the shame*, London: Temple Smith.

Campbell, A. (2007) *The Blair years: Extracts from the Alastair Campbell diaries*, London: Hutchinson.

Cloke, P. (1992) 'The countryside', in P. Cloke (ed) *Policy and change in Thatcher's Britain*, Oxford: Pergamon, pp 269-96.

Curtice, J. and Steed, M. (1982) 'Electoral choice and the production of government', *British Journal of Political Science*, vol 12, pp 249-98.

DETR/MAFF (Department of the Environment, Transport and the Regions/ Ministry of Agriculture, Fisheries and Food) (2000) *Our countryside: The future – a fair deal for rural England* (the Rural White Paper), Cm 4909, London: The Stationery Office.

Dixon, D. and Hapke, H. (2003) 'Cultivating discourse: the social construction of agricultural legislation', *Annals of the Association of American Geographers*, vol 93, pp 142-64.

DoE (Department of the Environment) (1995) *Rural England: A nation committed to a living countryside*, London: HMSO.

Edwards, B. and Woods, M. (2004) 'Mobilising the local: community, participation and governance', in L. Holloway and M. Kneafsey (eds) *Geographies of rural cultures and societies*, Aldershot: Ashgate, pp 173-96.

Edwards, B., Goodwin, M. and Woods, M. (2003) 'Citizenship, community and participation in small towns: a case study of regeneration partnerships', in R. Imrie and M. Raco (eds) *Urban renaissance? New Labour, community and urban policy*, Bristol: The Policy Press, pp 181-204.

Fairclough, N. (2000) *New Labour, new language?* London: Routledge.

Foucault, M. (1991) 'Governmentality', in G. Burchell, C. Gordon and P. Miller (eds) *The Foucault effect*, London: Harvester Wheatsheaf, pp 87-104.

Gamble, A. (2005) 'The meaning of the Third Way', in A. Seldon and D. Kavanagh (eds) *The Blair effect, 2001-5*, Cambridge: Cambridge University Press, pp 430-38.

Glendinning, C., Powell, M. and Rummery, K. (eds) (2002) *Partnerships, New Labour and the governance of welfare*, Bristol: The Policy Press.

Grant, W. (1983) 'The National Farmers Union: the classic case of incorporation?', in D. Marsh (ed) *Pressure politics*, London: Junction Books, pp 129-43.

Gray, J. (2000) 'The Common Agricultural Policy and the re-invention of the rural in the European Community', *Sociologia Ruralis*, vol 40, pp 30-52.

Greer, A. (1996) *Rural politics in Northern Ireland*, Aldershot: Avebury.

Greer, A. (2006) *Agricultural policy in Europe*, Manchester: Manchester University Press.

Griffiths, C. (2007) *Labour and the countryside: The politics of rural Britain, 1918–1939*, Oxford: Oxford University Press.

Halfacree, K. (1996) 'Out of place in the countryside: travellers and the "rural idyll"', *Antipode*, vol 29, pp 42-71.

Hodge, I. (1996) 'On penguins on icebergs: the Rural White Paper and the assumption of rural policy', *Journal of Rural Studies*, vol 12, pp 331-37.

Howkins, A. (1991) *Reshaping rural England: a social history, 1850-1925*, London: Routledge.

Imrie, R. and Raco, M. (eds) (2003) *Urban renaissance? New Labour, community and urban policy*, Bristol: The Policy Press.

Johnson, R.W. (1972) 'The nationalisation of English rural politics: Norfolk South West, 1945-70', *Parliamentary Affairs*, vol 26, pp 8-55.

Keating, M. and Stevenson, L. (2006) 'Rural policy in Scotland after devolution', *Regional Studies*, vol 40, pp 397-407.

Labour Party (1997) *New Labour: Because Britain deserves better*, Labour Party Manifesto, London: Labour Party.

Latour, B. (1990) 'Drawing things together', in S. Woolgar and M. Lynch (eds) *Representation in science*, Cambridge, MA: MIT Press, pp 19-68.

Lowe, P. and Ward, N. (2001) 'New Labour, new rural vision? Labour's Rural White Paper', *Political Quarterly*, vol 72, pp 386-90.

Matless, D. (1998) *Landscape and Englishness*, London: Reaktion.

Moore, S. (1991) 'The agrarian Conservative Party in parliament, 1920-1929', *Parliamentary History*, vol 10, pp 342-62.

Mosbacher, M. and Anderson, D. (eds) (1999) *Another country*, London: Social Affairs Unit.

Mougenot, C. and Mormont, M. (1988) *L'invention du rural*, Brussels: Vie Ouvrière.

Murdoch, J. (1997) 'The shifting territory of government: some insights from the Rural White Paper', *Area*, vol 29, pp 109-18.

Murdoch, J. and Lowe, P. (2003) 'The preservation paradox: modernism, environmentalism and the politics of spatial division', *Transactions of the Institute of British Geographers*, vol 28, pp 318-32.

Murdoch, J. and Ward, N. (1997) 'Governmentality and territoriality: the statistical manufacture of Britain's "national farm"', *Political Geography*, vol 16, pp 307-24.

NAfW (National Assembly for Wales) (2001) *Farming for the future*, Cardiff: National Assembly for Wales.

PIU (Performance and Innovation Unit of the Cabinet Office) (1999) *Rural economies*, London: The Stationery Office. (Also available at www.cabinetoffice. gov.uk/strategy/work_areas/rural_economies.aspx)

Rentoul, J. (2001) *Tony Blair: Prime Minister*, London: Little, Brown and Company.

RGLMP (Rural Group of Labour MPs) (1999) *Rural audit: a health check on rural Britain*, London: Rural Group of Labour MPs.

Richardson, T. (2000) 'Discourses of rurality in EU Spatial Policy: the European Spatial Development Perspective', *Sociologia Ruralis*, vol 40, pp 53-71.

Scottish Office (1995) *People, prosperity and partnership*, Edinburgh: HMSO.

Self, P. and Storing, H. (1962) *The state and the farmer*, London: George Allen and Unwin.

Smith, M. J. (1992) 'The agricultural policy community: maintaining a closed relationship', in D. Marsh and R. Rhodes (eds) *Policy networks in British governance*, Oxford: Oxford University Press, pp 27-50.

Smith, M. J. (1993) *Pressure, power and policy*, Hemel Hempstead: Harvester Wheatsheaf.

Ward, N. (2002) 'Representing rurality? New Labour and the electoral geography of rural Britain', *Area*, vol 34, pp 171-81.

Ward, N. and Lowe, P. (2007) 'Blairite modernisation and countryside policy', *Political Quarterly*, vol 78, pp 412-21.

Ward, N., Lowe, P. and Bridges, T. (2003) 'Rural and regional development: the role of regional development agencies in England', *Regional Studies*, vol 37, pp 201-14.

Welsh Office (1996) *A working countryside for Wales*, Cardiff: HMSO.

Winter, M. (1996) *Rural politics*, London: Routledge.

Wintour, P. (1998) 'Blair won over voters in the shires in 1997. And he won't desert them now', *The Observer*, 22 February, p 19.

Woods, M. (2002) 'Was there a rural rebellion? Labour and the countryside vote in the 2001 General Election', in L. Bennie, C. Rallings, J. Tonge and P. Webb (eds) *British Parties and Elections Review: Volume 12 – The 2001 general election*, London: Frank Cass, pp 206-28.

Woods, M. (2005) *Contesting rurality: Politics in the British countryside*, Aldershot: Ashgate.

Woods, M. (2006) 'Rural politics and governance', in J. Midgley (ed) *A new rural agenda*, Newcastle: IPPR North, pp 140-68.

TWO

Rethinking rural policy under New Labour

Neil Ward

Introduction: modernity and tradition

When New Labour swept to power in May 1997 it was on a manifesto that had little to say about rural areas or rural policy. The countryside was acknowledged as "a great natural asset, a part of our heritage which calls for special stewardship", but balanced with the "needs of people who live and work in rural areas" (Labour Party, 1997, pp 4 and 30). In contrast to Labour manifestos of old, there were no grand plans for land nationalisation, agricultural tenancy reform or investment in public services infrastructure. The proposals to establish a 'right to roam' across open country and to hold a free vote on outlawing hunting with hounds attracted much attention, but they did not amount to a rural policy and were redolent more of 'old' Labour rather than New.

The manifesto's mantra of 'modernisation' signalled the break with the past – but the focus was on the welfare state and the constitution. Having modernised the Labour Party, the manifesto promised "we will modernise Britain" (Labour Party, 1997, p 5). The process of modernisation had started with the reorientation of the Labour Party itself. Philip Gould, the Blairite pollster, had diagnosed the failings of old Labour as being "too rooted in trade unionism; too obsessive about public ownership; too tied to myth; too rooted in its past" (Gould, 1998, p 24). Instead, the manifesto promised a programme for "a new centre and centre-left politics" characterised by an approach "that differs both from the solutions of the old left and those of the Conservative right" (Labour Party, 1997, p 3).

The meaning of modernisation

If one word captured the essence of New Labour's ambitions in 1997 it was 'modernisation'. The word littered the general election manifesto and was deployed widely in Tony Blair's speeches (Fairclough, 2000, p 19). The meaning of modernisation is a source of rich debate. Is it simply the adoption of Thatcherism by the Labour Party, the continuation of the social democratic Gaitskellism of the 1950s and 1960s, or simply a superficial sheen to cover mere pragmatism and lack of ideology? Finlayson (2003, p 67) argues that to understand the meaning of modernisation, the term has to be considered from three angles: its rhetorical function, its concrete reference, and its use as a strategy of governance.

As a rhetorical device, modernisation is a positive, forward-looking term, implying progress, progressiveness and excitement. To be opposed to modernisation is to cling to outdated thinking. Because the same term is applied to a wide range of public policy issues, it helps to give a sense of overall coherence – a grand project. Modernisation serves as a code-word for 'what needs to be done', implying that the direction of change, however unpalatable to certain interests, is beyond dispute. The foundations for the modernising reforms under Blair had been laid in the party's Policy Review process between 1987 and 1992, which significantly shifted the party's outlook towards the market and the state. Central to this revisionism was a reconceptualisation of socialism as the creation of the social conditions to maximise individual liberty (Hattersley, 1987). New Labour discarded the old ideological commitment to public ownership and recast the role of the active state from a Keynesian demand management approach to one increasingly restricted to supply-side interventions. Markets, so the New Labour line of analysis went, were transforming the international conditions for economic activity, as well as fuelling revolutionary technological changes. Thus education and training became increasingly important to equip workers not only to cope with rapidly changing demands of the workplace, but also to innovate and participate in the enterprise culture of the 'new economy' of the information age (see Leadbeater, 1999). New Labour, crucially, took "the power of capital and the markets which empowered it" as a given, "merely a fact of life, a reality to be accommodated to, and not a problem, a force to be questioned and resisted" (Ruskin, 1998, p 11). That modernisation is so widely applied and often repeated adds to the sense of inevitability, universality and naturalisation.

> Forces are at work bringing about the need for modernisation. They are inevitable and clearly definable – technological transformation, the 'obvious' failure of the social-democratic welfare state and globalisation. Such forces are irreversible, the political challenge becomes construed as that of living up to them (as opposed to assessing them and deciding how politics should respond). (Finlayson, 2003, p 79)

Yet modernisation is about more than just a way of talking, and the term does imply specific tangible referents. Modern technologies, such as information and communication technologies (ICTs), are to be embraced. The elements of the 'knowledge economy', ranging from the arts and creative industries and software engineering through to the biosciences, are all part and parcel of modernising the economy. In more concrete terms, modernisation is essentially about seeing people as the key resource in economic growth and social harmony – in well-being. Information technology requires human skills in order to be useful, and so investing in skills is logical. At the same time, the new ICTs link people, businesses and communities in new networks through which knowledge flows.

Management theories of the knowledge economy emphasise the need to cope with perpetual change through innovation and knowledge acquisition in order to maintain competitiveness. New Labour's modernisation has been about applying new management and business theory to the business of government and to state institutions.

The concrete and rhetorical are not separate – the 'real' and the 'gloss' – but "function together and support each other" (Finlayson, 2003, p 68). As a strategy of governance, modernisation serves as a mechanism for diagnosing the problems of public services or institutions. If government functions through particular procedures of problem identification and generation then, for New Labour, modernisation has been a key strategy in problematisation – in picking the problems to address. Finlayson (2003) goes so far as to say that New Labour "practises not only the modernisation of governance but a kind of governance through modernisation" (p 69).

What did New Labour's modernising mission mean for its approach to rural policy? This chapter examines the government's handling of rural policy in three periods. The first, from taking office in 1997 to the production of the Rural White Paper in November 2000, sees the government seeking actively to apply its modernising approach to the rural question. The second, from 2001 to 2003, is dominated by the foot and mouth crisis and its aftermath, which resulted in a refocusing on agricultural concerns. Finally, the third period, from 2004 onwards, saw rural policy eclipsed within the new Department for Environment, Food and Rural Affairs (Defra), with the consequence that rural affairs was first marginalised and then effectively dismantled as a policy area of central government.

1997 to 2000: producing the Rural White Paper

Press speculation that the government intended to produce an overview of policies for the countryside began in spring 1998 after comments made by Michael Meacher in the aftermath of the Countryside March, although the formal announcement of the preparation of a Rural White Paper came several months later in November 1998. Preliminary work began in the Cabinet Office's new Performance and Innovation Unit (PIU). The PIU was intended to provide additional, research project-based capacity for the Prime Minister's Policy Unit, based in Number 10. It would seek to take a longer-term perspective in its analytical work, to complement the more short-term 'firefighting' role that occupied the Number 10 Policy Unit. A forerunner of this model was the Central Policy Review Staff, established by Edward Health in 1971 to advise the Cabinet on strategic policy issues and abolished by Mrs Thatcher in 1983 (see James, 1986; Blackstone and Plowden, 1988).

The PIU quickly became cast as being in the vanguard of efforts to improve 'joined-up government' and as "the Prime Minister's intellectual hit squad" (Beecham, 2000, p 22). The Unit reported directly to the Prime Minister and projects were carried out by small teams, including secondees from across government departments and beyond. The first set of projects dealt with e-commerce, the ageing society, the role of central government in regions and local areas, managing cross-cutting issues in Whitehall and rural economies. The Prime Minister had been presented with a list of 30 topics, and his selection of these five reveals that rural policy was seen as a priority issue for the government at the time.

The PIU Rural Team consisted of Greg Wilkinson (a public services specialist seconded from a management consultancy), myself (seconded from Newcastle University) and Sarah Thomas (seconded from the Welsh Office), assisted by other members of the PIU, including its Director, Suma Chakrabarti. Political leadership was provided by the project's sponsoring Minister Andrew Smith (then a minister in the Department of Education).[1] The project reviewed data about changes in rural areas in the light of the government's overall objectives, developed a new set of basic principles for rural policy, and then made recommendations for change to government policy. The PIU's analysis was inspired by academic studies of rural change and policy during the 1990s (see, for example, Marsden et al, 1993; Cloke et al, 1994) and earlier reviews conducted within or for government (UK Roundtable on Sustainable Development, 1998; Minister of Agriculture's Agricultural Advisory Group, 1999). The project team submitted a 188-page report containing 63 specific recommendations to the Prime Minister in July 1999.

Members of the Prime Minister's Policy Unit and Strategic Communications Unit were anxious about the scale and sensitivity of some of the recommendations, particularly following the public and media response to a leak of the report to *The Times*. Number 10 decided to treat the submitted report as an internal document and publish a sanitised version for public consumption, which would raise 'issues for discussion' rather than set out the PIU team's recommendations in detail. The internal report set out how the policy framework for rural areas and rural development had its roots in the post-war concerns about agricultural productivism and protectionism. It argued that times had changed and action was now needed on several fronts to modernise rural policy. The report characterised the government's role as helping rural areas to adapt to change. On economic issues, it contained recommendations on reducing restrictions on rural economic development, developing skills and infrastructure, improving business support and developing rural leisure and tourism. On the environment, it made recommendations on the functioning of the planning system, environmental taxes and agri-environmental schemes. On agriculture, it set out a path for an evolutionary approach to reform of the Common Agricultural Policy (CAP) through exploiting new opportunities for exercising national discretion, and particularly by switching support from direct payments to agri-environment and rural development measures. On rural communities, it argued for a new commitment to market towns and made recommendations for rural service provision, transport and housing.

Even the sanitised version of the PIU report (PIU, 1999), eventually published in early December 1999, caused quite a stir. Newspapers latched onto the suggestion that agricultural land should be released for development. In London, the *Evening Standard* ran with the headline "Shock new call to loosen green belt" (10 December 1999) and *The Times* in its leader (11 December 1999) welcomed 'blue skies thinking', but warned that development on Britain's green fields would not be welcome. The *Daily Mail* (11 December 1999) reported "outrage" under the headline "Labour accused of plot to concrete over countryside". *Country Life* was incandescent about the "fantasies of the townies in the Cabinet Office, who want every farm in England turned into a polystyrene nightmare of holiday villages and leisure amenities" (28 October 1999, p 49). Among rural policy specialists, the response was more sober. Michael Meacher, then Countryside Minister, welcomed the report as "an informed and strategic tour d'horizon" with "a number of radical ideas" (Meacher, 2000). The Countryside Agency commended the report for exposing "some fundamental issues which need to be settled before the White Paper" (Countryside Agency, 1999, p 1). The report was praised for its "unsentimental outlook" (Lowe, 2000, p 144), and the President of the Agricultural Economics Society described it as "an important milestone in the development of official thinking" (Thomson, 2001, p 3).

For a further 12 months following publication of the PIU's analysis, officials and ministers in the two lead government departments – the Department of the Environment, Transport and the Regions (DETR) and the Ministry of Agriculture, Fisheries and Food (MAFF) – continued to work on the Rural White Paper. When it was eventually published, at the end of November 2000, it contained a wide variety of measures, many of them taken from the PIU work. Like its urban counterpart, the Rural White Paper was a framework for spending the bonanza announced in the autumn of 2000 by the Chancellor. Overall, some £1 billion was allocated to rural programmes over the following three years, in addition to the increased support already announced for agricultural diversification and environmental schemes through the CAP.

The political outlook of the White Paper was inclusive. As John Prescott and Nick Brown declared in the Foreword, "we believe in a countryside for everyone". The outlook was also resolutely change-oriented. The ministers rejected preservationism – the "outdated, picture-postcard version" of rural England. Instead, the White Paper set out as its goal "to help people in rural areas to manage change, exploit the opportunities it brings, and enable them to create a more sustainable future" (DETR/MAFF, 2000, p 11).

Economically, the White Paper sought to encourage public and private investment in market towns and to strengthen their role as hubs for ICT, public transport and business, and public services for their surrounding hinterlands. It looked forward to further CAP reform, and farmers were urged to exploit the environmental economy – that is to "make the character of the countryside an economic as well as an environmental asset" (p 11) – through speciality foods, provision of environmental services and farm-based tourism and leisure.

Socially, the White Paper promised "A new deal on services" to ensure that rural communities would benefit from increased investment in public services and which tackled deprivation and social exclusion (p 31). It committed the government to doubling the Housing Corporation's programme in small settlements and better use of the planning system to secure more affordable homes in market towns and smaller settlements. A major expansion of funding for public and community transport was also promised, along with a commitment to maintain the rural Post Office network and to pilot new financial, community and ICT services through it.

In terms of governance, at the parish level, the White Paper introduced a quality test to which parish and town councils would be encouraged to aspire "to achieve a new status in local government as the voice of their community" (p 146). Parish councils that passed the test would then be encouraged to deliver more services on behalf of local authorities including provision of public information, management of facilities such as car parks, markets, or local amenities and maintenance of public space. Parish Plans were also encouraged, in the hope that they would make local authorities more responsive to the needs of rural communities. The White Paper also committed the government to explicit rural-proofing procedures, involving the Countryside Agency, to "ensure that our policies take account of specific rural needs" and to "strengthen the way in which we listen to the rural voice" (p 158).

At the regional level the thinking in the White Paper was less well developed. It set out a 'new rural vision' for Regional Development Agencies (RDAs) and charged them with various specific responsibilities to help rural businesses, overcome rural deprivation and promote sustainable development. At the same time, the rural dimension of the Government Offices for the Regions was strengthened through the incorporation of MAFF regional staff, and Government Offices were tasked with coordinating the delivery of rural policies and programmes and rural-proofing at the regional level. The ministers wrote in their Foreword, "We want a countryside which can shape its own future, with its voice heard by Government at all levels". The White Paper promised to "empower local communities so that decisions are taken with their active participation and ownership" (p 162). This socially inclusive, economically developmental and environmentally progressive vision for rural policy therefore came with a range of machinery of government reforms, from the parish to Whitehall.

2001 to 2003: the disruption of the foot and mouth crisis

With hindsight, the publication of the Rural White Paper in November 2000 represents the high point of New Labour's ambitions for reform of rural policy. Within three months of its publication, all hell was let loose with the outbreak of foot and mouth disease (FMD). Symptoms were spotted in pigs at an abattoir in Essex on 19 February 2001. The following day, FMD was confirmed and the European Commission quickly banned all meat and live animal exports from the UK. In the UK, this decision was immediately seen as yet another blow to an already beleaguered farming industry, even before the full extent of the epidemic was known. It took seven months for the disease to be wiped out. The last case of FMD in 2001 was confirmed on 30 September, with the final total of confirmed cases standing at over two thousand. Animals were also culled on contiguous premises. During the seven-month epidemic almost 6.5 million animals were slaughtered in all. The cost of the epidemic has been estimated at £5 billion to the private sector and £3 billion to the public sector (National Audit Office, 2002). This was the most damaging and destructive outbreak in a hitherto relatively FMD-free country anywhere in the world. The crisis delayed the calling of the 2001 General Election, which was eventually held on 7 June. Following his second landslide victory, Blair shuffled his cabinet and reorganised Whitehall. Unexpectedly, and to signal a break from the nightmare of FMD, he created a new department – the Department for Environment, Food and Rural Affairs (Defra) – to replace the old MAFF, and appointed Margaret Beckett to head it.

In August 2001 the government announced that three independent inquiries would examine issues related to the FMD outbreak, fulfilling an election manifesto commitment. One, by the Royal Society, involved a committee of 16 members with specialist scientific and industrial expertise who reviewed the scientific issues relating to the prevention and control of infectious diseases in livestock. A second, chaired by Dr Iain Anderson, involved a small Cabinet Office secretariat and focused on the government's handling of the crisis and the lessons to be learned. The third inquiry, chaired by Sir Don Curry, involved a Policy Commission of nine further members to advise the government on measures to improve the economic and environmental sustainability of the farming and food industries.

Don Curry's Policy Commission refocused the government's attention on agriculture. Curry was a livestock farmer with strong cooperative agri-business interests, and his Commission included prominent members of the environmental and consumer lobbies as well as the chief executive of one of the largest supermarket chains. The Commission was clearly intended to give direction to the new Defra. In some respects, its membership represented the Department's new political client base. Its recommendations put a seal of approval on a post-productivist consensus for agriculture. Indeed, despite the Commission's claim in its report to have produced something radically new, it was in fact the most recent in a succession of fundamental reviews (at least nine in all) of what to do about agriculture and rural policy since New Labour had come to power.

There was pre-existing political interest on the part of the Prime Minister in tackling agricultural production policy. Prior to FMD, he had held frequent farming summits and launched various action plans in an attempt to put farming policy on a new footing. For Blair, the overriding problem was how to make British farming more economically sustainable. It is revealing that within a week of the FMD outbreak, Blair had seen the crisis as an opportunity to 'grasp the nettle' and overhaul the domestic approach to agricultural policy, insofar as that could be achieved within the constraints of the CAP (*The Times*, 2 March 2001). His solution was to seek to improve the competitiveness of farming by weaning farmers off production subsidies. There was little interest now in recasting agriculture as a component of a wider and more territorial approach to rural development.

The Curry Commission returned to problems that the government had been re-characterising throughout its first term. The Commission was given a strong steer by the Prime Minister's Office that it was to focus on the economic and environmental sustainability of the food and farming industries, and not on the wider question of the role of these industries in rural development. This framing led the Commission to focus on a series of old solutions to past problems. Key among its recommendations was an extension of the UK's discretionary use of the modulation measures within the CAP to 'recycle' former farm production subsidies into environmental payments, for example. It also called for an expansion of agri-environmental schemes, and measures to strengthen the market orientation of farm businesses (Policy Commission on the Future of Farming and Food, 2002). These repeated the PIU's recommendations of two years earlier. Moreover, they had little to do with the FMD crisis. Rather, they were cast within a competitiveness imperative for the food and farming industry that stressed the need for farming to become weaned off production subsidies and be more closely connected with its markets and the food supply chain.

The Lessons to be Learned Inquiry reported in July 2002. The report focused on the poor state of contingency planning and the extent of animal movements, with particular attention paid to the use of science, calling in the army, the issue of whether to vaccinate, and the nature of communications and lines of responsibility among those managing the response to the outbreak. There was little detailed discussion of the wider rural economy impacts of the crisis, and this was mostly a reiteration of material from government and from the National Audit Office (Anderson, 2002).

The FMD crisis revealed the extent to which the countryside has changed since the 1960s and how out-of-date were the official and public conceptions of the position of agriculture in rural areas that prevailed in the crucial early days and weeks of the crisis. The Northumberland Committee that inquired into the previous FMD outbreak, more than 20 years earlier, considered solely its impact on the agricultural sector (Committee of Inquiry on Foot and Mouth Disease, 1969). In those days, farming played a much more important role in local rural economies. Much had changed since then, with the great growth in rural tourism and leisure, the urban–rural shift in population and employment and the diversification of farm household incomes. By 2001, fewer than 3% of jobs in England's rural districts were in farming. Yet public perceptions and official outlooks had not kept pace. MAFF, with its overly agriculturalist focus and risk-averse organisational culture, simply took an 'off-the-shelf' agriculturally oriented approach to tackling FMD (Ward et al, 2004). When it came to respond to the various FMD lesson-learning inquiries, the government pointed to the establishment of Defra as signalling a break with the past and an elevation of rural policy in government. It explained:

A fundamental difference in the way Government approached the delivery of rural economic and social policy was signalled by the creation of Defra, one of whose *central pillars* is the whole rural affairs agenda. (HM Government, 2002, p 13, emphasis added)

2004 onwards: the rural strategy and the eclipse of rural policy

Following the establishment of Defra, the government instigated a Rural Delivery Review, headed by Lord Haskins. As a new department, Defra had received a reasonably good settlement from the 2002 Spending Review and the Treasury was keen to see that the money was spent efficiently and in pursuit of a reform-oriented agenda. Lord Haskins was asked to suggest how to simplify the delivery of rural programmes and how to achieve Defra's rural priorities and targets cost-effectively. The birth of Defra had yielded a rather sprawling department sponsoring several agencies and there was a need for rationalisation. For the first time a single government department was given lead responsibility for policies aimed at meeting the economic, social and environmental needs of rural communities and rural areas. In seeking to streamline rural policy delivery, the review focused on Defra's Land Use and Rural Affairs Directorate and Rural Development Service, as well as the Countryside Agency and English Nature – quangos that had been transferred from the former Department of the Environment, Transport and the Regions (DETR).

Haskins' recommendations were based on what he referred to as "two fundamental cornerstones of good government" (Haskins, 2003, p 15) – the separation of policy development from delivery, and devolution. He was particularly adamant that "Defra's prime responsibility should be the development of policy" (p 111), and that it should arrange for the delivery of its policies through other national, regional and local agencies. He pointed out that "the multiplicity of delivery organisations, particularly at the national level, is most apparent in relation to sustainable land management" (p 63) and proposed therefore an amalgamation of organisations and bits of organisations to create "an integrated agency to promote sustainable use of land and the natural environment". The core of the new agency would be English Nature, to which would be added Defra's Rural Development Service (which manages the agri-environment schemes under the CAP), the landscape and recreational programmes of the Countryside Agency and possibly the operations of the Forestry Commission in England.

As an exercise in tidying up the machinery of government, particularly the relationship between Defra and its quangos, this could have been a worthwhile, if limited, exercise. But Haskins took a much wider swipe at the institutional landscape. While the report concentrated more narrowly on Defra and its agencies, it did not refrain from pontificating about what was in the best interest of rural communities and economies. Its central preoccupations were with agriculture and the rural environment, but it referred constantly to rural policy and rural delivery. This farm-centred view of the rural world put the clock back to the time before the Rural White Paper and the establishment of Defra. The promise of Defra was that farming would be integrated within a wider rural development perspective, and that Defra would become the champion of a more rounded rural policy which would be the counterpart of urban policy. Haskins helped to kill off this promise.

Haskins' report was not just blinkered towards the wider rural policy agenda, but showed antipathy towards it. The efforts of Defra to embrace a wider rural policy agenda were mocked and its rural Public Service Agreement target, agreed with the Treasury – to improve the relative productivity of poorly performing rural areas and improve the accessibility of services for rural people – was dismissed as "aspirational and woolly" and impractical (p 35). Haskins' clear intent was to clip Defra's wings. His review recommended carving up the Countryside Agency's functions, with some going to the new land management agency and others being absorbed by RDAs, local authorities, sub-regional partnerships and the voluntary sector. He also wanted to see rural social and economic programmes devolved to the regional and local levels. RDAs, for example, would be given overall responsibility for such matters as promoting farm diversification, the Vital Villages programme and funding of Rural Community Councils. The RDAs, in turn, would be expected to delegate the management of the delivery of most programmes. Local partnerships, local authorities and voluntary organisations would assume "the main responsibility for the delivery of schemes and services to rural communities" (p 57).

That, in fact, was already the case. Most rural delivery took place at the local and sub-regional levels. There was as much confusion here and overlap of roles and responsibilities as at the national level, as well as limited capacity. Haskins himself conceded that "The complexity at a national level in the delivery of rural targets further increases at the regional and local level" (p 23). In one region alone more than 70 regional or sub-regional strategies were recorded. However, the preoccupation of the review with national agencies and Whitehall meant a lack of critical attention to the regional and local level. Haskins' review was a strange mixture of factual evidence, assertion and blind faith. In key respects Haskins' inclinations were undoubtedly sound. Defra was overcentralised and needed to work more cooperatively with local and regional organisations; but then to propose dismantling the one agency in the Defra family – the Countryside Agency – with strong localistic instincts and knowledge seemed to be driven more by prejudice than analysis.

When the Review was published in November 2003, rather than announce its intentions there and then, the government instead recast the proposals as a contribution to a wider process – labelled the Modernising Delivery Review. This took several months and the Rural Strategy was eventually released in July 2004, during the final week of the parliamentary session (Defra, 2004). The Rural Strategy's response to Haskins was, likewise, more coherent in its treatment of farming and land management than of the socioeconomic dimensions to rural policy and rural development, where objectives and mechanisms remained ambiguous. The Strategy also failed to provide any greater clarity and coherence over how decentralisation might work. There was nothing on the role of local authorities, very little in the way of specific decentralising reforms, and many platitudes about decentralisation and public involvement that did not instil confidence.

Conceptually, the Strategy was also a step in killing off the idea of the entity 'rural England'. In emphasising that "there is no homogeneous rural England" (p 5) the Strategy helped to re-establish rural policy as a sub-category of regional policy. Rural social and economic problems came to be increasingly understood and handled as sub-regional problems, rather than as expressions of some national rural condition. However, under the new arrangements, at the regional level the responsibilities for primary economic and environmental policy delivery in rural areas was vested with separate organisations. Partnership working within a sustainable development framework, brokered by Government Offices and coordinated via strengthened Regional Rural Affairs Forums, is now expected to provide the necessary coordination, although this has proved to be a major challenge in most regions. At the regional level, there was little real sense of simplification and rationalisation in the Strategy.

As a result of the Rural Strategy, a great deal of energy among rural bodies had to be diverted into coping with institutional change. This was at a time of major strategic challenges. These included: the need to implement the new arrangements for the CAP in a bold and imaginative way so as to ensure the maximum public benefits; the major challenge of meeting the requirements of the Water Framework Directive, and the need to coordinate agri-environmental and land management measures more carefully with water quality management priorities; the government's regionalisation and new localism agendas; and the emphasis on public engagement and participation at the local level in public policy and service delivery. The Rural Strategy gave *institutional* change, when what was really needed was a clear strategy to cope with these major *policy* agendas.

Conclusions: New Labour, modernisation and the countryside

In his speech to the Party Conference in September 1999, Tony Blair proclaimed New Labour as "the new progressive force in British politics which can modernise the nation". He spelt out what he saw as "this historic mission ... to liberate Britain from the old class divisions, old structures, old prejudices, old ways of working". The 21st century, he argued, "will not be about the battle between capitalism and socialism but between the forces of progress and the forces of conservatism" (Blair, 1999). The battle lines seemed clear. On one side was the progressive force, "the new radicals, the Labour Party modernised". The foe were the 'forces of conservatism', found "not just in the Conservative Party but within us, within our nation" and among "the old elites, establishments that have run our professions and our country too long", with their "old air of superiority based on past glory".

As the speech was being delivered, outside the conference hall the Countryside Alliance was holding a demonstration to protest against proposals to ban hunting with hounds. Their campaigning had, for more than two years, sought to present the government as, at best, unsympathetic to, or naive about, what they called the 'rural way of life' and, at worst, actively opposed to it. The farming lobby also protested at the conference. For many commentators, these protesters were easily cast as an embodiment of the forces of conservatism. Indeed, the Prime Minister had joked about the Countryside Alliance protestors delaying the start of his speech, and had gone on to mock the Conservative Party as "the party of fox-hunting", to laughs in the Conference Hall.

Of course, the Countryside Alliance does not speak for all who live and work in rural areas,[2] but in the heady atmosphere of a party conference, the symbolism was important. The forces of progress were modern, meritocratic, radical, multicultural, feminist, and embracing of change. They were inside the hall. In contrast, the protestors outside were drawing on discourses of tradition and an anti-urbanism. It was difficult to see how else they might fit with the government's modernisation agenda. They could only be victims or opponents of it.

There were signs in the early years of the New Labour government of an appetite to apply its modernising zeal to the institutions and objectives of rural policy. Central to modernisation was that the role of agriculture should be rethought as an integral component of rural, that is territorial, development, rather than as a separate economic sector. The PIU review set out a path to bring agriculture within a rural development framework. The subsequent UK government decision to apply discretionary modulation to the financing of the CAP and its second pillar – the Rural Development Regulation – for the 2000–06 European funding period also implied greater emphasis on a rural development and agri-environmental rationale for CAP expenditure, to the detriment of direct compensation payments to farmers. Indeed, December 2000 was probably the high point of this more reformist, territorial approach to agriculture and rural development. Two months later, in early 2001, FMD struck and we have seen a retrenchment into a more sectoral approach to agriculture since then. After FMD, the Curry Commission presented a highly sectoral perspective on the future development of the farming industry. The subsequent *agricultural* White Paper, which took forward the Curry Commission recommendations, and a reorganisation of Defra nationally and in the regions reinforced this sectoral concern with the operation of food and farming supply chains and the competitiveness of the industry (Donaldson et al, 2006).

It is notable that the most bold, radical and imaginative bits of the Rural White Paper have run into the sand, been shelved, or led to disappointing outcomes. The area that was the least well thought-through – regionalisation – has been the agenda that has been most enthusiastically pursued and used to dismantle national rural policy, particularly after the vandalism of the Modernising Rural Delivery review and its aftermath.

Notes

[1] Andrew Smith went on to join the Cabinet in 2000, first as Chief Secretary to the Treasury and subsequently as Secretary of State for Work and Pensions. Suma Chakrabarti went on to become Permanent Secretary at the Department of International Development.

[2] Public opinion polling in the late 1990s continually revealed the proportions of people expressing opposition to hunting with hounds to be broadly similar between those people who live in rural areas and those in urban areas. For example, in a Gallup poll published in the *Daily Telegraph* on 11 August 1997, 77% of people who described themselves as 'country people' said they disapproved of hunting foxes with hounds (Campaign for the Protection of Hunted Animals, 1998).

References

Anderson, I. (2002) *Foot and mouth disease 2001: Lessons to be learned inquiry report*, Report by Dr Iain Anderson to the Prime Minister and the Secretary of State for Environment, Food and Rural Affairs, HC 888, London: The Stationery Office. (Also available at http://archive.cabinetoffice.gov.uk/fmd/fmd_report/index.htm)

Beecham, J. (2000) 'Warning shots from the front-line', *Guardian*, 31 March, p 22.

Blackstone, T. and Plowden, W. (1988) *Inside the Think Tank: Advising the Cabinet 1971-1983*, London: Heinemann.

Blair, T. (1999) Speech by Tony Blair MP, Prime Minister to the Labour Party Conference, 28 September (www.labour.org.uk, 30 September 1999).

Campaign for the Protection of Hunted Animals (1998) 'Anglers and riders support Foster Bill to ban hunting with dogs', Press release, 3 February, London: Campaign for the Protection of Hunted Animals.

Cloke, P., Millbourne, P. and Thomas, C. (1994) *Lifestyles in rural England*, London: Rural Development Commission.

Committee of Inquiry on Foot and Mouth Disease (the 'Northumberland Committee') (1969) *Report of the Committee of Inquiry on Foot and Mouth Disease, 1968*, London: HMSO.

Countryside Agency (1999) 'Radical approach to government rural policy', Countryside Agency news release, 10 December.

Defra (Department for Environment, Food and Rural Affairs) (2004) *Rural strategy*, London: Defra. (Also available at www.defra.gov.uk/rural/pdfs/strategy/rural_strategy_2004.pdf)

DETR/MAFF (Department of the Environment, Transport and the Regions/Ministry of Agriculture, Fisheries and Food) (2000) *Our countryside: The future – a fair deal for rural England* (the Rural White Paper), Cm 4909, London: The Stationery Office.

Donaldson, A., Lee, R., Ward, N. and Wilkinson, K. (2006) *Foot and mouth – five years on: The legacy of the 2001 foot and mouth disease crisis for farming and the British countryside*, Centre for Rural Economy Discussion Paper No 6, Newcastle: University of Newcastle upon Tyne.

Fairclough, N. (2000) *New Labour, new language*, London: Routledge.

Finlayson, A. (2003) *Making sense of New Labour*, London: Lawrence and Wishart.

Gould, P. (1998) *The unfinished revolution: How the modernisers saved the Labour Party*, London: Abacus.

Haskins, C. (2003) *Rural delivery review: A report on the delivery of government policies in rural England*, London: Defra. (Also available at www.defra.gov.uk/rural/pdfs/ruraldelivery/haskins_full_report.pdf)

Hattersley, R. (1987) *Choose freedom: The future for democratic socialism*, London: Harmondsworth.

HM Government (2002) *Response to the reports of the foot and mouth disease inquiries*, Cm 5637, London: The Stationery Office.

James, S. (1986) 'The Central Policy Review Staff, 1970-1983', *Political Studies*, vol 34, pp 423-40.

Labour Party (1997) *New Labour – because Britain deserves better* (General Election manifesto), London: Labour Party.

Leadbeater, C. (1999) *Living on thin air: The new economy*, London: Viking.

Lowe, P. (2000) 'Labour's rural policy', *Town and Country Planning*, vol 69, pp 143-5.

Marsden, T., Murdoch, J., Lowe, P., Munton, R. and Flynn, A. (1993) *Constructing the countryside*, London: UCL Press.

Meacher, M. (2000) Evidence to the House of Commons Environment, Transport and the Regions Select Committee, 12 January 2000, Q 501.

Minister of Agriculture's Agricultural Advisory Group (1999) *Europe's agriculture: the case for change*, London: Ministry of Agriculture, Fisheries and Food.

National Audit Office (2002) *The 2001 outbreak of foot and mouth disease*, HC 939, Session 2001-02, London: The Stationery Office.

Performance and Innovation Unit (of the Cabinet Office) (1999) *Rural economies*, London: The Stationery Office. (Also available at www.cabinetoffice.gov.uk/strategy/work_areas/rural_economies.aspx)

Policy Commission on the Future of Farming and Food (2002) *Farming and food: A sustainable future*, London: The Stationery Office. (Also available at http://archive.cabinetoffice.gov.uk/farming/pdf/PCReport2.pdf)

Ruskin, M. (1998) 'The New Labour project', *Soundings*, vol 8, p 11.

Thomson, K. (2001) 'Agricultural economics and rural development: marriage or divorce? Presidential address', *Journal of Agricultural Economics*, vol 52, pp 1-10.

UK Round Table on Sustainable Development (1998) *Aspects of sustainable agriculture and rural policy*, London: UK Round Table on Sustainable Development.

Ward, N., Donaldson, A. and Lowe, P. (2004) 'Policy framing and learning the lessons from the UK's foot and mouth disease crisis', *Environment and Planning C: Government and Policy*, vol 22, pp 291–306.

THREE

Rural governance, devolution and policy delivery

Mark Goodwin

Introduction

This chapter examines the institutions and structures through which rural policy is devised and delivered at national, regional and local scales. The institutional map of rural policy forged through three successive New Labour governments is markedly different from that which they inherited from the Conservatives in 1997. Perhaps this is not surprising, for as Jamie Peck (2001, p 449) has reminded us the state is, after all, a "political process in motion". As new governments come into office, consolidate their power and attempt to deliver their own political strategies they can be expected to alter the institutions through which they govern. What is perhaps less expected is the extent and pace of change – especially in an area of policy not traditionally identified as a major concern for the Labour Party. For in less than a decade since taking power, New Labour has utterly transformed the structures and institutions of rural policy.

This chapter traces these transformations. It does so by exposing the dialectic that lies at their heart – that between the general concern of New Labour with reforming the constitutional and political structure of the UK state (known as its 'Devolution Settlement'), and its particular response to a series of political, economic, social and cultural pressures emanating from the countryside. It is at this intersection between the broader processes of devolution and the specific responses to rural change that we find the driver for the transformation of the structures and institutions of rural policy under New Labour. The chapter will first explore the outcomes of this dialectic in England, before moving on to look at rural policy in the other devolved territories of the UK.

New Labour's regional agenda and its impact on rural policy

The first impetus for change in the development and delivery of England's rural policy came from New Labour's devolution agenda. In Scotland this agenda resulted in the establishment of a new Parliament, and in Wales and Northern Ireland it led to newly elected Assemblies. As will be seen, rural policy was one of the areas devolved to these new institutions. In England, however, devolution was a fairly restricted activity, being administrative rather than electoral (with the exception of London) and solely focused on the regional level.

However, despite its limited scope, the statutory powers and functions of the Regional Development Agencies (RDAs) in particular had significant implications for rural policy. The RDAs were charged with promoting economic competitiveness, efficiency, investment, employment and skills within their region, and as Ward et al point out, "much of the parliamentary debate on the Regional Development Agencies Bill was spent arguing about the ways in which the RDAs should encompass rural concerns" (2003, p 203). In some ways the answer was very straightforward. In the words of the 1997 RDA White Paper:

> The Government are committed to promoting the interests of rural areas. Rural needs and institutions may be different, but many of the same concerns ... are common across each region. We need to understand the particular needs of rural areas, but to address them within an overall framework for the region as a whole. (DETR, 1997, p 24)

This was effectively calling for the rural to "be embedded in the regional" (Ward et al, 2003, p 203). However, this proved easier said than done. RDAs were new institutions with staff drawn from a range of existing agencies, including the Rural Development Commission (RDC) (see Jones et al, 2004, on the difficulties of settling new personnel into RDAs). Indeed, New Labour's devolution agenda signalled the end for the RDC, which had been promoting rural development since 1909 (Rogers, 1999). Its economic functions went to the RDAs, while its social and community remits were transferred to the new Countryside Agency. The Countryside Commission was also dismantled, with its own social and community operations going to the Countryside Agency and its conservation remit passing to English Nature.

Amid this institutional flux, the RDAs were expected to develop policies to promote rural regeneration. Initially they had to work with ring-fenced funding, and with a set of programmes inherited from the RDC, which limited their ability to fully embed the rural within a wider regional agenda. The opportunity to do this came with the publication of the RDAs' new Regional Strategies later in 1999, but, as Ward et al (2003) detail, the coverage of rural issues was extremely variable across the eight RDAs. However, the regionalisation of rural development policy had been established, and the RDC and the Countryside Commission had been abolished, all within two years of New Labour coming to power.

The regionalisation of rural policy was given further force with the publication in 2000 of the Rural White Paper for England, *Our countryside: The future – a fair deal for rural England* (DETR/MAFF, 2000). This set out New Labour's full rural affairs agenda for England for the first time, and here we can clearly discern the intersection between the devolution agenda and the rural policy agenda. The White Paper stressed the interdependence of urban and rural areas, and in so doing reinforced the regional agenda. It confirmed the RDAs' role with respect to rural issues, and charged them "with various specific responsibilities to help rural businesses, to overcome rural deprivation and to promote sustainable development" (Ward et al, 2003, p 204). The general vision of the White Paper promoted sustainable development for rural areas through four major themes: a living countryside with thriving rural communities and access to high quality public services; a working countryside, with a diverse economy giving high and stable levels of employment; a protected countryside in which the environment is sustained and enhanced, and which all can enjoy; and a vibrant countryside that can shape its own future with its voice heard by government at all levels. Quite how this vision was to be achieved leads us on to the next phase of New Labour's rural policy development.

Problematising the rural as an object of government

The publication of the White Paper marked the final stage in New Labour's initial redefinition of rural policy. Woods (2006) notes that the first serious political challenge to the new government came from the 120,000 people who gathered in Hyde Park for the Countryside Rally in July 1997, barely two months after New Labour's election victory. The Rally was sparked by New Labour's manifesto commitment to hold a free vote on the future of hunting with hounds, but the hunting lobby managed to reinvent itself as the Countryside Alliance and mobilise "a broad coalition of protest against the perceived threat to the countryside of the new 'urban-centric' government" (Woods, 2006, p 140). In response, New Labour sought to reclaim control of the rural political agenda by "challenging the protesters' representation of the countryside and promoting its own distinctive rural policies" (Woods, 2006, p 141).

This process began with the commissioning of the *Rural audit* by the Rural Group of Labour MPs (RGLMP). This was billed as a 'health check on rural Britain', and contained an extensive analysis of various components of rural life, including crime, deprivation, employment, social change and family life (RGLMP, 1999). Launched in Westminster by the Agriculture Minister, Nick Brown, it acted as a position statement for around 180 rural Labour MPs, many of whom had unexpectedly won rural and semi-rural seats. At the same time as the *Rural audit* was being written for Labour MPs, the Prime Minister's Performance and Innovation Unit in the Cabinet Office was producing two major reports on the rural economy (PIU, 1999, 2000). These reviewed the objectives of rural policy and provided a set of statistical indices of socioeconomic conditions in the countryside. The 'evidence' provided in these publications – of a countryside where agriculture was in decline, where in-migration was on the increase, and where social and economic diversity was the norm – informed the preparation of the Rural White Paper, and enabled New Labour to identify a series of policy priorities for rural areas. Crucially, these were not "farming and the future of hunting, but healthcare, education, employment, crime and public transport"

(Woods, 2006, pp 141-2). They were, of course, also issues that were common to both urban and rural areas, and policy areas where the Labour Party had a traditional strength (Woods, 2006).

One way to interpret these shifts in the definition of rural concerns is to see them as part of a redefinition of the rural as a specific object of governance. Rose and Miller (1992, p 179) point out how the language that constitutes political discourse is more than just rhetoric, but "should be seen, rather as a kind of intellectual machinery, or apparatus for rendering reality thinkable in such a way that it is amenable to political deliberations".

With this in mind, what we can see happening over the first few years of the New Labour government is the rural being 'rendered thinkable' in a different manner, so that it is amenable to a new form of political deliberation. For much of the post-war period, in policy terms the rural had been drawn fairly narrowly and largely equated with the agricultural and the environmental. Now it was being made thinkable in a different guise, with an emphasis placed on economic diversity, social change and urban–rural integration.

Rose and Miller (1992, p 183) go on to note that government programmes and strategies "presuppose that the real is programmable, that it is a domain subject to certain determinants, rules, norms and processes that can be acted upon and improved by authorities. They make the objects of government thinkable in such a way that their ills appear susceptible to diagnosis, prescription and cure by calculating and normalising intervention".

With the publication of the Rural White Paper we were able see just how the ills of the rural were made susceptible to "calculating and normalising intervention" (p 183). For example, one of the noticeable features of the document was its concern with setting and monitoring a range of targets, commitments and service standards: the second chapter set out minimum standards and targets covering access to, and the delivery of, public services in rural areas. This chapter outlined commitments to rural access to services where they are additional to or different from national commitments, or especially significant to people living in rural areas. It also explained how national or local entitlements to services apply in rural areas. In all, the White Paper contained 261 separate commitments, covering funding regimes, pilots, evaluations, annual activity, legislative requirements, consultations, and dissemination of information or best practice. These were accompanied by the setting of 15 'headline' rural indicators, which when taken together were designed to track progress towards achieving the government's 'vision' for rural England as set out in the White Paper.

What is interesting is the fact that, once set, these targets then led to a host of monitoring arrangements, which in turn have fed through to policy delivery. Monitoring progress towards meeting the 15 headline indicators was devolved to the Countryside Agency, which provided a commentary through its annual State of the Countryside report. The 261 commitments in the White Paper were monitored via the White Paper Implementation Plan, which reported three times a year and was first published in March 2001. The Rural Service Standards were monitored annually through the Cabinet Committee on Rural Affairs, in the light of advice from the Countryside Agency and national and regional stakeholder panels.

These targets, indicators and standards represent a further phase in the process of rendering the rural thinkable. Through them, New Labour's rural policy priorities of education, health, employment, crime and public transport were reduced to a set of manageable statistical indices. The core rural service standards, for instance, are set out in Box 3.1.

Two things are immediately noticeable. The first is the range of government departments involved in meeting these targets. In fact none of the standards are the responsibility of the 'rural' ministry, the Department for Environment, Food and Rural Affairs (Defra), and all rely on activity elsewhere in the government. The second noticeable aspect is the link that is drawn between targets and policy delivery. For by publishing the standards in this manner, they will, by definition, skew activity towards outputs that are able to meet the targets. Rose and Miller (1992, p 181) have written that "government is a problematising activity: it poses the obligations of rulers in terms of the problems they seek to address. The ideals of government are intrinsically linked to the problems around which it circulates, the failings it seeks to rectify, the ills it seeks to cure. Indeed, the history of government might well be written as a history of problematisations".

The array of targets, standards and commitments set out in the White Paper, and measured and assessed through subsequent practice, are examples of the way government activity is couched in, and circulates around, particular sets of problems. Once written down and codified, these become the 'rural problems' which policy seeks to address. This is not to deny that the issues covered are not problematical in a very real sense for a great many rural people. It is just to point out that these targets are a selective problematisation of the rural, and that there are other sets of 'ills' and 'failings' – to do perhaps with income levels, or employment rates, or homelessness – which the government has chosen not to codify and rectify in this very direct manner.

Modernising the delivery of rural policy

The White Paper had barely been published when the institutional structure of rural policy was thrown into sharp relief by the outbreak of foot and mouth disease (FMD), which began in February 2001. According to Ward et al (2003, p 205), this outbreak "triggered a crisis not only in the agricultural sector, but also amongst non-agricultural firms in rural areas, especially those dependent upon tourism and passing trade". Some six million animals were slaughtered on almost 14,000 farms, and whole swathes of the countryside were effectively sealed off to prevent spread of the disease. The government's response to the outbreak revealed a signal lack of coordination between government departments and with other rural agencies. In particular, the Ministry of Agriculture, Fisheries and Food (MAFF) worked closely with farming organisations to promote a response based

Box 3.1: The 11 core rural service standards

1) By 2006, all rural LEAs to have at least one full-service-type Extended School offering a core of services, including health and social care, childcare, study support, parenting support, adult education and family learning, ICT access and arts and sports facilities.

2) By March 2006, Sure Start children's centres will be established in the 20% most disadvantaged areas, providing good quality childcare with early education, family and health services and training employment advice, and offering services to at least 650,000 local children and their families.

3) A presumption against closure of rural schools: published guidance requires that the need to preserve access to a local school for rural communities is taken into account in considering closure proposals.

4) Improve the quality of life and independence of vulnerable older people by supporting them to live in their own homes, where possible, by: increasing the proportion of older people being supported to live in their own homes by 1% annually in 2007 and 2008; and increasing by 2008 the proportion of those supported intensively to live at home to 34% of those being supported at home or in residential care.

5) All schools will have broadband connectivity by 2006. (By the end of March 2004, the proportion stood at 60%.)

6) Formal requirement on the Post Office to maintain the rural network of post offices and to prevent any avoidable closures of rural post offices until 2006.

7) By December 2005, all hospital appointments will be booked for the convenience of the patient, making it easier for patients and their GPs to choose the hospital and consultant that best meets their needs. By December 2005, patients will be able to choose from at least four to five different healthcare providers for planned hospital care, paid for by the NHS.

8) All patients, including those living in rural areas, can expect to be offered an appointment to see a primary care professional within 24 hours or a GP within 48 hours.

9) To ensure that everyone who wants it has access to the internet by 2005.

10) Emergency services:

10a) The NHS ambulance service is required to respond to immediately life-threatening calls (Category A) within 8 minutes in 75% of cases, irrespective of location. Other emergency calls that are not immediately life-threatening (Categories B/C) should be responded to 95% of the time within 14 minutes in urban areas and 19 minutes in rural areas.

10b) With the introduction of Integrated Risk Management plans, each fire authority is now responsible for determining: the number of appliances sent to an incident; and target times for attendance. This applies to the whole range of calls to which the Fire and Rescue Service is called and is not limited to their response to fires.

10c) Each police force sets response times locally and has targets that they deem appropriate to reflect the circumstances of their area.

11) A target for the proportion of the rural population living within about 10 minutes' walk of an hourly or better bus service to increase from 37% to 50% by 2010, with an intermediate milestone of 42% by 2004.

Source: Defra, 2004a.

on restricting movement around the countryside. The consequences of this for the rural economy more widely were initially ignored in an effort to protect farming exports (see Woods, 2006). But as the outbreak continued, there was a gradual realisation of its widespread impact. When in March 2001 the government set up a Rural Task Force to advise on how best to limit the damage to the wider economy, it was located in the Department of the Environment, Transport and the Regions (DETR), not in MAFF. The Task Force asked the RDAs to manage a Business Recovery Fund, and when Lord Haskins was asked to report on the mechanisms for promoting rural recovery in the aftermath of FMD, his report recommended that RDAs "should be the catalyst for overseeing and targeting support for all sections of the rural economy" (Haskins, 2001, p 9). Here again we see the intersection of the rural policy and devolution agendas.

Even more importantly in the longer run, FMD also triggered the demise of MAFF. When New Labour won a second general election victory in June 2001, Tony Blair immediately used a wider government reshuffle to abolish MAFF and subsume its responsibilities within a new Department for Environment Food and Rural Affairs (Defra). As Woods (2005, p 157) has noted, "the absence of any explicit reference to agriculture in the title was highly symbolic, signifying that the countryside was to be constructed in new terms". Once more we can interpret this as another stage in the continuing process of rendering the rural thinkable – with even less visibility for agriculture.

Within 18 months of Defra's inception, Margaret Beckett, Secretary of State for Environment, Food and Rural Affairs, invited Lord Haskins to carry out a fundamental review of the arrangements for delivering government rural policies in England. Haskins, a Labour peer with a background in the agri-food business who had previously reported on rural recovery mechanisms after the crisis of FMD, was asked to make recommendations on: simplifying responsibilities for rural delivery; maximising value for money; providing better, more streamlined services and helping to deliver Defra's rural priorities and the Public Service Agreement targets in a cost-effective manner. Although the establishment of the brand new department was used to justify the root and branch review, Haskins' task was given added political impetus by the continuing debates over the (lack of) government response to the impacts of FMD. The White Paper had also contained a commitment that overall progress towards its targets would be reviewed, and Haskins' Rural Delivery Review was designed to run in parallel with the White Paper review (see Defra, 2004b) in order to give an overall picture of progress made and future delivery plans. The Haskins Review examined rural delivery arrangements at national, regional and local levels. As well as focusing on relevant parts of Defra, Lord Haskins and his team (drawn from Defra civil servants) were asked to consider the rural delivery activities of other agencies, including the Countryside Agency, English Nature (in so far as its work related to the delivery of Defra's rural policies), National Park authorities, Areas of Outstanding Natural Beauty teams, RDAs, Government Offices for the Regions, the Forestry Commission, the Small Business Service, British Waterways, and local authorities.

The remit was thus broadly drawn, and not surprisingly the final report was also wide in scope. The Rural Delivery Review report (Haskins, 2003) was published in November 2003 and contained 33 separate recommendations for improving the delivery of rural policies. These were grouped around four main themes:

- Improving accountability through a clearer separation of responsibility for policy and delivery functions.
- Devolving greater power for delivery to regional and local organisations in order to bring delivery closer to the customer.
- Developing a more integrated approach to regulation and service delivery.
- Reporting regularly on the implementation of the recommendations.

Following the report the government established a Modernising Rural Delivery Programme, led by Defra, in order to set out a framework for the new rural delivery landscape. This included a review of rural funding streams. The new framework was published in the government's 2004 Rural Strategy (Defra, 2004c), which identified key priorities for rural policy over three to five years and set out the specific actions in support of these.

The Rural Strategy contained three priorities for rural policy:

- Economic and Social Regeneration – supporting enterprise across rural England, but targeting greater resources at areas of greatest need.
- Social Justice for All – tackling rural social exclusion wherever it occurs and providing fair access to services and opportunities for all rural people.
- Enhancing the Value of our Countryside – protecting the natural environment for this and future generations.

In pursuit of these priorities, and building on the Haskins report, the 2004 Rural Strategy promised to modernise delivery arrangements in order to:

- Rationalise funding programmes and provide more professional and streamlined support for rural people, targeted on their needs.
- Devolve decision-making and delivery closer to the community, and ensure clear responsibility and accountability for policy and delivery.
- Achieve more coherent and effective environmental outcomes through organisational streamlining.

If we look at the Rural Delivery Review and the Rural Strategy together, what stands out is a growing concern with what we might describe as the mechanics and technologies of rural governance at the expense of policy content. In other words there is a focus on the 'how' rather than the 'what' of rural policy, encompassing a further engagement with targets, monitoring, reporting, rationalising, integrating, devolving and streamlining.

Indeed the major policy shifts are themselves signalled by organisational change, for at the heart of this 'modernisation' was the intention to establish a new 'integrated agency' to deliver the environmental, landscape and recreation aspects of rural policy. Natural England, which was formally established in October 2006, brings together English Nature, the Landscape, Access and Recreation division of the Countryside Agency and most of the Rural Development Service (responsible for the agri-environmental aspects of the European Rural Development Programme funded by the EU). Natural England acts as a single independent statutory organisation, covering the policy areas of resource management, nature conservation, biodiversity, landscape, access and recreation, and is planned to have some 2,300 staff, in national, regional and local teams. In many ways this fulfils one of the aims of the Rural Delivery Review in providing a more integrated approach, but this is limited to an environmental remit.

The social aspects of rural policy have come out of the delivery review less well, and indeed the Countryside Agency – only founded in 1999 – has been dismantled. Its social and community remit has now passed to the Commission for Rural Communities (CRC) established in 2005. The aim of the Commission is to act as rural advocate, adviser and watchdog – freed from the delivery functions of the former Countryside Agency, which have been transferred to Natural England and the RDAs. The former Prime Minister Tony Blair emphasised that the role of the CRC "is to champion and mainstream the concerns and interests of rural communities, particularly, but not solely, with central and local government" (CRC, no date). Interestingly, in the same letter of support, Mr Blair reaffirmed New Labour's stance that "the overall challenges facing our urban and rural communities are, for the most part, very similar".

This view of the similarities facing urban and rural communities partly explains the decisions taken in the Rural Strategy with respect to the economic aspects of rural policy. Responsibility for these has been transferred to regional and local delivery bodies, in particular the RDAs and the Government Offices for the Regions (GOs). At the time of writing in 2007 the RDAs have been given an extra £21 million in funding from Defra, and Defra's contribution to the RDAs' 'Single Pot' of funding now totals £72 million. An extra £2 million has also been given to Business Links for rural areas to help provide business advice. RDAs have also been given control over the socioeconomic elements of the European Rural Development Programme (ERDP). The eight GOs have been given lead responsibility for brokering a regional level rural delivery framework through a new Regional Rural Priorities Board that will prioritise and pull together existing plans and actions. Regional Rural Affairs Forums will be 'refreshed' to ensure local voices are heard in these new frameworks, and the chairs of these forums are also expected to meet quarterly with the Rural Minister and with the CRC's new rural advocate.

One final aspect of Defra's Rural Strategy concerns the continued devolution agenda, this time at the local level. A series of eight local authority-led 'pathfinder projects' have been set up across rural England, one in each RDA area in order to experiment with, and test, ways of achieving more joined-up delivery of rural services at the local level, stressing the prioritisation of resources, innovation and best practice. The overall aim is to mainstream best practice in order to inform the development of the Regional Rural Delivery Frameworks. Each pathfinder has been given a grant of £100,000 to support its work.

Taken as a whole, the Modernising Rural Delivery Agenda has transformed the structure of rural policy making in England. New institutions have been established, others have been dismantled, and the regional scale is becoming increasingly significant for rural policy formulation and delivery. In less than a decade New Labour has completely transformed the institutional landscape of rural policy in England. It has also rendered the rural thinkable in entirely new terms. However, its broader devolution agenda has opened up the possibility for other parts of the UK to pursue different trajectories and it is to these that we now turn.

Devolution and rural policy beyond England

New Labour came to power in 1997 accompanied by manifesto commitments which promised devolution for Northern Ireland, Scotland and Wales. The programme of devolution that gained legislative support over the next two years has been labelled as "one of the most significant features" of New Labour's first term in office (Driver and Martell, 2002, p 54). Essentially, under the devolution programme (enshrined in separate Acts for Scotland, Wales and Northern Ireland), the government set down the powers which were 'reserved' for the Westminster Parliament to take decisions on, including matters of defence, international relations, fiscal and monetary policy, immigration and social security. Other matters were then devolved to a new Parliament in Scotland, and to Assemblies in Wales and Northern Ireland, which were established in 1999, following positive referenda in 1997. Rural policy was one of the areas for which responsibility was devolved, along with matters such as health, housing, planning, transport, economic development, sport and the arts (see Keating, 2002, for details). This laid the basis for separate trajectories of rural policy in each of the UK's devolved territories.

The devolved administrations wasted little time in putting in place new institutional and political structures. All three set up new government departments to develop and oversee rural policy, headed by ministers and scrutinised and advised by formal parliamentary and assembly committees. In Northern Ireland and Wales Departments of Agriculture and Rural Development were established, whilst Scotland set up a Department of Rural Affairs. While these all located agriculture and broader rural development issues within the same department, the rural policy networks and wider political cultures of each country ensured that agriculture became the main focus of rural policy in each of the devolved administrations. Indeed, Woods (2005, p 145) points out that agriculture was the single most debated item within the Welsh Assembly during its first year in office. The context for such debates was often provided by a discursive manoeuvre that equated the agricultural recession of the time with a 'rural crisis' and then with a 'national crisis'. Thus the Welsh Assembly's first major policy paper on rural issues (*Farming for the future*) stated that "the family farm defines the character of Welsh rural society and its sense of identity" (National Assembly for Wales, 2001, p 7), despite the fact, as Woods notes, that the farm population "constitutes less than 10 per cent of the Welsh rural population" (2006, p 146). Even before the outbreak of FMD in 2001, Woods claims that rural Wales "had already been constructed as a 'space in crisis'" (2005, p 145). The power of the farming networks and agricultural lobbying groups meant that the incoming Labour administration was unable to present an alternative representation of rural Wales. In this instance, rural Wales had been 'rendered thinkable' as a policy space largely through the lens of an agriculturally derived rural crisis. A policy focus on farming was legitimised as a result. The types of representational shifts described earlier that were occurring in England could not be performed in Wales due to the "deep-seated cultural association between farming, rurality and national identity" (Woods, 2006, p 146), and the rural was problematised in a different form.

A similar situation held in Northern Ireland, only here the cultural and political dominance of agriculture was overlain by the special features of sectarian politics. Ellis and Neill (2006, p 133) note that in relation to rural development, "fundamental issues related to sustainability, service efficiency and economic development performance are suppressed for fear of exposing tender questions of ethnic geography". Both Unionist and Nationalist parties are reluctant to challenge the agricultural dominance of the rural agenda "because Northern Irish rural society continues to be a repository of political power and moreover cultural imagination for both sides of the sectarian divide" (Ellis and Neill, 2006, p 132). A confirmation of the political importance of this imagination came when Ian Paisley, then outspoken leader of the Democratic Unionist Party, took up the chair of the Assembly's Agriculture and Rural Development Committee himself.

In Scotland, the situation is slightly different in that wider rural development and social justice issues have been able to be inserted into the rural policy agenda, especially around land reform, but Keating and Stevenson (2006, p 401) argue that although "there has been some progress in extending the rural policy community beyond farming ... change is limited and gradual". A discussion paper *Rural Scotland: A new approach* (Scottish Executive, 2000) was issued at the same time as the White Paper in England, but this has been described as "shorter, more reflective and less conclusive" (Keating and Stevenson, 2006, p 402). In many ways this was the start of a process of thinking about rurality, and an emphasis was placed on social inclusion as well as on economic development. Unlike England, there were no service delivery targets, and the paper emphasised that agriculture remained at the core of the rural economy.

The 2003 elections to the devolved administrations in Scotland and Wales opened up some political space for institutional change. Although this was not an option in Northern Ireland, where the breakdown of the Belfast Agreement had caused the Assembly to be suspended in October 2002, similar reforms were carried out in the other two territories. In Scotland, the political and administrative structures were reformed by placing the environment portfolio from the former Department of Transport and Environment together with the Department of Rural Affairs to form a new Scottish Executive Environment and Rural Affairs Department (SEERAD). In Wales, the reform of the Assembly's structures resulted in a new Environment, Planning and Countryside Department. Despite these institutional changes, the agricultural focus remains. Keating and Stevenson claim that "farming groups still enjoy the strongest position within the SEERAD networks" resulting in "a strong emphasis on keeping agriculture going" (2006, p 406). Scotland has not had the FMD-inspired 'rural crisis' that triggered the overhaul of English rural policy making, whereas in Wales the power of the agricultural groups ensured that responses to the outbreak were centred on the needs of farmers. Woods concludes that following the 2003 elections the Labour government in Wales "has further marginalised rural social issues, with many Labour Assembly members unconvinced that the problems of rural Wales are as pressing as the clear and visible deprivation of the Valleys communities" (2006, p 146).

Concluding comments: on constructing rural policy in a devolved environment

What we witness in this unfolding process of institutional reform is the constant intersection between New Labour's devolution agenda and the shifting concerns of rural policy. Devolution has opened up new political spaces where these concerns can be played out differently in different parts of the UK, and it has also allowed the creation of new organisations which are able to act over new territories and at new scales. This in turn means that a new array of political actors and social groups are able to gain access to the rural policy agenda, adding further layers of complexity. The end result is that there are now well over 20 key spaces where rural policy is derived and implemented – if we include England as a whole: the eight RDAs and Government Office for the Regions, the devolved administrations and national level organisations such as Natural England and the Commission for Rural Communities.

A key point, as we have seen, is that the rural is rendered thinkable in different ways in each of these different policy spaces. To a certain extent the eight sets of regional institutions in England work within centrally prescribed frameworks, but even here we can discern differences in the way the 'rural' is problematised and treated. As a result some parts of the UK are addressing rural concerns through a continued emphasis on agriculture and farming, while others are prioritising regional linkages with urban areas. New Labour has developed a set of institutional structures that are capable of producing different policy trajectories across the UK. This may not necessarily matter, and indeed the Labour Party has always defended its devolution agenda on the grounds that distinctive parts of the UK should be able to pursue the policies that they feel are best suited to local circumstances. However, this does mean that we have an institutional structure that promotes very different understandings of the rural and of rural policy. Woods has recently called for progressive forces to "articulate a clear vision of the countryside ... that can unite rather than divide in setting out a programme for rural governance in the twenty-first century" (2006, p 165). In many respects the devolved institutional structures which are able to respond to an increasingly "differentiated countryside" (Murdoch et al, 2003) make it that much harder to articulate a clear and unified vision for rural governance and policy delivery.

References

Commission for Rural Communities (no date) 'Message of Support from the Prime Minister' (Available at www.ruralcommunities.gov.uk/content/messageofsupportfromtheprimeminister)

Defra (Department for Environment, Food and Rural Affairs) (2004a) *Rural service review: Reviewing standards, 2004*, London: Defra. (Available at www.defra.gov.uk/rural/pdfs/services/rural_services_review.pdf)

Defra (2004b) *Review of the Rural White Paper, Our countryside: the future*, London: Defra.

Defra (2004c) *Rural strategy*, London: Defra. (Also available at www.defra.gov.uk/rural/pdfs/strategy/rural_strategy_2004.pdf)

DETR (Department of the Environment, Transport and the Regions) (1997) *Building partnerships for prosperity: Sustainable growth, competitiveness and employment in the English regions*, Cm 3814, London: HMSO.

DETR/MAFF (Department of the Environment, Transport and the Regions/Ministry of Agriculture, Fisheries and Food) (2000) *Our countryside: The future – a fair deal for rural England* (the Rural White Paper), Cm 4909, London: The Stationery Office.

Driver L. and Martell S. (2002) *Blair's Britain*, Cambridge: Polity.

Ellis, G. and Neill, W. (2006) 'Spatial governance in contested territory: the case of Northern/North of Ireland', in M. Tewdwr-Jones and P. Allmendinger (eds) *Territory, identity and spatial planning*, London: Routledge, pp 123-38.

Haskins, C. (2001) *Rural recovery after foot and mouth disease*, London: Defra.

Haskins, C. (2003) *Rural delivery review: A report on the delivery of government policies in rural England*, London: Defra. (Also available at www.defra.gov.uk/rural/pdfs/ruraldelivery/haskins_full_report.pdf)

Jones, R., Goodwin, M., Jones, M. and Simpson, G. (2004) 'Devolution, state personnel and the production of new territories of governance in the United Kingdom', *Environment and Planning A*, vol 36, pp 89-109.

Keating, M. (2002) 'Devolution and public policy in the United Kingdom: divergence or convergence?' in J. Adams and P. Robinson (eds) *Devolution in practice: Public policy difference in the UK*, London: IPPR/ESRC, pp 3-21.

Keating, M. and Stevenson, L. (2006) 'Rural policy in Scotland after devolution', *Regional Studies*, vol 40, no 3, pp 397-407.

Murdoch, J., Lowe, P., Ward, N. and Marsden, T. (2003) *The differentiated countryside*, London: Routledge.

National Assembly for Wales (2001) *Farming for the future*, Cardiff: National Assembly for Wales.

Peck, J. (2001) 'Neoliberalizing states: thin policies/hard outcomes', *Progress in Human Geography*, vol 25, pp 445-55.

PIU (Performance and Innovation Unit of the Cabinet Office) (1999) *Rural economies*, London: The Stationery Office. (Also available at www.cabinetoffice. gov.uk/strategy/work_areas/rural_economies.aspx)

RGLMP (Rural Group of Labour MPs) (1999) *Rural audit: A health check on rural Britain*, London: RGLMP.

Rogers, A. (1999) *The most revolutionary measure: A history of the Rural Development Commission 1909-1999*, London, Rural Development Commission.

Rose, N. and Miller, P. (1992) 'Political power beyond the state: problematics of government', *British Journal of Sociology*, vol 43, no 2, pp 172-205.

Scottish Executive (2000) *Rural Scotland: a new approach*, Edinburgh: Scottish Executive.

Ward, N., Lowe, P. and Bridges, T. (2003) 'Rural and regional development: the role of regional development agencies in England', *Regional Studies*, vol 37, no 2, pp 201-14.

Woods, M. (2005) *Contesting rurality: Politics in the British countryside*, Aldershot: Ashgate.

Woods, M. (2006) 'Rural politics and governance', in J. Midgley (ed) *A new rural agenda*, Newcastle: IPPR North, pp 140-68.

FOUR

New Labour's countryside in international perspective

Mark Shucksmith

Introduction

In international perspective, rural Britain appears something of a paradox: Britain's rural areas differ in many respects from those of other countries, and yet they are strongly subject to similar international forces and influences, notably from the EU. The New Labour project itself was born partly out of an international perspective. Giddens (2002) sees its origins in Labour's recognition of the need to rethink leftist doctrines in the light of the big changes happening in the world – globalisation, the emergence of the knowledge economy, the rise of individualism and 'postmaterialist' concerns, the 'dysfunctions' of the welfare state, and the emergence of new risks such as climate change – as well as the electoral need to reach beyond working-class votes.

When the Labour government came to power in 1997, ministers and policy advisers had had a long period in opposition to consider this changing international context, as well as approaches to social and economic policy in other countries and their relevance to Britain. While Bill Clinton's 'New Democrats' offered models for welfare reform and 'third way' thinking, European social democracies struggled to sustain strong welfare states in the face of rising unemployment, prompting new discourses of 'social exclusion'. Once the New Labour approach was in place, its architects sought to reassert Britain's international influence by promoting their 'modernising' and 'third way' approaches through supra-national forums, such as the European Union, G8, the Organisation for Economic Co-operation and Development (OECD) and the World Trade Organization. This has included New Labour's proposals for agricultural and rural policies.

Critics of New Labour have presented their 'third way' as essentially vacuous, "an escape from self-definition – a butterfly always on the wing" (Toynbee, 2001). But the broad lines and intellectual underpinnings of New Labour's thinking were set out in the 1994 Report of the Commission on Social Justice (Borrie, 1994), established by John Smith under the auspices of the Institute of Public Policy Research (IPPR) think tank[1] and described by Tony Blair as "essential reading for everyone who wants a new way forward for our country". Not only did the state have to change because the world had changed, as Giddens argues, but policy renewal would itself change Britain's place in the world (Borrie, 1994, p 91).

The report argued that policy needed to engage with worldwide economic, social and political revolutions that faced all advanced industrialised countries. There could be, it said, no return to the post-war consensus whose foundations had been destroyed by national and international change, notably the collapse of the Bretton Woods system, the rise of the Organization of Petroleum Exporting Countries (OPEC), rising unemployment and inflation, the weakening of the nuclear family and the curtailing of the autonomous powers of the nation state.

The economic revolution was seen as "a global revolution of finance, competition, skill and technology in which the UK is being left behind" (Borrie, 1994, p 64). Economic globalisation had curtailed the power of individual nation states, shown most starkly on 'Black Wednesday' when the Conservative government was forced by currency speculation to leave the European exchange rate mechanism. Part of the remedy was increased international cooperation. Moreover, global economic competition demanded more innovation, higher productivity, higher skills and investment in human, social and physical capital if the UK was to maintain or improve its standard of living. The state should invest and enable, but could only seek to regulate through international action.

The social revolution was seen as "a revolution of women's life-chances, of family structures and of demography" (Borrie, 1994, p 77). A shrinking proportion of the population now lives in a traditional nuclear family, society is ageing and more multicultural, women are increasingly engaged in more flexible labour markets, and redundancy from old traditional industries has impacted especially on older men. While many of the changes in society were welcomed, the main concern was growing social exclusion, still predominantly class-based but also related to gender, race and disability. The remedy would be to build an inclusive society, "where rights carry responsibilities, and individuals have the chance to realise their potential" (p 3).

The political revolution was seen as "a challenge to old assumptions of Parliamentary sovereignty, and to the growing centralisation of government power" (Borrie, 1994, p 84). In a "double-shift", the national arena in advanced industrial societies had become "too small for the large problems and too large for the small problems" (p 87). Government should be "decentralised and democratised" (p 3), in more participative ways, so that people could have more say about the things that are important in their lives. This would constitute a fundamental reorientation of the relationship between those who govern and those who are governed – 'better government' not 'less government'. In essence, government should use its power to devolve responsibility to individuals and communities, as well as playing a more positive and active role in the EU.

The authors of the report took pains to distance themselves from neoliberalism, which had swept across North America, much of Europe, Australia and New Zealand, rejecting this as misconceived and "even worse than the disease" (Borrie, 1994, p 12). Instead they sought to build the New Labour project on explicit values of social justice. These were listed as: the equal worth of all citizens; their equal right to be able to meet their basic needs; the need to spread opportunities and life-chances as widely as possible; and where possible to eliminate unjustified inequalities. "Social justice stands against fanatics of the free market economy; but it also demands and promotes economic success. The two go together" (p 1) . This was the basis of third way thinking.

This chapter considers how these international perspectives have been reflected in New Labour's policies as they have affected the British countryside. The chapter is broadly structured around the themes of the three revolutions – economic, social and political – identified in 1994 by the Commission on Social Justice.

International economic change and the British countryside

Much recent writing in rural sociology has employed the concepts of 'late modernity' (Giddens, 1991) and 'risk society' (Beck, 1992) to help understand the complex and less certain world in which we live at the start of the 21st century. Giddens has identified particular features of modernity which have fostered an international division of labour within a global system of nation states operating in a world capitalist economy, including time–space distantiation; the disembedding of social relations out of local contexts of interaction, notably through trust in money and expertise; and reflexivity – examining, questioning and reviewing one's behaviour. These forces have transformed rural and urban areas alike, through the pace, totality and interconnectivity of change (Woods, 2005).

Much has been written about the globalisation of production, the move towards flexible specialisation and a global division of tasks across huge distances. A core of workers is highly paid, while others (often in other countries) are made 'flexible' through low wages, insecure contracts and casualisation. The key orientation is towards flexibility and the production of tailored, specialised products using 'just-in-time' production systems. For any given locality in late modernity (rural or urban), future prosperity may be profoundly affected by the manner in which global capital seeks to exploit local resources such as land and labour, unless local capital itself is able to underpin development. Rural areas characterised by low wages, a compliant, non-unionised workforce, and lower levels of regulation, may be particularly prone to exploitation by international capital, leading to increased dependency and peripherality. On the other hand, rural areas with highly educated and skilled populations, strong institutions and social capital may be sites of innovation, prosperity and security. In the US, Richard Florida (2002) has shown that some areas may attract a 'creative class' whose presence then underpins these fortunate areas' economic performance: there is some evidence that accessible rural areas of England might be characterised in this way (Hepworth, 2006). Another scenario is that local, rather than global, capital may underpin successful local economies, seeking to develop products which depend upon a local identity for their market niche, so 'selling the local to the global'.

Woods (2005, p 33) has stated that "globalisation is therefore, in essence, about power – about the lack of power of rural regions to control their own futures, and about the increasing subjection of rural regions to networks and processes of power that are produced, reproduced and executed on a global scale". However, as Woods also recognises, people and policy-makers in rural areas are not entirely passive in the face of global forces, with many opportunities to resist and negotiate these forces, so seeking to exert agency and remain competitive in a globalised world.

This emphasis on global competitiveness in a world where localities are increasingly interconnected and interdependent is the main thrust of the EU's Lisbon Strategy and of the UK government's economic policies, as was explicitly stated in a European Commission report (CEC, 2004, p 2): "The whole of the Union faces challenges arising from a likely acceleration in economic restructuring as a result of globalisation, trade opening, the technological revolution, the development of the knowledge economy and society, an ageing population and a growth in immigration."

The Lisbon Strategy accordingly sets out the EU's aspiration to become the most competitive and dynamic knowledge-based economy, capable of sustainable economic growth with more and better jobs and greater social cohesion. These priorities have been restated on many occasions by the UK Chancellor of the Exchequer. But how does this translate into rural policy, especially in the UK?

Agriculture is still the main object of EU and UK rural policy, dominating both the EU's overall budget and the economic development spending of UK administrations. For example, in the West Midlands region single farm payments to farmers exceed the total budget of the Regional Development Agency for rural and urban areas combined (Pearce et al, 2005). Yet there is now widespread agreement that this spending contributes little towards the Lisbon Strategy's aspiration of competitive and knowledge-based rural economies. A recent report by the European Court of Auditors (2006) concluded that the EU's rural development policy is an ineffective means of supporting rural economies, because the Commission places too much emphasis on agriculture and member states pay too little attention to the specific characteristics of rural areas. Lowe (2006) has argued that while agri-environment payments to farmers may help to provide the broader conditions for sustainable rural development, by maintaining a region's landscape and habitats, they do not directly promote the economic competitiveness of rural areas. This is because, as the OECD (2006) puts it in its report calling for "a new rural paradigm", these and other payments under the Common Agricultural Policy (CAP) are predominantly *subsidies* rather than investments, and they are *sectoral* rather than territorial in their nature. As Lowe (2006) observed, "If the goal is to widen the base and vitality of the economies of rural areas, it is surely important that the crucial, consistent and largely non-agricultural drivers that are revitalising rural economies are supported" (p 42).

For a brief period, from 1997 to 2000, it appeared that New Labour would promote just such a redirection of rural policy away from subsidies to farmers and landowners and towards promoting the global economic competitiveness of rural areas. This period saw, for example, a Cabinet Office Performance and Innovation Unit (PIU) report on rural economies which proposed a reorientation of policy away from farming, and the decision to apply voluntary modulation from direct payments to farmers in favour of rural development spending (PIU, 1999). Sadly, as Ward observed (2006, p 49), "December 2000 was probably the high point of this more reformist, territorial approach to agriculture and rural development. Two months later, in early 2001, Foot and Mouth Disease (FMD) struck, and there has been a retrenchment into a more sectoral approach to agriculture since then". This change in approach was somewhat paradoxical, since the FMD crisis had revealed just how much more important other sectors of rural economies are than agriculture.

Expectations of a more territorial approach were raised by the replacement of the Ministry of Agriculture, Fisheries and Food (MAFF) by a new ministry, the Department for Environment, Food and Rural Affairs (Defra), which omitted the words 'farming' or 'agriculture' from its title. Furthermore, the Curry Commission on the Future of Farming and Food recommended radical reforms to connect farmers once again to markets and consumers, precisely so that they could adjust to global competition, and it recommended even higher (20%) levels of voluntary modulation. However, another report established in the wake of FMD, the Haskins Report on the delivery of rural policy, took quite a different tack, reflecting Haskins' own background in agri-business. He proposed reorganising the institutional structure surrounding rural policy in England to suit the *customer* (that is, farmers), rather than the *citizens* of rural areas and their economic and social welfare (Haskins, 2003). His recommendations reoriented the direction of English rural policy towards agricultural retrenchment and natural environments, partly because rural policy was driven overwhelmingly by the EU Council of Ministers, where agricultural interests dominate, and partly because (against all expectations) rural policy became the poor relation within Defra itself, as environmental issues interested ministers more. The IPPR (Midgley, 2006) estimated that Defra planned to spend no more than 3% of its total budget on rural policy in 2007–08, and it is many years since a Secretary of State made a speech on rural policy.

A further factor is the model which New Labour has of urban–rural relationships, which underlies much of their 'city-regions' policy (and also the European Spatial Development Perspective, it should be noted). This, in essence, views urban centres as the nodes of growth – the locomotives of economic competitiveness pulling the rural 'carriages' passively along behind them; rural areas are viewed primarily as pastoral backwaters whose function is to look attractive, for recreation (of many) and perhaps for residence (of a few), but which will benefit from adjacent urban vitality. As Ward (2006) has argued, such a view of rural areas as passive beneficiaries of urban-focused strategies "assumes that rural areas will benefit from overall regional growth, and that any interventions focused on city-regions will bring trickle-out benefits to wider rural areas" (p 52). Empirical research does not tend to support this view. First, such evidence as there is suggests that trickle-out does not work and, on the contrary, that urban centres gain from such policies at the expense of rural hinterlands (Cloke, 1979). Second, there is plenty of evidence that rural areas are just as likely as urban areas to be sites of autonomous growth – the State of the Cities Report, for example, showed faster rates of economic growth in rural localities than urban nodes, and the European Commission and the OECD have both noted that many rural areas are growing through the developed world (CEC, 1988; OECD, 2006).

If, instead, one views "rural areas and their assets as active contributors to the development of cities, city-regions and even national territories" (Ward, 2006, p 52), then the issue becomes how to promote growth in rural areas. In the Highlands and Islands of Scotland, for example, Highlands and Islands Enterprise (HIE, 2005, p 2) recognised the "huge economic, political, environmental and technological changes" sweeping across the globe, and has devised a strategy for a "smart, successful Highlands and Islands" to meet this challenge and seize the new opportunities created. Broadly the HIE strategy seeks to change gear to a higher-value economy, attracting substantial numbers of skilled migrants to the region (particularly from the new member states of the EU) – taking the population from 300,000 in 1971 to a target of half a million – and pursuing an ecological modernisation approach to build on the region's natural and cultural assets. Key elements are investment in science and technology, and seeking University status for the region's higher education institutions. Furthermore, investment is not to be focused on Inverness, but rather "the HIE Network operates on the principle of balanced development across the entire Highlands and Islands" (p 24) including the smallest communities. The general acceptance that "encouraging more people to live, work and study in the Highlands will improve prosperity and quality of life for everyone" (p 6) contrasts starkly with the anti-growth views expressed by residents of much of rural England.

The question of how to promote growth in rural areas has been the subject of a recent study, the Dynamics of Rural Areas (DORA), which explored the factors underlying the differential economic performance of rural areas across Europe (Bryden and Hart, 2004). The study essentially compared eight matched pairs of study areas in Scotland, Sweden, Germany and Greece, focusing both on tangible and less tangible factors. Six main themes were found to underlie differences in economic performance: cultural traditions and social arrangements; peripherality and infrastructure; governance, institutions and public investment; entrepreneurship; economic structures and organisation; and human resources and demography. Similar conclusions were reached in the RUREMPLO project (Terluin and Post, 2000; Terluin, 2003).

The principal conclusion is that successful local responses to globalisation derive essentially from cultural and social factors, although these can be encouraged/discouraged by styles of governance, institutional arrangements and forms of organisation that encourage or undermine self-determination, independence and local identity. Policy should focus on the improvement of governance and economic structures, and facilitating community and individual action. More specifically, as Bryden and Hart have stated:

> local enterprise can be stimulated by:
>
> * Widespread or community ownership of land and housing;
> * Good local institutional autonomy and governance;
> * Investment in appropriate public goods;
> * Strong local identity and market positioning;
> * Good education, health and other service provision and access; and
> * Cultural and environmental attributes and a 'can do' entrepreneurial approach. (Bryden and Hart, 2004).

These are the very arguments now embraced and proposed by the OECD's Territorial Development Working Group in their report *The new rural paradigm* (OECD, 2006). In Britain, within the constraints of the EU's CAP (Shucksmith et al, 2005), it seems that these ideas have been adopted enthusiastically in the Highlands and Islands of Scotland, but in England a short-lived tendency in this direction has been fought off by agricultural interests in the wake of FMD. So far as broader competitiveness is pursued in rural England, this is now the responsibility of the Regional Development Agencies (RDAs), most of which have a primary orientation towards urban regeneration. As a result it appears that rural policy in most of Britain remains little informed by the UK government's economic policies or the EU's Lisbon Strategy – as is also the case for rural policies in Europe. For this to change requires not only a reorientation of rural economic policy within Britain, challenging vested interests, but also more effective engagement at supra-national level in decisions about the reform of the CAP, the EU's broader spending priorities and world trade.

International social change and the British countryside

One of the principal themes of the New Labour government since 1997 has been 'welfare reform', and this has been energetically pursued, by Chancellor Gordon Brown in particular, drawing variously on European, Scandinavian and US influences. This range of influences might be thought curious, since each may appear to derive from different models of the welfare state, but Giddens (1998) argues that this in fact is the whole point of the 'third way'.

International studies of social welfare policy have tended to follow Esping-Andersen (1991) in identifying three ideal types of welfare state regime in advanced capitalist societies, each related to the historical development of those societies. The 'liberal' welfare state regimes of the US, Canada and Australia emphasise the market rather than social solidarity, with modest means-tested assistance, strict entitlement rules and few universal benefits. The welfare state essentially provides a safety net for the poorest members of society, but benefits are limited so as to avoid disincentives to work which might interfere with the assumed efficiency of markets. Levels of inequality are high. A second 'corporatist' or 'conservative' model, deriving from the Church, typifies several continental European countries, including Germany, France, Italy and the Netherlands. This emphasises traditional family values, rather than markets, and so offers weak social services but well-resourced benefits in other respects, financed from social insurance contributions and employment. Third, there is the 'social democratic' model, typified by Sweden, Denmark and Norway, which emphasises social solidarity and a paternalistic, pervasive role for the state, taking care of its citizens 'from cradle to grave'. This is characterised by universal benefits, high rates of taxation and low levels of inequality. Britain is seen by Esping-Anderson, and by others, as having shifted from a social democratic model in the immediate post-war years towards a position intermediate between liberal and corporatist models by the 1990s, reflecting the 'dry' (neoliberal) and 'wet' (conservative) wings of Conservative Party thinking.

When New Labour came to power in 1997, key influences were the 'welfare to work' and neighbourhood renewal policies introduced by the Clinton administration, the French discourse of 'social exclusion' which had become dominant through the EU during the 1990s, and the adjustments being made to welfare state regimes by the Scandinavian social democracies in the face of global economic change.

In 1996 the Clinton administration introduced policies which emphasised work as the solution to persistent poverty, on the one hand placing time-limits on families receiving welfare benefits while on the other offering a variety of state programmes to assist individuals back into employment. On the surface the UK's welfare reforms may appear to be similar, viewing work as the best form of welfare, but underneath the surface they were premised on a different concept of the underlying problem and on a continuing commitment to a strong welfare state.

The underlying problem was viewed in terms of 'social exclusion' – an analysis which primarily adopts systemic explanations rather than placing the blame on individuals themselves for their poverty. To help fulfil his promise that there would be "no forgotten people and no no-hope areas" (Toynbee and Walker, 2001, p 10), Tony Blair established a Social Exclusion Unit which produced a series of high-quality reports on truancy, school exclusion, rough sleepers, teenage pregnancy, children leaving care, problem housing estates and other issues which led in turn to a suite of area-based initiatives for neighbourhood renewal. A series of New Deal programmes was also launched to help specific vulnerable groups into work, beginning with young people (NDYP), and including lone parents, disabled people, older people over 50, and other target groups. Pre-school education and the Sure Start programme were introduced as early interventions which would reduce inherited inequalities. Meanwhile Chancellor Gordon Brown developed a series of modifications to tax and benefit policies, designed systematically to offer greater incentives to move into employment while at the same time targeting benefits more effectively, notably through the generously funded Working Families Tax Credit. A National Minimum Wage, already adopted by all other EU member states, was introduced in 1999. The Child Tax Credit and Working Tax Credit were introduced in 2003, effectively offering a Minimum Income Guarantee, which lifted many children and pensioners out of poverty. But perhaps most importantly these measures have all been accompanied by strong and continuous economic growth, reducing the level of unemployment substantially while also providing the growth in tax revenues needed to finance them.

These policies have had significant impacts in rural areas of the UK, as in urban areas, although no formal studies have been undertaken of their rural incidence and it is not clear to what degree they have been 'rural-proofed'. The National Minimum Wage, for example, has increased the wages of around 6%-7% of the lowest-paid workers (Social Exclusion Unit, 2004) and is thought to have prevented wages being depressed by in-migration from the new member states of the EU. Research undertaken prior to its introduction (Gilbert et al, 2001), using the British Household Panel Survey, anticipated its potential impacts would be greatest in remote rural areas, but no evaluations have been undertaken of its actual impact in rural areas. Shucksmith (2000b) reviewed evidence that the New Deal faced particular obstacles and challenges in rural areas, notably arising from the small size of rural firms, the distances involved, and the low levels of skills required. There are also challenges in delivering personal counselling (the gateway to the New Deal) in some rural areas.

Similarly, the reforms to benefits and tax credits have had a marked impact, reducing the proportion of pensioner households in poverty from 29% in 1996/97 to 17% in 2005/06, and the rate of child poverty from 34% to 30% (DWP, 2007). The government has recently published a rural/urban breakdown of its estimates of changes in pensioner poverty and child poverty from 1996-97 to 2004-05, drawn from the Family Resources Survey for district council areas.[2] In the most rural districts (R80) child poverty (after housing costs) has fallen from 26% to 22%, and in other rural districts (R50) from 25% to 20%. The decline in poverty among pensioner households is even greater, in the most rural districts (R80) from 27% to 21%, and in other rural districts (R50) from 26% to 18%. Against the trends of rising child and pensioner poverty pre-1997, these are considerable achievements. In neither case, however, has there been any formal evaluation of the impact of the policy reforms on rural households.

One other important social change has been proceeding in the British countryside. Between 1991 and 2001 there was an average annual net migration of 30,000 people into rural areas, consisting of 420,000 people moving into rural areas and 390,000 moving in the other direction each year. As a result, the population of rural England grew by 14.4% between 1981 and 2003, while urban areas grew only by 1.9% over the same period. It can readily be seen that England's rural areas are generally areas of high demand for houses, and unusually in international terms a house in the country denotes higher social status and is something to which most people aspire. Those able to realise their aspiration of moving into rural England tend to be older and wealthier owner-occupiers (notably the professional and managerial classes), while those moving to urban areas by choice or necessity tend to be younger and poorer, containing a disproportionate number from the skilled and unskilled working classes. Housing market processes are heavily implicated in this selective migration (Shucksmith, 1990, 2000; CRC, 2006a, 2006b).

This strong demand for rural living interacts with planning policies intended to prevent house-building and other development in the countryside, so restricting the supply of houses in rural areas and forcing rural house prices ever higher. Probably uniquely in international terms, the average price of a house in rural England is substantially higher than that in urban areas. Research undertaken for the CRC (Roger Tym and Partners, 2006) indicated that across all rural England (settlements below 10,000 population) only 55% of newly forming households projected over the next five years would be able to afford a house in their own ward, leaving an affordable housing need of 22,800 homes per annum, on top of a backlog of a further 40,000 houses already required to meet existing needs. In the South East, South West and East regions of England the proportion unable to find market solutions to their housing need is expected to be nearer 70%. Research for Defra (ARHC, 2006) shows that average rural earnings of £17,400 would be sufficient to fund the purchase of a home in only 28% of rural wards, compared with 53% of urban wards.

Meanwhile the supply of social rented housing is focused on larger, urban settlements, further narrowing opportunities and life-chances in smaller rural settlements. Only around 10% of the housing stock in villages, and 5% in smaller settlements, is in social rented tenure. The opportunities for people on lower and middle incomes to find affordable housing in rural communities are therefore few and far between. This is not only an issue of social injustice (inequality of opportunity) and social exclusion, but has the consequence of spatial exclusion of poorer and middle income groups from rural communities as these become exclusively colonised by higher income groups (Shucksmith, 2000a, 2000b; Best and Shucksmith, 2006). It is this which led the government to establish an Affordable Rural Housing Commission (ARHC, 2006) to recommend practical solutions for meeting affordable housing needs in rural areas, in the context of sustainable rural communities. At the time of writing, two years after the ARHC delivered its report, the government has responded to several of that report's recommendations but investment still appears too small and planning policies at local level are still used to prevent the necessary housing being built.

International political change and the British countryside

Alongside these changes in economic and social policies as they affect rural areas, there have been strong international influences on the governance of rural areas of Britain. Changing economic functions and a diversity of rural experiences across

Europe have been a catalyst for rethinking rural development at both European and national political levels. Many commentators have argued that for policies to meet diverse needs and circumstances there has to be a mobilisation of local actors, supported by partnership structures and arrangements. This chimes well with the analysis of New Labour's Commission on Social Justice, which identified a need for a double-shift in governance: on the one hand playing a more positive and active role in the EU, and on the other hand moving towards more participative modes with power and responsibility increasingly devolved towards individuals and communities.

What has come to the fore has been the casting of local actors as the catalysts for change through collective, neo-endogenous action (see for example Ward and Ray, 2004). These approaches rely upon resources and actors being mobilised to reassert the identity of place and self. While not exclusive to rural policy, such notions of 'bottom-up' development build upon the notion of cooperative social relations (*gemeinschaft*), frequently associated with rural areas. Often these initiatives have been encouraged through EU policies – in particular LEADER (to be discussed later).

As Ward (2002) has noted, "the mid-1980s saw increasing interest at the European level in the need to develop a new model of rural development support" as agricultural surpluses and growing environmental concerns challenged the identity of the rural with the agricultural (CEC, 1988). In direct opposition to the *sectoral* basis of rural policy, Integrated Rural Development (IRD) was presented as essentially *territorial* and "became fashionable in the early 1980s in European countries such as the UK as part of the struggles to reform discredited support policies" (Ward, 2002, p 2).

From 1989, the EU's structural funds were able to target particular rural regions in the 'most need' of policy help (Ray, 1998, p 30) and development of these was pursued through a territorial approach, involving partnership both between sectors and between levels of government. These funds are administered through a programming approach in which the EU Commission, member states and other regional and local actors together identify the problems and potential of the area and propose a strategy in the form of a Single Programming Document. In the LEADER Community Initiative, actors and organisations from the target areas themselves were invited to contribute to the design of the strategy, and towards its implementation. The EU Commission (1988, p 62) argued that this incorporation of local knowledge would avoid "errors of diagnosis" and also would create a network of rural development agents which could "play a stimulating, mobilising and coordinating role". In practice, local interests complained of a 'top-down' approach in which central government set the parameters too tightly and exercised control (Ward and McNicholas, 1997).

The neo-endogenous, territorial approach in EU policy, for many, is exemplified by the LEADER Community Initiative. The EU's declared objective for LEADER was for local actors to work together to find innovative solutions to rural problems which could reflect what was best suited to their areas and could also serve as models for developing rural areas elsewhere. Ray (2000) identifies three aspects to this approach: a territorial basis (as opposed to sectoral); the use of local resources; and local contextualisation through active public participation. The approach held out the prospect of "local areas assuming greater control of development by reorienting development around local resources and by setting up structures to sustain the local development momentum after the initial 'official' intervention" (Ray, 2000, p 166). The LEADER model, then, is seen as offering a territorial alternative to sectoral policies, promoting neo-endogenous development as a means of building the capacity of people in rural localities to resist broader forces of global competition, fiscal crisis or social exclusion (see Ray, 1999a, 1999b; Shucksmith, 2000a, 2000b).

Such tendencies must also be viewed in the context of what is widely seen as a shift from *government* towards *governance*. Governance, as discussed elsewhere in this volume, "refers to the development of governing styles in which boundaries between and within public and private sectors have become blurred" (Stoker, 1996, p 2). It is generally understood to imply a shift from state sponsorship of economic and social programmes and projects, as in the original IRD model, towards the delivery of these through partnerships involving both governmental and non-governmental organisations and perhaps other actors. According to Goodwin (2003, p 2), the increasing use of this term "indicates a significant change in the processes by which rural society is governed and rural policy is delivered". Features of this style include a new role for the state as coordinator, manager or enabler rather than as provider and director; the formation of tangled hierarchies, flexible alliances and networks through which to govern; the inclusion of new partners, notably from the private and voluntary sectors; and indeed 'government at a distance' (Goodwin, 1998). Mackinnon (2002, p 321), for example, shows how a 'governmentality' approach "provides a framework for connecting notions of community-led rural development to a broader shift in the dominant mode of state intervention, away from welfarism and social democracy to a more selective and indirect emphasis on 'governing through community'". As Stoker (1995, p 4) has put it, these are the elements of "managing a nobody-in-charge world".

One reason which has been put forward for these developments is the argument that the modern state can no longer govern national spaces in an all-inclusive fashion, but since it does not wish to be seen as exclusionary it has been forced to promote self-government instead. On the one hand this may be seen positively as an opportunity for participation and empowerment, leading to capacity-building. But on the other hand this may be seen as an abdication of the state's role and responsibilities, and even as an extension of flexibilisation and casualisation to government itself. Often there is a tension between the concern to promote local participation and 'civic renewal' and the reliance on a set of managerial technologies such as targeting, auditing and financial control that are deployed to ensure that local institutions are accountable to (central) government (Mackinnon, 2002). Critical questions emerge both over the effectiveness of these new styles of governance, and also over who has been involved, who has not, and why (see

Shucksmith, 2000a, 2000b; Ellis, 2003; Shortall, 2004) – in short about power relations.

The tendency towards new styles of governance and towards collaborative planning has relied upon partnerships as a central component, along with advocacy of citizen participation and stakeholder involvement, even if these have been unevenly realised in practice. Echoing the New Labour espousal of 'double devolution', the 1996 Cork Declaration, for example, asserted that new rural policy "must be as decentralised as possible and based on partnership and co-operation between all levels concerned" (European Conference on Rural Development, 1996).

This approach to rural governance may be viewed in essence as a combination of Europeanisation (Shortall and Shucksmith, 1998) and 'new localism' (Ray, 2000). It is clear that the imperative of accessing funds from the EU's structural funds encouraged member states' adoption not only of European agendas of neo-endogenous territorial development (in both rural and urban contexts) but also of many of the EU's programming and partnership structures. Ideologically and symbolically, this has also incorporated the new localism agenda of citizen participation and the passing of responsibility down to communities of place. For example, as has already been discussed, the European Commission wanted local actors in its LEADER programme to work together in a community-based approach to find innovative solutions to rural problems which could reflect what is best suited to their areas and could also serve as models for developing rural areas elsewhere. Very rarely, however, has this communitarian logic been extended to the passing of individual resources and property rights into community ownership. Yet, as Bryden and Geisler (2004) have argued, "devolution of responsibility and stewardship without entitlement is a contradiction. It is symbolic devolution at best, and is likely to be dysfunctional".

This is one aspect of the community-based rural development approach where Britain has gone further than any other country, namely in the *community-based land reform* enacted in Scotland in 2003. This is arguably the most radical and notable aspect of New Labour's rural policies from an international perspective, despite little attention being paid to this measure (or to Scotland in general) by the rest of the UK.

During one of the 1970s' seminars organised by the Arkleton Trust for people engaged in rural policy in Europe and North America to learn from rural development activists in the South, one expert from India was amazed after a brief tour of rural Britain: "your experts come to our countries and you are hardly off the plane before you tell us we need land reform, and now I discover you need it more than any of us!"

While still a taboo subject in England, political agitation for land reform in the Highlands of Scotland has continued for more than a century since the people who worked the land were dispossessed during the notorious Clearances (Hunter, 1976; Devine, 1994; Mackenzie, 1998). As a result, Scotland had the highest level of concentration of land ownership anywhere in Europe, with 1,200 landowners owning two thirds of Scotland's land (Wightman, 1999). Often absentee landlords obstructed attempts at community and regional development and managed their land against the broader community interest (eg HIDB, 1979; Wightman, 1996). Meanwhile a growing community movement was developing a shared vision of community ownership of land (see Bryden and Geisler, 2004), and in 1997 New Labour was elected with a manifesto commitment to enact land reform in Scotland.

In essence, the 2003 Land Reform (Scotland) Act gave communities a first option to purchase feudal estates of which they were a part (The 'Community Right to Buy'). Beyond this, crofting communities were given the power to exercise a pre-emptive, or hostile, right-to-buy the landlord's interest in land under crofting tenure, where a majority of both crofters and the community are in favour and where this promotes sustainable rural development (The 'Crofting Community Right to Buy'). A Community Land Unit was established by Highlands and Islands Enterprise to assist communities in the purchase and management of land, and a Scottish Land Fund (initially of £10 million, later increased to £15 million) was set up with UK Lottery Money to assist rural communities to acquire and develop land and buildings. Communities typically establish a democratic and locally controlled body (usually a company limited by guarantee) to acquire the land. According to Bryden and Geisler (2007, p 30), the Community Land Unit and Scottish Land Fund have been "vital tools for community empowerment and enterprise in fragile rural areas of Scotland – for example, since acquisition about 13 new enterprises have started on Gigha and the number of families and children on the island has increased significantly. A small local housing enterprise has started, and housing improvements in the existing housing stock are under way." Now, three wind turbines produce electricity which is sold by the Gigha community to the national grid. Such wind-farms are becoming a common community enterprise on such estates, offering hope of sustainable rural development in several senses. More than half the land area of the Western Isles is now in community ownership.

Mackenzie (2006) sees this community-centred land reform not only as a movement towards collective ownership with strong historical resonances but also as the removal of land from circuits of global capital, in turn permitting a re-visioning of the political possibilities of place and a commitment to social justice and sustainability. While the move towards collective ownership is borne out of historical (genealogical) claims to the land, rights are now defined in terms of the community of place rather than the community of interest: "genealogy is 'denaturalised' as a marker of belonging now defined in terms of place-based residence" (p 395). This redefinition of community rights to land opens up rights to those who previously had none and is therefore inclusionary. Moreover, people are 'written into the land' through the reconstitution of nature as well as by the exercise of collective rights. Colonising discourses of wilderness, serving the sporting interests of a landed class or the environmental designations of non-local conservationists, are disputed and overturned through the performance of community stewardship and dismantling the class basis of stalking, for example. And community wind-farms also reproduce nature as a worked landscape, while their inescapable complicity with capitalism is "mediated through a local and collective rather than global and corporate or private ethic" (Mackenzie, 2006, p 396) such that the wind's commodification becomes part and parcel of the community's rights to the land and of their post-colonial resistance. As Mackenzie (2006, p 396) concludes: "the wind becomes the means through which the 'local' – place – is not set in opposition to the 'global', but through which 'the very mechanisms of the global' are altered. It becomes a key means through which the potential for collective rights to land to contribute to the sustainability of local livelihoods may be realised."

This is one, exceptional, way in which New Labour has acted to fulfil the vision of the Commission on Social Justice towards community empowerment. Arguably, however, they have also made other important strides towards rescaling governance and towards their aspiration of a 'double-shift', notably through the devolution of powers to the Scottish Parliament and Welsh Assembly, through attempts to establish regional assemblies and other regional bodies in England (Pearce et al, 2005), through attempts to reinvigorate parish and town councils, and through pursuit of supra-national agreements on CAP reform and world trade, for example.

Conclusion

How far, then, have New Labour's policies for rural areas been informed by the internationalist perspectives of the Commission on Social Justice in 1994? How far have they addressed the economic, social and political revolutions recognised by the authors of that report, and so changed rural Britain's 'place in the world'?

It is in the economic sphere that New Labour's rural policies have perhaps fallen furthest short of their ambitions, even though many rural areas have prospered. While its macroeconomic policies have fostered continuous growth, shared by (and sometimes led by) rural areas, New Labour's economic policies for rural areas remain stubbornly agricultural and outdated, rather than introducing rural economic development policies which promote the international competitiveness of rural areas. Partly this is because the UK has been unable to persuade its EU partners to reform the CAP, away from agricultural protectionism and towards rural development, and to revise its expenditure priorities towards science, research and development, and regional development. But partly this has also been due to a reassertion of agricultural interests in England, following the FMD crisis, so frustrating the brief tendency towards a more territorial rural policy. The more innovative approach of Highlands and Islands Enterprise in Scotland suggests what might have been.

In addressing social exclusion in rural areas, New Labour can demonstrate impressive reductions in poverty, notably among children and pensioners. Again, these and other improvements stem largely from national, rather than rural, policies – such as the National Minimum Wage, the New Deal and Sure Start programmes, and especially changes to tax and benefit regimes. Indeed, New Labour's Social Exclusion Unit, and relevant ministries (such as the Treasury, the Department for Work and Pensions and the Department for Communities and Local Government), have shown little interest in social exclusion in rural areas compared with the attention given to poor urban neighbourhoods. One could argue that this is an appropriate response to poverty and social exclusion which is less concentrated and area-based. Yet there are rural dimensions to social exclusion and there are ways in which policies could address these more effectively, as the CRC has documented (CRC, 2006a, 2006b). Notwithstanding this, New Labour's innovative ways of addressing social exclusion, deriving from ideas in both the US and the EU, have been one of its successes.

New Labour has also made some progress towards their aspiration of a 'double-shift' in the governance of rural areas, notably through the devolution of powers to the Scottish Parliament and Welsh Assembly, through attempts to establish regional assemblies and other regional bodies in England, through attempts to reinvigorate parish and town councils, and through pursuit of supra-national agreements on CAP reform, world trade and climate change.

David Miliband, secretary to the Commission on Social Justice in 1994 and more recently Secretary of State for Environment, Food and Rural Affairs, has returned to these themes to offer a renewed vision for Labour politics:

> My judgement is that successful countries in the future will be marked by three things. They will put more power into the hands of citizens and communities. They will promote open and meritocratic social structures. They will recognise global interdependence through strong networks that link individuals, companies, cities and countries. Labour has real strengths in addressing this agenda. The collectivist impulse was designed for an age of interdependence. The recognition of community was designed for an era of mutual responsibility. (Miliband, 2007, p 24)

And he went on to say "while leadership comes from government, innovation and mobilisation come from the bottom up" (p 24). Perhaps, largely unknown to him, community-based land reform in the Highlands and Islands of Scotland may be the biggest step New Labour has made in this direction.

Notes
[1] With David Miliband, then of the Institute of Public Policy Research (IPPR), as secretary to the Commission.

[2] These rural estimates (available at http://www.defra.gov.uk/rural/ruralstats/ofa. htm) are not strictly comparable with the Department for Work and Pensions

(DWP) figures, since they are relative to the GB median household income, not the English median used by the DWP.

References

ARHC (2006) *Affordable Rural Housing Commission: Final report*, London: Defra.

Beck, U. (1992) *The risk society*, London: Sage.

Best, R. and Shucksmith, M. (2006) *Homes for rural communities*, York: Joseph Rowntree Foundation.

Borrie, G. (1994) *The report of the Commission on Social Justice*, Harmondsworth: Penguin.

Bryden, J. and Geisler, C. (2007) 'Community-based land reform: lessons from Scotland', *Land Use Policy*, vol 24, no 1, pp 24-34.

Bryden, J.M. and Hart, J.K. (2004) *Why local economies differ? The dynamics of rural areas in the European Union.* Lampeter: The Edwin Mellen Press.

CEC (Commission of the European Communities) (1988) *The future of rural societies*, COM (1988) 501 Final, Brussels.

CEC (2004) *Third Report on Economic and Social Cohesion*, COM (2004) 107 final, Luxembourg.

Cloke, P. (1979) *Key settlements in rural areas*, London: Methuen.

CRC (Commission for Rural Communities) (2006a) *Rural disadvantage: priorities for action.* (Available at http://www.ruralcommunities.gov.uk/publications/crc29priorities)

CRC (2006b) *Evidence to the Affordable Rural Housing Commission.* (Available at http://www.ruralcommunities.gov.uk/publications/ourevidencetothearhc)

Devine, T. (1994) *Clanship to crofters' war: The social transformation of the Scottish Highlands*, Manchester: Manchester University Press.

DWP (Department for Work and Pensions) (2007) *Households below average income.*(Available at http://www.dwp.gov.uk/asd/hbai/hbai2006/excel_files/chapters/chapter_4_excel_hbai07.xls http://www.dwp.gov.uk/asd/hbai/hbai2006/excel_files/chapters/chapter_6_excel_hbai07.xls).

Ellis, A. (2003) *Power and exclusion in rural community development: The case of LEADER2 in Wales*, PhD thesis, Department of Geography, University of Swansea.

Esping-Andersen, G. (1990) *The three worlds of welfare capitalism*, Cambridge: Polity.

European Conference on Rural Development (1996) *The Cork Declaration: A lving countryside*, 7-9 December 1996, Cork.

European Court of Auditors (2006) *Rural Development Investments: Do they effectively address the problems of rural areas?* (Available at www.eca.europa.eu/audit_reports/special_reports/docs/2006/rs07_06en.pdf)

Florida, R. (2002) *The rise of the creative class*, New York: Basic Books.

Giddens, A. (1991) *Modernity and self-identity: Self and society in the late modern age*, Cambridge: Polity.

Giddens, A. (1998) *The Third Way: The renewal of social democracy*, Cambridge: Polity.

Giddens, A. (2002) *Where now for New Labour?*, Cambridge: Polity.

Gilbert, A., Phimister, E. and Theodossiou, N. (2001) 'The potential impact of the National Minimum Wage in rural Areas', *Regional Studies*, vol 35, no 8, pp 765-70.

Goodwin, M. (1998) 'The governance of rural areas: some emerging research issues and agendas', *Journal of Rural Studies*, vol 14, pp 5-12.

Goodwin, M. (2003) *Partnership working and rural governance: Issues of community involvement and participation*, report to Defra/CA and ESRC, London: Defra.

Haskins, C. (2003) *Rural delivery review: A report on the delivery of government policies in rural England*, London: Defra.

Hepworth, M. (2004) *The knowledge economy in rural England*, London: Defra.

HIE (Highlands and Islands Enterprise) (2005) *A smart, successful Highlands & Islands*, Inverness: HIE.

Hunter, J. (1976) *The making of the crofting community*, Edinburgh: John Donald.

Lowe, P. (2006) 'European agricultural and rural development policies for the 21st century', in J. Midgley (ed) *A new rural agenda*, Newcastle: IPPR North, pp 29-45.

Mackenzie, F. (1998) 'The cheviot, the stag ... and the white, white rock? Community, identity and environmental threat on the Isle of Harris', *Environment and Planning D: Society and Space*, vol 16, pp 509-32.

Mackenzie, F. (2006) 'A working land: crofting communities, place and the politics of the possible in post-Land Reform Scotland', *Transactions of the Institute of British Geographers, NS*, vol 31, pp 383-98.

Mackinnon, D. (2002) 'Rural governance and local involvement: assessing state-community relations in the Scottish Highlands', *Journal of Rural Studies*, vol 18, pp 307-24

Midgley, J. (ed) (2006) *A new rural agenda*, Newcastle, IPPR North.

Miliband, D. (2007) 'Out with the old, in with the new', *The Observer*, 25 March Review Section, p 24.

Murdoch, J. and Abram, S. (1998) 'Defining the limits of community governance', *Journal of Rural Studies*, vol 14, pp 41-50.

OECD (Organisation for Economic Co-operation and Development) (2006) *The new rural paradigm: Policies and governance*, Paris: OECD.

Pearce, G., Ayres, S. and Tricker, M. (2005) 'Decentralisation and devolution to the English regions: assessing the implications for rural policy and delivery, *Journal of Rural Studies*, vol 21, no 2, pp 197-212.

PIU (Performance and Innovation Unit of the Cabinet Office) (1999) *Rural economies*, London: The Stationery Office. (Also available at www.cabinetoffice. gov.uk/strategy/work_areas/rural_economies.aspx)

Ray, C. (1998) 'Culture, intellectual property and territorial rural development', *Sociologia Ruralis*, vol 38, no 1, pp 3-20.

Ray, C. (1999a) 'Endogenous development in an era o. reflexive modernity', *Journal of Rural Studies*, vol 15, no 3, pp 257-67.

Ray, C. (1999b) 'Towards a meta-framework of endogenous development: repertoires, paths, democracy and rights', *Sociologia Ruralis*, vol 39, no 4, pp 521-37.

Ray, C. (2000) 'The EU LEADER programme: rural development laboratory', Introduction to special issue of *Sociologia Ruralis*, vol 40, no 2, pp 163-71.

Roger Tym and Partners (2006) *Calculating housing needs in rural England*, London: Commission for Rural Communities.

Shortall, S. (2004) 'Social or economic goals, civic inclusion or exclusion? An analysis of rural development theory and practice', *Sociologia Ruralis*, vol 44, no 1, pp 109-23.

Shortall, S. and Shucksmith, M. (1998) 'Integrated rural development in practice: the Scottish experience', *European Planning Studies*, vol 6, no 1, 73-88.

Shucksmith, M. (1990) *Housebuilding in Britain's countryside*, London: Routledge.

Shucksmith, M. (2000a) 'Endogenous development, social capital and social inclusion', *Sociologia Ruralis*, vol 40, no 2, pp 208-18.

Shucksmith, M. (2000b) *Exclusive countryside? Social inclusion and regeneration in rural Britain*, York: Joseph Rowntree Foundation.

Shucksmith, M., Thomson, K. and Roberts, D. (2005) *The CAP and the regions: The territorial impact of the Common Agricultural Policy*, Oxford: CABI.

Social Exclusion Unit (2004) *Breaking the cycle: Taking stock of progress and priorities for the future*, London: The Stationery Office.

Stoker, G. (1996) 'Public–private partnerships and urban governance', in G. Stoker (ed) *Partners in urban governance: European and American experience*, London: Macmillan.

Terluin, I. (2003) 'Differences in economic development in rural regions of advanced countries: an overview and critical analysis of theories', *Journal of Rural Studies*, vol 19, pp 327-44.

Terluin, I. and Post, J. (2000) *Employment dynamics in rural Europe*, Oxford: CABI.

Toynbee, P. (2001) 'This is Blair's new road map, but it leads nowhere?', *Guardian*, 28 February.

Toynbee, P. and Walker, D. (2001) *Did things get better? An audit of Labour's successes and failures*, Harmondsworth: Penguin.

Ward, N. (2002) *Integrated rural development – a review of the literature*, Centre for Rural Research, Trondheim: University of Trondheim.

Ward, N. (2006) 'Rural development and the economies of rural areas', in J. Midgley (ed) *A new rural agenda*, Newcastle: IPPR North, pp 46-67.

Ward, N. and McNicholas, K. (1998) 'Reconfiguring rural development in the UK: Objective 5b and the new rural governance', *Journal of Rural Studies*, vol 14, pp 27-39.

Ward, N. and Ray, C. (2004) *Future analysis, public policy and rural studies*, CRE Working Paper 74, Centre for Rural Economy, Newcastle: University of Newcastle.

Wightman, A (1996) *Who owns Scotland?* Edinburgh: Canongate.

Wightman, A. (1999) *Scotland: Land and power, the agenda for land reform*, Edinburgh: Luath.

Woods, M. (2005) *Rural geography*, London: Sage.

Woods, M. (2006) 'Rural politics and governance', in J. Midgley (ed) *A new rural agenda*, Newcastle: IPPR North, pp 140-68.

Part Two
The key debates

FIVE

The foot and mouth crisis

Michael Winter

Introduction

Whilst New Labour might have anticipated one particular difficult rural issue as providing a challenge in their first administration, namely hunting, they can hardly have anticipated a second. Yet in February 2001, the government was confronted with one of its most serious domestic crises so far. The epidemic of foot and mouth disease (FMD) was the first in Britain since 1968, apart from an isolated outbreak, affecting just one farm, on the Isle of Wight in 1981. It brought far-reaching consequences not only for biosecurity practices and policies, but also for our understanding of agri-food sustainability and of the changing nature of the rural economy, and in the institutional arrangements for rural policy. Paradoxically, the FMD crisis brought agriculture to the centre of political and media attention for many months at the same time as driving home the message that farming had long since ceased to be the dominant economic and social force within rural communities. The story is of an old disease in a radically new countryside, new in terms of its socioeconomic profile and its farming practices.

FMD had been prevalent in Britain well into the 20th century with major epidemics in 1922, 1924, 1954 and 1968, and only two totally FMD-free years between 1922 and 1967 (Anderson, 2002). But most of these earlier outbreaks were locally contained, as farms were smaller and more likely to trade locally even in the late 1960s. The disease itself is debilitating rather than necessarily fatal but, being highly infectious, has potentially disastrous economic and animal welfare implications if allowed to become established. The policy of slaughtering was pushed in the late 19th century by pedigree breeders with their obvious particular interests in protecting high value stock (Woods, 2002) but few would deny that it was a policy that eventually achieved a long period of FMD-free status for Britain with corresponding economic and welfare benefits. However, the slaughter policy was based on *local* containment and a more localised agricultural industry than had become the norm. The meat supply chain by 2001 had become predominantly national rather than local. A combination of improvements in road transport, the concentration of slaughtering facilities, and Common Agricultural Policy (CAP) livestock payment rules had led to movements of animals over greater distances in the period between 1968 and 2001 (Law, 2006; Winter et al, 2002).

Thus an outbreak that was discovered in Essex on 19 February 2001, originating in Northumberland, had probably already spread to between 50 and 100 destinations from sheep traded at Hexham market. Certainly within days cases were confirmed as far afield as Devon, Cumbria, Scotland and Wales. Thirty-two weeks later, after the final confirmed case, there had been cases in 44 counties, unitary authorities and metropolitan districts in the United Kingdom, with over 2,000 premises infected, and pre-emptive culling on a further 8,000 holdings. Over six million animals had been slaughtered with approximate direct public expenditure of £3 billion (National Audit Office, 2002), and estimated total economic losses of £9 billion (Anderson, 2002). The government was criticised for its management of the epidemic, its policy described by Campbell and Lee (2003a) as taking "the empirical form of incompetence, irrationality, enormous waste and barbaric cruelty" (p 448). The government commissioned a series of separate reports, inquiries and policy reviews in its aftermath but never a full public inquiry.

This chapter outlines and analyses the government's response to the FMD epidemic, both during and after the crisis, and assesses its implications for the subsequent development of agricultural policy and for rural policy more broadly. The chapter draws on a range of responses to FMD including official and academic papers. In places the chapter has also drawn on the author's own experience of FMD as a resident in one of the worst affected communities in West Devon, a participant-observation method of research that is explained and deployed in two other papers touching on the crisis (Winter, 2003, 2006).

'Carnage by computer': dealing with an epidemic

The title for this section is taken from a searing condemnation of the government's handling of the epidemic by David Campbell and Robert Lee (2003a), who argue that the FMD crisis provides "an object lesson in how not to regulate" (p 426). They in turn are quoting from the evidence submitted by a local vet to Devon County Council's FMD inquiry (Mercer, 2002). Campbell and Lee point to the abject failure of the government and its agencies to recognise the gravity of the problem in the early days of the crisis with a failure to release sufficient staff to deal with the problem. The failings of the Ministry of Agriculture, Fisheries and Food (MAFF) were such that just five weeks into the crisis control was transferred to the ad hoc committee convened to deal with national emergencies – COBR – based in the Cabinet Office. One of COBR's first acts was to introduce contiguous culling, or carnage by computer, requiring the slaughter of animals on farms adjacent to outbreaks, supposedly within 48 hours, to form a firewall around infected farm holdings. In some parts of the country this was extended to include all livestock within a 3 km radius of an infected holding.

The legality of this was in dispute from the outset, and has been argued to be ultra vires by Campbell and Lee (2003b); nor was the policy seen by many veterinarians to be either practical or efficacious. It originated from the FMD Science Group convened by MAFF for this purpose, but the practitioners in this group were not experts in either agriculture or non-human epidemiology (Campbell and Lee, 2003a), and their use of a deterministic as opposed to stochastic modelling mitigated against sensitive local application (Keeling and Woolhouse, 2001; Bickerstaff and Simmons, 2004). There were also serious grounds for questioning the quality of some of the agricultural census data used (Morris et al, 2001; The Royal Society, 2002; Bickerstaff and Simons, 2004), not least the false assumption that agricultural holdings, as defined in the census, are spatially defined.

Almost immediately the contiguous policy was subject to vigorous challenges from veterinary scientists and practitioners and, notably, from the government's own Institute of Animal Health, which appealed for local risk assessments based on levels of likely contact (Donaldson et al, 2001). As Bickerstaff and Simmons (2004) have convincingly demonstrated, a dispute on the appropriateness of competing areas of scientific expertise, not unusual in scientific circles but usually confined to the pages of learned journals, in this instance became a matter of long-lasting policy and political significance. The choice was between the predictive epidemiological modelling utilised by the FMD Science Group and largely drawing on science based at Imperial College, as against traditional veterinarian approaches to containment, based on local assessment of the disease on the ground. The fact that COBR chose the epidemiological approach was a direct result of the diminution in the standing of MAFF and its scientists as a result of the bovine spongiform encephalopathy (BSE) crisis (Forbes, 2004). The BSE Inquiry (Phillips et al, 2000) had criticised veterinary training and veterinary epidemiology, and this had lasting knock-on effects which now influenced the policy related to FMD (Bickerstaff and Simmons, 2004). Of course, there were stark differences between BSE and FMD. BSE was a new disease, invariably fatal, and seemingly transferable to humans. FMD is none of those things. The BSE experience should not have influenced the government's treatment of FMD, other than to have provided a salutary lesson in the need for considerable care in the use of scientific evidence. Instead COBR chose to adopt one particular scientific approach that, of course, was consistent with a more centralised policy style once the crisis was moved under the control of the Cabinet Office: "the spatial practices of the veterinarians and the greater sensitivity to local circumstances they argued for, did not offer the degree of generalisability and predictability demanded by policymakers set on imposing central control on the problem" (Bickerstaff and Simmons, 2004, p 410).

The degree of centralised panic was understandable. The speed of the geographical spread of FMD, unprecedented in earlier 20th-century outbreaks, suggested to some a nightmare scenario of escalation. Of particular concern was growing evidence of unacceptable delays between diagnosis and slaughter, and delays in disposal of carcasses. Both sets of delays served to increase the risk of further spread. As clearly stated in the Anderson Report, the situation by mid-March was that "the logistical machinery for dealing with the epidemic was inadequate for the task" (Anderson. 2002, p 79). Disputes, confusion and contradictory information about the operation of the so-called contiguous cull served only to heighten concern about MAFF from within the farming community and its political representatives. This was accompanied by growing wider public disquiet about the slaughter policy and disposal practices. In truth, centralised policy coordination and scientific practice were not matched by effective implementation on the ground. In effect, the FMD epidemic was not a single entity but a large number of local epidemics occurring in widely varying farming and rural socioeconomic conditions:

> The Science Group's model took no heed of concrete information about the likelihood of the transmission of disease beyond the original suspicion of infection. It took no account whatsoever of the possible variable conditions of spread according to factors such as geography. It made no allowance for natural barriers which might restrict spread. It made no distinction between infected species, let alone infected herds or individual animals. It almost certainly overestimated long-range wind-spread ... it made no distinction between different farming practices in different regions, and allowed no assertion that a farmer had exercised rigorous biosecurity measures. Typically, any farm which shared a boundary with a premesis declared infected ... had all its animals culled in a process of 'postcode slaughter'. (Campbell and Lee, 2003a, pp 435-36).

An example of the absurdities that could arise from this centralised approach, is the case of a dairy farm scheduled for slaughter because of an infection in sheep half a mile away with the two farms separated by woodland. The 'shared boundary' was just a few metres in length. All the dairy cows had been housed throughout the epidemic, strict biosecurity measures had been deployed, and there were no signs of infection. The cows were saved not because of these salient facts though, but because the two farmers both denied ownership of the very small strip of scrub woodland that apparently joined their properties. Neither sets of deeds included the strip of land in question and no ownership could be proved. MAFF could not prove contiguity and the cull was avoided.

But in most cases no such legal loophole was available. The contiguous cull was widely pursued, although slaughter within 48 hours, as required by COBR, was achieved in less than 50% of cases (Anderson, 2002). Although MAFF's successor department – the Department for Environment, Food and Rural Affairs (Defra) – has claimed the contiguous cull was successful, it is not possible to prove this conclusively (Campbell and Lee, 2003a).

FMD and the politics of resistance

In this section, we examine the several ways in which the crisis became a totemic political issue serving to galvanise rural opposition to MAFF/Defra, in particular, and more generally to New Labour. On the ground, the adoption of the contiguous cull policy did nothing to improve political relations between MAFF and local farming and rural communities. Indeed, one of the political consequences of MAFF's slow start in dealing with the crisis followed by its rapid introduction of the blunt instrument of the contiguous cull was a strong and lasting antagonism to MAFF/Defra. In the author's own ethnographic work on the response to the FMD crisis in the Hatherleigh area of West Devon he found that the introduction of the contiguous cull marked a turning point in the community's experience of the disaster (Winter, 2003). Hitherto its anger and despair had been directed against the impersonal agency of the virus itself. There had been much talk of the nature and characteristics of the virus, debate over how it was spread, its durability, its impact. The contiguous cull introduced by government edict along with the officials charged with enforcing it became, in many eyes, an alien antagonistic force. It became clear that there were three main opinions with regard to the cull. Some came to radically challenge the cull and saw it as unnecessary and evil. Conspiracy theories began to take hold in which the government was accused of wishing to destroy the UK livestock industry with the cull as a convenient tool for this end. The beleaguered and 'victim' mentality of farmers noted elsewhere (Reed et al, 2002) contributed to this. Given that the National Farmers' Union (NFU) nationally, and for the main part regionally, accepted the need for the cull, it is not surprising that the groundswell of opposition to the cull and to MAFF's entire handling of the crisis should have led to a new expression of farming opinion, known as 'The Heart of Devon', established and funded by a local landowner and TV personality. The Heart of Devon launched a vigorous press and website campaign which was relentlessly antagonistic to MAFF/Defra and the Labour government.

Alongside the controversy surrounding the means of controlling the spread of the disease, were equally difficult challenges surrounding the disposal of carcasses. In the early weeks of the crisis, carcass disposal was largely undertaken through burning on gigantic funeral pyres. The extent of the burning was in contrast to the greater use of burial, including use of lime to accelerate decomposition, in 1968. In 2001, burial was judged environmentally risky, itself a comment on the changing balance of political interests in the interim. But fears grew that pyres were becoming questionable in terms of efficiency, impractical because of lack of burning fuel and unacceptable because of their symbolic power to deter tourists. In response, MAFF developed ideas for mass burial sites with procedures in place to protect groundwater.

Wherever these were proposed and/or implemented local public concerns emerged rapidly in relation to public health and environmental impact. Again the Hatherleigh case can act as an example: a large burial site was chosen three miles from Hatherleigh at Ash Moor, and a vociferous pressure group opposed to the Ash Moor Pit emerged (STAMP). Protest marches were held, a 24-hour vigil was held for many weeks at the entrance to the site, and public meetings, petitions and lobbying all took place. Notwithstanding the reassurances provided by both MAFF and the Environment Agency that the risks were minimal and the site was only a contingency measure that hopefully would not be needed, rumours in the community were rife. These reached a pitch during the general election campaign of May/June 2001. STAMP campaigners opined that a mass cull would be put in place covering all sheep on Dartmoor and Exmoor immediately after the election. By this stage, blood-testing was taking place throughout the country and the reports from MAFF and vets on the ground were that very few positive results were being found. These views were flatly contradicted by STAMP campaigners. Not surprisingly, and despite a general criticism of MAFF, not everyone in the community shared this analysis. Some were reassured by MAFF and, more significantly, some felt that the control of disease and farmers' interests in rapid carcass disposal were of paramount concern. Intra-community conflict was inevitable.

How should the Ash Moor incident be interpreted? At one level STAMP is a classic example of a spontaneous local environmental pressure group, although the lack of involvement of mainstream environmental pressure groups is notable. The strength of feeling and the high level of distrust of MAFF/Defra and the Environment Agency meant that any constructive and participative engagement was almost impossible to promote. Whatever the rights and wrongs of the scientific argument surrounding the site, it seems clear that Ash Moor Pit provided the catalyst for an outburst of anger directed at the authorities perceived to be, in some measure, responsible for the FMD disaster. Ash Moor became a symbol for those critical of the manner in which the FMD epidemic had been handled. It was a small step from criticising a particular mode of carcass disposal to attacking the extent and nature of the cull. Here STAMP was able both to contribute to, and draw on, a wider critique of the contiguous cull. Because of these links, it would be simplistic to see the Ash Moor dispute as instigating or reinforcing a rift between farming and non-farming interests. On the contrary, the Ash Moor dispute took place at a time when the agricultural consensus on how to approach the disease was itself breaking down. A critique of the contiguous cull from farmers found particular expression in other emergent local politics surrounding The Heart of Devon campaign as well as in the growing dissent from the organic farming community.

There can be little doubt that the strength of opinion represented in STAMP and The Heart of Devon contributed towards a growing local and regional dimension to the politics of FMD. These processes were replicated in the NFU regionally, where there was a growing distance between the local and regional NFU position and the Union's central policy generally in support of the contiguous cull and opposed to vaccination. FMD also served to focus attention on a more generalised critique of the agri-food system. For example, the extent of livestock movements is often (not entirely correctly) blamed on the loss of abattoirs. As Law (2006) has explained, there is both an anti-EU version of this story, with prohibitive EU regulations imposed on British abattoirs, and an anti-UK government version, which sees MAFF/Defra using these regulations for their own purposes. In both cases, the antagonism to government is reinforced.

The lack of trust in the government encountered in ethnographic research in West Devon was supported by a comparative study between Norwich and Bude (20 miles west of Hatherleigh) conducted at the height of the crisis. Some key results are shown in Table 5.1.

Table 5.1: Average trust in various information sources to tell the truth about the FMD outbreak (scale ranges from 1 'distrust a lot' to 5 'trust a lot')

	Norwich (N = 229)	Bude (N= 244)	Overall (N = 473)
Veterinary surgeons	4.18	4.28	4.23
Farmers	3.62	3.92	3.78
Friends and family	3.63	3.89	3.76
Consumer organisations	3.56	3.48	3.52
Environmental organisations	3.51	3.52	3.51
The Food Standards Agency (FSA)	3.62	3.37	3.50
The media (TV, radio, newspapers)	3.38	3.53	3.46
MAFF/Defra	3.22	2.94	3.07
The Internet	2.85	3.06	2.96
Supermarkets	2.69	2.64	2.66
Food manufacturers	2.63	2.57	2.60
The European Union (EU)	2.46	2.18	2.32
Government ministers	2.40	2.11	2.25

Source: Adapted from Poortinga et al (2004, p 84)

To conclude this section, the unfolding FMD crisis, and the widespread perception that the government's response was inept and inadequate, served to build up a local politics of resistance and antagonism to New Labour that readily found expression in a deep-rooted suspicion of MAFF/Defra both within and outside the farming community. This cannot be attributed to FMD alone. The BSE crisis, the threat to hunting, and fuel taxes had already served to undermine the government's credibility in significant sections of the rural community (Woods, 2005).

Learning the lessons

The learning of appropriate lessons is critically dependent upon the particular diagnoses adopted. Law (2006) argues that these can be divided into two distinct types, one associated with the failures of policy making and the other with systems failure. In the first, exemplified by Ward et al (2004), the failures are largely seen as a consequence of the narrow agri-centric focus of the policy community, especially in neglecting the overall consequence of the measures adopted for the rural economy. Law prefers the second explanation of systems failure as developed in the work by Poortinga et al (2003). In truth, the two diagnoses are not incompatible. They are merely oriented at different aspects of the same problem. Moreover, a proper policy-making process requires awareness of systems issues and a systems approach inevitably has implications for policy.

The rural economy diagnosis is based on the contention that the measures taken to deal with the crisis were inappropriate because they failed to recognise the knock-on effects of agricultural disease control measures on the wider rural economy and therefore did not deal with all the true victims of the outbreak. For example, the closure of public footpaths and access to open country had a devastating affect on tourism businesses, particularly in Cumbria and Devon. As assessments and predictions of the economic impact of FMD began to emerge within a matter of weeks of the outset of the epidemic, so it became clear that the financial impact on tourism was likely to outweigh by far the cost to agriculture itself. For example, Newcastle University's Centre for Rural Economy (CRE), in its evidence to the Anderson Committee, estimated a loss of revenue to conventional agriculture in Cumbria of £150 million and a loss to tourism of £400 million. Subsequently it has been estimated by the National Audit Office and Treasury that UK agriculture, the food chain and supporting services lost £0.6 billion, and tourism and supporting services between £4.5 and £5.4 billion (although the total net economic loss, due to displacement of economic activity to other sectors of the economy, was perhaps as low as £2 billion). The human dimension of this was spelled out by Phillipson et al (2004) in a paper examining in detail the impacts of the crisis on a wide range of non-agricultural businesses in the North-East of England (see also work on Scotland by Kenyon and Gilbert, 2005). Phillipson et al (2004) showed how coping with the economic downturn across a wide range of businesses led to considerable pressures within businesses and households of a social as well as an economic nature.

The reasons for the impacts on non-agricultural businesses are primarily as a consequence of the 'closure of the countryside' to tourism and recreation activities. Notwithstanding a wide acceptance of this in both academic circles and in the rural and regional development policy communities, the official responses to the crisis have granted only limited attention to this. It warranted only minimum coverage by the Anderson Committee, although it did recommend a cost–benefit analysis of FMD control strategies. This was subsequently undertaken and influenced Defra's current FMD contingency plan. The contingency plan shows an awareness of the wider economic issues and recognises that vaccination may be necessary because of this. It seeks to mitigate some of the impacts on tourism, for example by stating that footpaths would only be closed on infected premises and within a 3 km Protection Zone. But it insists on the possibility of culling of other susceptible livestock and pre-emptive or 'firebreak' culling of animals not on infected premises, not dangerous contacts or not necessarily exposed to the disease, in order to prevent the wider spread of the disease within an area. The 2002 Animal Health Act gives the Secretary of State new and enlarged powers to kill 'any' animal in the interest of disease control, suggesting a continued silo mentality surrounds the issue.

Law's systems approach argues for a much greater degree of radicalism than is possible in the policy-framing approach, which, as shown in the amended contingency planning, is liable to incrementalism and even uncertainty as to what would actually happen in the event of another outbreak. Law, drawing on Perrow (1999), argues that the modern agri-food system has become a system of flows which are both quick and complex:

> In a complex system with rapid flows, normal accidents are always waiting to happen. … What happens if we apply the whole argument to the various material flows of agriculture: to beasts, micro-organisms, people, money, trucks, and feed? These various flows are certainly complex, indeed unknowably so, and often they move fast too, too fast for intervention. The barriers holding them apart are unpredictably reliable. … The foot and mouth outbreak *is* a normal accident. (Law, 2006, pp 236-7)

For Law, as for many in the organic and alternative agriculture movements, "if the consequences of a failing system and its escaping flows are dangerous then … we need to take a political decision not to create such a system in the first place" (Law. 2006, p 236). But the various government reports and inquiries did not even consider radical solutions. This was avoided by the way the UK government chose to divide its response between the science of the disease (The Royal Society, 2002), the manner in which the epidemic was dealt with (Anderson, 2002), and a third report into the future for farming and food (Policy Commission on the Future of Farming and Food, 2002). Arguably, the Commission, chaired by Sir Don Curry, had the greatest opportunity to take a radical systems approach to the agri-food sector. Instead it produced something of a 'lucky dip' mix of policy prescriptions and pleas – excellent and forward-looking in parts but lacking a coherent vision. The government's response was to adopt most of the ideas without any attempt to resolve some of the inherent tensions, still less to relate back to some of the emerging issues from the FMD crisis. As a direct response to the Policy Commission's report, *The strategy for sustainable farming and food*, subtitled 'Facing the future', was published in 2002 (Defra, 2002). The Strategy, which covers England (there were similar initiatives elsewhere in the UK), envisages for the agri-food industry and government "a new relationship – a new settlement – in which in the long-term farming and food may be unsubsidised but not unsupported" (p 8).

The Strategy is implicitly built around three models for the future of farming and the rural economy which are not explicitly recognised. The three models are of farmers as producers of food commodities in a global free market; farmers as multifunctional – producers of public goods for which there is not an existing market; and farmers as land-based entrepreneurs within a diversified rural economy (Winter, 2006).The Strategy's specific policies flow from these three models: first, it reaffirms the UK's position as the leading exponent in Europe of World Trade Organization (WTO) compliance and CAP reform through the principles of decoupling and the removal of trade barriers; second, it justifies support for farmers for the provision of public goods, primarily through agri-environment schemes; and, third, it seeks to facilitate diverse rural economic development. It seems a big step removed from real lessons learned.

New policies and institutions for farming, food and the rural economy

As set out by the author in earlier papers, one of the consequences of the crisis was to instigate a lasting change to the architecture of rural governance (Winter, 2003, 2006). The crisis brought MAFF under unprecedented and continuous scrutiny by the media, public and farmers. Government departments may withstand criticism if measures are taken which are seen to be successful, however painful, or if the criticisms are quite clearly from a narrow sectional interest. But as the previous sections have demonstrated, this was not the case in 2001. MAFF was under attack on a wide range of fronts and could not claim any early successes in its strategy to cope with the epidemic.

MAFF's fate was sealed by some of the wider implications of the problem, particularly the impact FMD was having on the wider rural economy, especially tourism, as discussed in the previous section. MAFF came under implicit or explicit criticism, not least from local and regional authorities, for its failure to recognise the wider rural economy. It was this sense of a ministry institutionally divorced from significant sectors clearly affected by its actions, and actively promoting only narrow sectional interests, that drew fresh attention to the definition of MAFF's remit and responsibilities.Thus, FMD provided the stimulus to the 'architectural' changes that took place after the June 2001 general election, but the emergence of a new ministry (the Department for Environment, Food and Rural Affairs – Defra) was the culmination of a series of steps over two decades broadening the role of MAFF.

The main change to the institutional architecture heralded by the creation of Defra was the bringing together of the agricultural and rural development responsibilities of the former MAFF with the environmental and rural development responsibilities of the former Department of the Environment, Transport and the Regions (DETR), in particular the work of the Environment Agency, the Countryside Agency and English Nature.This, it was hoped, would lead to a greater coordination and integration of policies across agriculture and the environment.There had been suggestions in the past that aspects of food policy might be transferred to the Departments of Health and/or Trade and Industry.

However, by retaining food within the department with lead responsibility for rural policy, policy integration within the agri-food chain remains an important policy goal, and this is highly relevant to the post-FMD agenda for sustainable agriculture.

However, if the formation of Defra potentially improves the prospects for a more integrated and coordinated delivery of rural policy, some other changes arguably make the task more difficult. The new Department for Transport, Local Government and the Regions, while retaining responsibility for local government, including the local authorities' critical town and country planning functions, ceded responsibility for the Regional Development Agencies (RDAs) to the Department of Trade and Industry. Moreover, tourism remained under the Department for Culture, Media and Sport. Thus, while the new architecture of government reinforced a long-standing shift of policy from agricultural to rural, real anomalies and tensions remained. In particular, these revolved around how the rural economy was to be conceptualised in policy terms and the structures and mechanisms for its planning and regeneration. Thus the formation of Defra, while clearly a more radical step than the incremental shifts that might have occurred in the absence of FMD, retained a rather narrow focus on agriculture. Defra's broader remit, in terms of both its environmental focus and rural development under the terms of the EU's Rural Development Regulation, remained largely rooted in the land-based sector. Rural development was equated with diversifying agriculture rather than with any sense of a highly diverse rural economy and society in which farming per se is no longer the economic linchpin.

If the demise of MAFF was designed to appease rural opinion in the light of the criticisms of the department that emerged during the FMD crisis, then the response from the countryside must have disappointed government. In some ways departmental reorganisation occurred too rapidly, for FMD was still rampant and almost inevitably the new department became embroiled in the same set of concerns over the handling of the disease as had its predecessor. Moreover, as the disease receded in the autumn of 2001, the clamour for a public inquiry increased and this was consistently resisted by Defra ministers. The absence of the word 'agriculture' from the new departmental title caused consternation in some sections of the farming and countryside lobby, reinforcing accusations of a government betrayal of farming. Thus in many ways the new structure served to focus even more political criticism on the responsible department than was previously the case. One aspect of the reorganisation brought the new department into particular contention: the vexed issue of hunting was transferred into the new department from the Home Office. Thus the Liberty and Livelihood March in London on 22 September 2002 could focus its ire over hunting, the fortunes of farming and the handling of FMD on a single department of state.

Arguably, more profound and lasting policy impacts of FMD than the changes to national institutional arrangements were the changes at the sub-national level which took place remarkably early in the crisis. With MAFF so absorbed in dealing with the disease itself and with little inclination or capacity to deal with wider social and economic effects, the RDAs and local authorities spotted a policy vacuum with regard to the wider economic implications of FMD. They grasped the initiative and made much of the running in developing strategies for dealing with the resulting issues. In the South West, for example, the RDA (SWRDA) commissioned research on the economic impacts of FMD, convened both an economic and a social summit on FMD, gave crucial support to the establishment of a new Chamber of Rural Enterprise, funded some early local recovery projects, and extended the Market and Coastal Town Initiative to cover some of the hardest-hit market towns. Devon County Council held its own independent inquiry on FMD, produced a Rural Recovery Plan and subsequently helped to establish a Devon Rural Task Group under the aegis of Devon Strategic Partnership. This subsequently became the Devon Rural Network (DRN), with the food and farming agenda featuring highly. The Devon FMD Recovery Plan alone resulted in over £16 million of funding being drawn down to implement the Plan's actions, which included £415,000 from SWRDA for projects to enable tourism business associations to rebuild bookings, local food businesses to increase sales and community organisations to lead regeneration initiatives; £600,000 to extend and expand the Devon Food Links project for three years; and £4 million for community regeneration initiatives from EU LEADER+ and SWRDA's Market and Coastal Town Initiative.

Conclusions

In some respects the concerns and fears of the Labour government on food and farming came to a head in the FMD crisis. Much as Margaret Thatcher took the issue of the CAP to the heart of government in the early 1980s, so FMD prompted Tony Blair to attempt to assert his authority in both Whitehall and the countryside. Dealing with the disease was the pretext for intervention, but Labour's longer-term goal appears to have been to bring the rural sector into line with wider supply-chain efficiencies while responding to environmental, animal welfare and other public pressures. The result has been an inconsistent and conflicting set of policy outcomes and continued uncertainty in the agri-food sector. It is far from clear that lessons have been properly learned or that another outbreak of FMD would be handled significantly differently.

References

Anderson, I. (2002) *Foot and mouth disease 2001: Lessons to be learned inquiry report*, Report by Dr Iain Anderson to the Prime Minister and the Secretary of State for Environment, Food and Rural Affairs, HC 888, London: The Stationery Office. (Also available at http://archive.cabinetoffice.gov.uk/fmd/fmd_report/index.htm)

Bickerstaff, K. and Simmons, P. (2004) 'The right tool for the job? modelling, spatial relationships, and styles of scientific practice in the UK foot and mouth crisis', *Environment and Planning D: Society and Space*, vol 22, pp 393-412.

Campbell, D. and Lee, R. (2003a) '"Carnage by computer": the blackboard economics of the 2001 foot and mouth epidemic', *Social and Legal Studies*, vol 12, no 4, pp 425-59.

Campbell, D. and Lee, R. (2003b) 'The power to panic: the Animal Health Act 2002', *Public Law*, pp 382-96.

Defra (Department for Environment, Food and Rural Affairs) (2002) *The strategy for sustainable farming and food: Facing the future*, London: Defra.

Donaldson, A.I., Alexandersen, S., Sørensen, J.H. and Mikkelsen, T. (2001) 'Relative risks of the uncontrollable (airborne) spread of FMD by different species', *Veterinary Record*, vol 148, pp 602-4.

Forbes, I. (2004) 'Making a crisis out of a drama: the political analysis of BSE policy-making in the UK', *Political Studies*, vol 52, pp 342-57.

Keeling, M. and Woolhouse, M. (2001) 'Dynamics of the 2001 UK foot and mouth epidemic: stochastic dispersal in a heterogeneous landscape', *Science*, vol 294, pp 813-17.

Kenyon, W. and Gilbert, A. (2005) 'Business reactions to the 2001 foot and mouth disease outbreak in Scotland', *Local Economy*, vol 20, pp 372-88.

Law, J. (2006) 'Disaster in agriculture: or foot and mouth mobilities', *Environment and Planning: A*, vol 38, pp 227-39.

Mercer, I. (2002) *Crisis and opportunity: final report of the Devon foot and mouth inquiry*, Tiverton: Devon Books.

Morris, R., Wilesmith, J., Stern, M., Sanson, R. and Stevenson, M. (2001) 'Predictive spatial modelling of alternative control strategies for the foot and mouth disease epidemic in Great Britain, 2001', *Veterinary Record*, vol 149, pp 137-44.

National Audit Office (2002) *The 2001 outbreak of foot and mouth disease*, HC 939, Session 2001–2002, London: The Stationery Office.

Perrow, C. (1999) *Normal accidents: living with high risk technologies*, Princeton, NJ: Princeton University Press.

Phillips of Worth Matravers, Bridgeman, J. and Ferguson-Smith, M. (2000) *The BSE inquiry report*, London: The Stationery Office.

Phillipson, J., Bennett, K. and Lowe, P. (2004) 'Adaptive responses and asset strategies: the experience of rural micro-firms and Fot and Mouth Disease', *Journal of Rural Studies*, vol 20, issue 2, pp 227-43.

Policy Commission on the Future of Farming and Food (2002) *Farming and food: A sustainable future* (the Curry Report), London: The Stationery Office. (Also available at http://archive.cabinetoffice.gov.uk/farming/pdf/PCReport2.pdf)

Poortinga, W., Bickerstaff, K., Langford, I., Niewohner, J. and Pidgeon, N. (2003) 'The British foot and mouth crisis: a comparative study of public risk perceptions, trust and beliefs about government policy in two communities', *Journal of Risk Research*, vol 6, pp 73-90.

Reed, M., Lobley, M., Winter, M. and Chandler, J. (2002) *Family farmers on the edge: Adaptability and change in farm households*, Report by University of Plymouth and University of Exeter to the Countryside Agency.

The Royal Society (2002) *Infectious diseases in livestock*, Policy Report 19/02.

Ward, N., Donaldson, A. and Lowe, P. (2004) 'Policy framing and learning the lessons from the UK foot and mouth disease crisis', *Environment and Planning: C*, vol 22, pp 291-306.

Winter, M. (2003) 'Some ethnographic reflections on the 2001 foot and mouth disease epidemic: a case study from Devon', *CRR Annual Review*, University of Exeter, pp 7-14.

Winter, M. (2006) 'Rescaling rurality: multilevel governance of the agro-food sector', *Political Geography*, vol 25, pp 735-51.

Winter, M., Turner, M., Palmer, M., Whitehead, I. and Millard, N. (2002) *Desk research on developments in farming policy and practice 1967–2002*, Report to Anderson Inquiry, London.

Woods, A. (2002) *Foot and mouth disease: an evaluation of the current control policy from a historical perspective*, Wellcome Unit for the History of Medicine, University of Manchester. (Available at www.sheepdrove.com/fam_disease.htm)

Woods, M. (2005) *Contesting rurality: Politics in the British countryside*, Aldershot: Ashgate.

SIX

Hunting: New Labour success or New Labour failure?

Michael Woods

Introduction

In a special supplement marking ten years of Tony Blair's premiership, *The Observer* newspaper heralded the ban of fox-hunting as the second most significant 'defining Blair moment', behind only the war with Iraq (*The Observer*, 2007). The hunting ban arguably qualifies for this elevated status on a number of grounds. It is one of the truly historic achievements of the New Labour government, criminalising an activity that had been part of rural tradition for several centuries and which was regarded by many as an icon of Englishness, as well as concluding a century-old campaign for its prohibition. The hunting ban was also a notable instance of New Labour enacting a long-standing 'old' Labour commitment and adopting a clearly left-wing position that distinguished it from the Conservative Party. Furthermore, consuming over 700 hours of parliamentary time between 1997 and 2004, the hunting issue was a recurrent preoccupation of Blair's first two terms of office, and the source of the first significant popular challenge to his authority. From the Countryside Rally in July 1997 to the invasion of the House of Commons chamber during the passage of the final Hunting Bill in September 2004, the prospect of a ban on hunting galvanised an unprecedented wave of rural protests that at times arguably formed the most vocal opposition to the Labour government.

Yet, at the same time, the ban on the hunting of wild mammals with hounds eventually introduced in February 2005 has about it something of the air of an accidental policy outcome. For seven years the Blair administration vacillated in its support for a hunting ban between lukewarm endorsement and government-sponsored legislation. It repeatedly searched for a compromise or a way out, but its attempts at evidence-based policy making fell foul of baser political machinations. As such, the policy process that led to the ban eludes rationality-based models of policy making, and rather encapsulates Flyvbjerg's (1998) contention that power defines rationality, not the reverse.

This chapter traces the development of the hunting debate between New Labour's election in May 1997 and the passing of the Hunting Act in November 2004. It divides this trajectory into three periods: the sparking of the debate by the Foster Bill in 1997 and efforts to neutralise the hunting issue during the first term; the workings of the Burns Inquiry as an attempted move towards evidence-based policy making; and the search for compromise in Labour's second term and the eventual success of the Hunting Bill. First, however, the chapter maps out the background to New Labour's hunting legislation by following Labour's historical engagement with hunting as an issue over the last century.

Labour and hunting in historical perspective

Hunting with hounds has been the focus of political campaigning in Britain for nearly a hundred years, and throughout that period the Labour Party has been consistently positioned on the side of the anti-hunting campaign. At the start of the 20th century hunting was, as Newby (1987) describes, "the gentry's particular delight ... [that] developed into more than a mere sport to become almost a celebration of the gentry's ideal of the rural community" (p 65). Although all classes of rural society were involved in hunting, participation was structured by a rigid hierarchy, such that hunting embodied and enacted discourses of a 'natural order' in the countryside (Woods, 1997). The hunting field was a meeting place for the rural elite and a seedbed for political careers, contributing to the reproduction of elite power (Woods, 1997, 2005).

For left-wing radicals, therefore, hunting was both a symbol and a practical component of class inequality, and the campaign to ban hunting was positioned as an extension of political reform in much the same way as the struggle for a right to roam (see Chapter 8 in this volume). Opposition to hunting also came on grounds of animal cruelty from liberal humanitarians, who founded the Humanitarian League in 1891 and the League Against Cruel Sports (LACS) in 1924 (Thomas, 1983; George, 1999). While liberal humanitarians were not necessarily socialists, the growing Labour Party provided a more accommodating political home than the Conservative or Liberal parties with their ties to the rural landowning elite (Tichelar, 2007).

A number of parliamentary attempts to ban or restrict certain types of hunting were unsuccessfully launched from 1893 onwards, usually sponsored by the Humanitarian League or the Royal Society for the Prevention of Cruelty to Animals (RSPCA), but all were heavily defeated (Thomas, 1983). The growth of the Labour Party in the inter-war period provoked increased optimism among anti-hunting campaigners, especially after the 1929 Labour manifesto included a commitment to opposing cruelty in the name of sport (Tichelar, 2007). It was, however, the election of a majority Labour government in 1945 that raised the first prospect of successful legislation on hunting. Yet, as in 1997, hunting did not form part of the government's legislative programme, being left instead to Private Member's Bills. In late 1948 the Labour MP for Broxtowe, Seymour Cocks, introduced the Prohibition of Hunting and Coursing Bill, which was debated in February 1949 (Clayton, 2004). The Cocks Bill was limited to stag-hunting and hare-coursing, but a second Bill aimed at banning fox-hunting was prepared to be introduced by another Labour MP, Frank Fairhurst, should the first Bill pass its Second Reading (Tichelar, 2007). The Bill provoked the first significant pro-hunting protests, with 1.2 million supporters signing a 'Countryman's and Sportsman's Pledge' and hunters from the Midlands riding through the West End of London in the so-called 'Piccadilly Hunt' (Clayton, 2004).

However, the Labour Party in 1949 was not united on hunting. The 1945 cohort of Labour MPs, including a significant number representing rural constituencies and 'miners' hunts', were important to the culture of the Labour heartland of the South Wales Valleys. Equally importantly, the government was at the time laying the foundations for the productivist agricultural regime to address food shortages and was working closely with the National Farmers' Union (NFU), which supported hunting. In an influential intervention in the Second Reading of the Cocks Bill, the Minister of Agriculture, Tom Williams, questioned the cruelty of hunting and emphasised the importance of hunting to farmers. Moreover, he warned, "since this party has been given the power to govern the nation, I believe we have a record of achievement of which we ought to be proud, and I hope we are not going to forfeit the goodwill we have so rightly earned to go down in history as a party anxious to abolish the pleasure of others" (quoted by Clayton, 2004, p 236). The Bill was defeated by 214 votes to 101, and the Bill to prohibit fox-hunting was withdrawn (see also Tichelar, 2007).

Instead, the government appointed a Committee of Inquiry into the cruelty of hunting, chaired by Mr Justice Scott Henderson, but with a membership that was perceived by opponents to be dominated by pro-hunting interests (Tichelar, 2007). The committee reported in 1951, concluding that hunting with hounds was the 'least cruel' form of control of foxes and other vermin. The Scott Henderson Report, together with the return of a Conservative government, stilled parliamentary opposition to hunting for a while and prompted a change of tactics by anti-hunting campaigners with the emergence of the hunt saboteurs movement (Thomas, 1983). Further unsuccessful Bills to ban stag-hunting were debated in 1958 and 1965, but the focus of the Labour government elected in 1964 was concentrated on hare-coursing. A Bill prepared by the LACS and introduced by the Labour MP Eric Heffer in 1967 gained the support of Prime Minister Harold Wilson, but was talked out by pro-hunting MPs. Thirteen other Bills to ban hare-coursing either ran out of time or were defeated in the House of Lords between 1967 and 1975 (George, 1999; Clayton, 2004).

Labour's opposition to hunting was reinvigorated in the late 1970s, in part due to the increasing influence of the 'New Left' concerned with broader social and cultural issues as well as economic struggle, and in part reflecting hardening public attitudes. Public opinion surveys had found majorities in favour of banning both stag-hunting and fox-hunting as early as 1958, and by 1978 an opinion poll recorded 60% of respondents in favour of banning fox-hunting, and 74% supporting a ban on stag-hunting (George, 1999). The LACS had also strengthened its ties with the Labour Party, working closely with the Co-operative movement and donating £80,000 to the party in 1979. A resolution to ban all forms of hunting was passed by the Labour Party Conference in 1977, yet some senior party figures, including the Prime Minister James Callaghan, were concerned that the policy would lose rural votes, and the 1979 manifesto included only promises of legislation on stag-hunting and hare-coursing (Thomas, 1983; George, 1999).

In contrast, Labour fought both the 1983 and 1987 elections with a manifesto pledge to ban all forms of hunting with hounds. Although out of power nationally, Labour remained at the forefront of the anti-hunting campaign during the 1980s and early 1990s. Labour councillors, together with Liberal Democrat councillors, took advantage of weakened Conservative representation in local government to pass anti-hunting motions on councils across the country, most commonly bans on hunting on council-owned land (Woods, 1998; George, 1999; Clayton, 2004). In 1986, the Labour MP Kevin McNamara presented a Ten Minute Rule Bill to ban hunting with hounds, gaining the support of 133 MPs – 123 of them Labour (George, 1999). In 1992, McNamara tried again with a Private Member's Bill, which was narrowly defeated at its Second Reading by 187 votes to 175 (Clayton, 2004). A further attempt was made by another Labour MP, John McFall, in 1994. The McFall Bill was either cleverly or ineptly drafted, depending on your point of view, including a clause that sought to ban "kicking, beating or torture" of wild animals. Unwilling to vote against this clause, pro-hunting MPs abstained on the Second Reading vote, allowing the Bill to be passed by 253 votes to 0 (Clayton, 2004). Without government support, however, the McFall Bill ran out of parliamentary time.

Shortly before the 1997 general election, Labour received a donation of £1 million from the Political Animal Lobby, a group associated with the International Fund for Animal Welfare (IFAW), which had become increasingly involved in the anti-hunting campaign in Britain (George, 1999). A year earlier, in 1996, the LACS had confidently announced that a Labour government would ban hunting on Ministry of Defence and Forestry Commission land on taking office (George, 1999). Yet, at the same time, Labour's official position on hunting was actually weakened. Its policy document *A working countryside*, published in 1995, pledged not government legislation, but government time for a Private Member's Bill on banning stag-hunting, fox-hunting and hare-coursing (Pye-Smith, 2006). The commitment was diluted still further in the 1997 manifesto which stated simply that "we have advocated new measures to promote animal welfare, including a free vote in Parliament on whether hunting with hounds should be banned by legislation" (Labour Party, 1997, p 30), with no explicit promise of government time.

The Foster Bill

The election of the Labour government with a landslide majority in May 1997 raised expectations of an imminent move to ban hunting with hounds. This expectation was held not only by anti-hunting campaigners, but also by supporters of hunting, who had started to plan for such an eventuality in early 1997 as a

Labour government became seemingly inevitable. The main pro-hunting lobby group, the British Field Sports Society (BFSS), had initiated arrangements for a mass rally of supporters in London in the summer of 1997 as early as January, soon bolstered by grassroots organising by hunting supporters across the country. In April 1997, on the eve of the election, the BFSS formed a coalition with two other pro-hunting groups, the Countryside Movement and the Country Business Group, under the title of the Countryside Alliance. Later confirmed by a formal amalgamation, the merger reflected unease at the BFSS's image as 'the Tory party on horseback' and the need to forge an organisation that would have greater credibility with Labour (George, 1999).

In June 1997, the newly elected Labour MP for Worcester, Michael Foster, won first place in the ballot for Private Member's Bills, and was persuaded to introduce a Bill to ban the hunting of wild mammals with hounds. The news was greeted somewhat ambivalently by the government. Downing Street sources had been briefing journalists that they did not want a hunting Bill so early in the new parliament, fearing that it would consume parliamentary time and distract attention away from other flagship legislation. However, it was also announced that the Prime Minister would support the Foster Bill.

On 14 June, four days before the Foster Bill received its First Reading, a group of hunt supporters left the Cumbrian town of Caldbeck at the start of a protest march to London. Nearly a month later, on 10 July, they converged with marchers from Wales and the West Country to parade into Hyde Park where they joined over 120,000 hunting supporters assembled for the Countryside Rally (Hart Davis, 1997). Assisted by a largely sympathetic press, the Countryside Rally received extensive media coverage and became an early landmark for the New Labour administration. The protest was the first significant challenge to the new government and suggested a political cleavage between city and countryside that threatened New Labour's consensual approach.

The size of the Countryside Rally and the passion of its participants certainly rattled the government. *The Daily Telegraph* political editor George Jones judged that Labour had been "outmanoeuvred and outgunned on a popular issue", although he also warned that the hunting lobby "may have won the first skirmish, but a year long parliamentary battle lies ahead before they can be sure of victory" (George, 1999, p 127). Downing Street press briefings sought to distance the government from the proposed legislation, emphasising that it was a Private Member's Bill and that no government time would be made available.

Nonetheless, the Bill's supporters were undeterred, buoyed by opinion polls that suggested that a ban was backed by around 70% of voters, and confident of a large majority in parliament. The Foster Bill received its Second Reading on 28 November 1997, with 411 MPs voting in favour and 151 against. With no prospect of government time, both supporters and opponents of the Bill attempted to play parliamentary procedure to their advantage. Supporters of the Bill initially sought to prolong the Bill's passage through the Committee Stage, hence blocking the progress of other Bills and potentially gaining more time for the Foster Bill in the chamber. However, when the Bill did return to the House of Commons in March 1998, it was talked out of time by opponents.

The Foster Bill, or more correctly the Wild Mammals (Hunting with Dogs) Bill, would have made hunting fox, deer, hare and mink with hounds a criminal offence subject to a maximum fine of £5,000 or imprisonment for up to six months. An amendment in the drafting stage had exempted the flushing out of foxes from cover by dogs, as commonly practised by Welsh farmers' hunts. The emphasis of the Bill, the speeches of its supporters, and the supporting campaign publicity, was on animal welfare. The claims and evidence advanced were disputed by hunting supporters, drawing on veterinary reports and appealing back to the Scott Henderson Report (see Woods, 2000). Concerns that a ban on hunting would lead to indiscriminate shooting of foxes by farmers were reinforced by staged photographs from Somerset (where stag-hunting on the Quantock Hills had been effectively ended by a ban on hunting on National Trust land) that showed the piled-up antlers of deer shot by farmers.

This had been the structure of debates about hunting for the previous 40 years. However, the strategy of the Countryside Alliance was to shift the debate onto new discursive terrain. As well as presenting the threat to hunting as an urban assault on the countryside, the pro-hunting campaign played with the ambiguities of New Labour's ideological position. On the one hand, they targeted Labour's modernising zeal, portraying the proposed hunting ban as showing disregard for tradition and gradual change; on the other hand, they suggested that to ban hunting would be to curtail personal liberties and demonstrate intolerance towards a minority, in apparent contradiction of Labour's social liberalism.

This latter argument, in particular, was taken up by opponents of the Bill within Labour, who coalesced in a new group 'Leave Country Sports Alone'. These included the only two Labour MPs to speak against the Foster Bill in the Second Reading debate, Kate Hoey and Llin Golding (both of whom represented urban constituencies), and the Labour peer Baroness Mallalieu, who became President of the Countryside Alliance. The themes of liberty, tradition and tolerance were also highlighted by the Conservatives, who saw the hunting debate as an opportunity to align themselves with a popular protest movement against the government. As the Conservative Leader, William Hague, wrote in *The Daily Telegraph* prior to the 1998 Countryside March:

> The reason why Sunday's march is so important is that the Government's attack on the countryside is also an attack on many peculiarly British values, which city-dwellers feel as keenly as rural dwellers. (Hague, 1998)

The problem for the Conservatives, however, was that this attempt to build a broader coalition fell on largely deaf ears. The majority of protesters were already Conservative supporters (79% of participants in the Countryside March told MORI that they would vote Conservative), and in adopting a cause that was popularly perceived as an elitist and outdated tradition, the Conservatives in fact appeared to be retreating to their core base. The first test of the electoral significance of hunting came with the Eddisbury by-election in July 1999, a rural Conservative-held seat that was home to the historic Cheshire Hunt. The Conservatives hoped that pro-hunting sentiment would help to significantly increase their majority of just 1,185, while the Labour candidate prominently emphasised her support for a ban on hunting in the campaign. In the event, the Conservatives only marginally increased their majority and the Labour vote-share increased. Moreover, an opinion poll in the constituency during the by-election campaign found that only 10% of voters said that they were more likely to vote for a candidate who was strongly pro-hunting, whilst 39% said that they would be less likely to support a pro-hunting candidate (MORI, 1999).

By this stage, Labour had fulfilled the letter of its manifesto commitment by permitting a free vote on hunting. However, there was a strong opinion among anti-hunting backbench Labour MPs that the Foster Bill had demonstrated the will of parliament, and that as a Private Member's Bill was unlikely to provide a viable vehicle for a ban, the government itself should now sponsor legislation. This view was repeatedly expressed to party leaders, including to a sceptical Home Secretary, Jack Straw, by a packed meeting of the backbench committee on Home Affairs (Cowley and Stuart, 2005).

The position of Tony Blair himself, however, was enigmatic. Blair had publicly expressed his support for a hunting ban, and had voted for the McNamara Bill in 1992. He was absent in Northern Ireland for the Foster Bill Second Reading, although he later mistakenly claimed to have voted in favour. Privately, though, Blair frequently expressed his exasperation at the prominence of hunting as an issue and the time that it consumed. His former Press Secretary, Alastair Campbell, in his published diaries records several such occasions, noting on one that Blair's "problem with [a hunting ban] was that he felt it was basically illiberal, and not him" (Campbell, 2007, p 488). On another occasion, Blair reportedly confided in his mentor, Roy Jenkins, "Roy, I wish I had never heard the word hunting. We are in such as mess. I do not know how we are going to get out of it" (*The Times*, 1 March 2003, quoted by Pye-Smith, 2006, p 29).

Yet, Blair was also astute enough as a politician to realise that hunting could be an important bargaining tool with his own party. The clearest evidence of this came in early summer 1999, as the government experienced backbench unrest over military action in Kosovo and concerns about the direction of the domestic agenda. To widespread surprise, Blair announced on the BBC's *Question Time* programme on 8 July 1999 that legislation to ban hunting would be introduced "as soon as possible" (Clayton, 2004, p 254). Although Blair's advisors initially believed the promise to be an unintended slip (Price, 2005), the commitment was reinforced by Blair at the Labour Party Conference in September 1999 when he positioned "Today's Tory Party – the party of fox-hunting, Pinochet and hereditary peers: the uneatable, the unspeakable and the unelectable" among the 'forces of conservatism' that his government was pledged to sweep away (BBC News, 1999).

The government assuming responsibility for hunting legislation did not, however, result in a new Bill before the 2001 election, as some had believed Blair's statement implied. Instead, it marked the start of an attempt to construct a distinctively New Labour approach to hunting. The first step in this process replicated the response of the 1945 Labour government to the Cocks Bill when Home Secretary Jack Straw announced in November 1999 the establishment of an independent inquiry into the significance of hunting to the rural economy.

The Burns Inquiry

The Committee of Inquiry into Hunting with Dogs in England and Wales was formally constituted on 9 December 1999, having been announced by the Home Secretary, Jack Straw, on 11 November. Straw's statement, which was delivered as the response to a parliamentary question from Michael Foster, was the product of five months of deliberation by the government as to how to take forward the hunting issue following Blair's pledge on *Question Time*. Carefully worded, the statement noted that Labour had fulfilled its manifesto pledge, but also reaffirmed a commitment to produce enabling legislation to ban hunting, while also making a case for the rational and objective examination of the evidence on hunting:

> The Government have decided that there should first be an inquiry. This will be a committee of inquiry not into whether hunting is right or wrong, which is a matter for Parliament to decide. Instead, the inquiry will be put in place better to inform the debate. The inquiry will look at the practical issues involved in hunting with dogs, how a ban could be implemented and what the consequences of a ban would be. It will provide an opportunity for the facts about hunting properly to be considered. (Home Secretary Jack Straw, Answer to parliamentary question, 11 November 1999)

Politically, therefore, the establishment of the inquiry performed a number of purposes. First, it was a useful delaying tactic. As noted above, the government had come under intense pressure from backbenchers to take up the cause of a ban on hunting, in spite of the scepticism of a number of senior ministers, including not only Blair, but also Robin Cook, Peter Mandelson and Jack Straw himself. By announcing the inquiry in tandem with a reaffirmed commitment to support hunting legislation, the government gave the impression of moving forward whilst effectively ruling out legislation for at least a year.

Second, the commissioning of the inquiry permitted the government to distance itself from the emotive arguments which had dominated previous debates on hunting and attempt to present itself as an independent arbitrator acting on the objective analysis of the 'facts'. In this aim it can be positioned as part of a wider

New Labour emphasis on 'evidence-based policy making' (to be discussed later), as well as part of a New Labour penchant for drafting in 'independent' establishment figures to advise on controversial issues (for example, the Haskins Report on rural delivery and the Barker Report on housing, etc).

Third, by explicitly including examination of a ban on hunting on the rural economy and society in the terms of reference, the inquiry also allowed the government to claim that they had listened to the concerns of the countryside protesters, while at the same time gathering evidence that might allow the Countryside Alliance's representation of the significance of hunting to the countryside to be challenged.

The committee of inquiry was chaired by Lord Terry Burns, a former Permanent Secretary at the Treasury, with four members from academic backgrounds, Dr Victoria Edwards, Professor Sir John Marsh, Lord Soulsby of Swaffam Prior and Professor Michael Winter. The inquiry's terms of reference instructed it to inquire into:

> the practical aspects of different types of hunting with dogs and its impact on the rural economy, agriculture and pest control, the social and cultural life of the countryside, the management and conservation of wildlife, and animal welfare in particular areas of England and Wales; the consequences for these issues of any ban on hunting with dogs; and how any ban might be implemented. (Burns, 2000, p 1)

References to the implementation and consequences of a ban led some in the hunting community to believe that the inquiry presupposed that a ban would be introduced and was aimed solely at constructing a justification (Clayton, 2004). Of arguably greater significance, however, was the exclusion from the terms of reference of any consideration of whether hunting with hounds was 'cruel', and the absence of a requirement on the committee to make a recommendation about the future of hunting.

The inquiry was hence positioned as an exercise in gathering and analysing evidence, which would subsequently inform decision-making. The inquiry invited the submission of written evidence in two stages, receiving 351 submissions from organisations and individuals in stage one, and 108 submissions in stage two (Table 6.1); heard oral evidence from the two key lobby groups, the Countryside Alliance and Deadline 2000; and organised by-invitation meetings with supporters of both sides. Committee members also made a number of field visits, organised by both hunt supporters and hunt opponents, and commissioned seven research studies.

As such, the Burns Inquiry could be regarded as a prime example of evidence-based policy making, which has become a key tool of governmentality under New Labour. As a Civil Service summary of the approach explains, evidence-based policy making is premised on the assertion that:

Table 6.1: Submissions to the Burns Inquiry, by source

	Stage 1 submissions	Stage 2 submissions
Hunts and Hunt Supporters Clubs	80	13
Individuals	48	42
Businesses	45	3
Other field sports organisations	41	11
Animal welfare groups	27	14
Equestrian organisations	24	3
Pro-hunting pressure groups	12	5
Anti-hunting pressure groups	11	5
Agricultural organisations	10	2
Other rural groups	8	1
Parish and town councils	7	1
Environmental organisations	6	2
Estates	6	2
Statutory bodies	4	1
Veterinary organisations	2	1
Other	20	2

Source: www.huntinginquiry.gov.uk

> the opinions and judgements of experts that are based upon up-
> to-date scientific research clearly constitute high quality valid and
> reliable evidence. Those opinions that are not based upon such
> scientific evidence, but are unsubstantiated, subjective and opinionated
> viewpoints do not constitute high quality, valid and reliable evidence.
> (Civil Service Policy Hub, 2006)

Evidence-based policy making is hence intended to progressively replace 'opinion-based decision-making', producing a more 'rational' form of governance (Gray, 1997). As the Department for Environment, Food and Rural Affairs (Defra) suggests:

> The key benefit of evidence-based policy making is better policy. The
> recent increase in interest in evidence-based policy making comes
> in response to a perception that Government needs to improve the
> quality of decision-making.... Many critics argued in the past that
> policy decisions were too often driven by inertia or by short-term
> political pressures. (Defra, 2006)

The Burns Inquiry was intended to redress the shortage of hard scientific evidence available to support 'effective' and rational decision-making on the future of hunting. Yet, if the government believed that the committee could isolate and remove itself from the deeply entrenched politics of hunting, it had grossly miscalculated. The committee members were subjected to severe pressure from both sides, found their backgrounds trawled and every contact with actors involved on each side scrutinised for any indication of bias. Hunting supporters and opponents alike questioned the independence of committee members, while at the same time picking selectively from the evidence considered by the inquiry to makes claims supporting their own case. Thus, rather than removing the politics from the hunting question, the Burns Inquiry became embroiled in the power-play of hunting politics as campaigners sought to influence the 'rationality' that it had been charged with constructing.

Moreover, if the government had hoped that the inquiry would provide clear guidance on which legislation could be based, it was again to be disappointed. Conscious of the extreme political sensitivity of its work, the committee adhered to a strict interpretation of its terms of reference, and spelled this out carefully in its report. The inquiry presented findings and conclusions rather than recommendations, and many of these were equivocal in nature, reflecting the complexity of the issues under consideration. In the covering letter to the Home Secretary, Jack Straw, the committee members observed:

> Without doubt, conducting the inquiry has been a challenging experience. This is a complex issue that is full of paradoxes. We were helped by the terms of reference, which asked us to concentrate on the factual and analytical background to hunting. We have addressed those issues and we have not attempted to answer the question of whether or not hunting should be banned. In particular, we have not sought to find a compromise solution, which we regarded as outside our terms of reference. ... The result is a report that might appear long on analysis and short on solutions. (Burns, 2000, p 1)

The publication of the Burns Report in June 2000 was perhaps predictably seized upon by both the pro- and anti-hunting lobbies as vindicating their positions. The LACS and the RSPCA contended that the report showed that hunting with dogs was cruel, and supported the case for a complete ban. Simon Hart, the director of the Countryside Alliance's Campaign for Hunting, in contrast, asserted that the report "confirms our view that hunting is a legitimate activity in the countryside and nothing suggests that it is worthy of criminal sanction" (Clover and Jones, 2000, p 2). However, if the Burns Inquiry failed to bring objective clarity to the hunting impasse, the report's publication marked the entry of the debate into its final stage.

The political endgame

Presenting the report of the Burns Inquiry to the House of Commons, Jack Straw announced that the government intended to introduce a Bill in the autumn of 2000 setting out a series of options on the future of hunting ranging from a complete ban to self-regulation. As *The Daily Telegraph* observed, "Mr Straw's statement amounted to a significant declaration of intent by Labour to ensure that a ban – a fiercely fought issue in Parliament for 50 years – was finally brought to fruition" (Clover and Jones, 2000, p 1). With this signal, the political endgame of the hunting debate commenced.

The drama that unfolded over the next four years was in essence centred not around the struggle between supporters and opponents of hunting, but around a tension within the Labour Party – between political tribalism and 'third way' consensus-building. The latter was reflected in the government's approach to the legislation, and in its decision to present not a clear Bill to ban hunting, but rather an 'Options Bill', giving parliament a choice of three ways forward:

- self-regulation by hunts, supervised by an independent authority;
- establishment of an independent government-appointed authority to regulate hunting;
- an outright ban.

The appearance of the second option indicated the growing influence of the Middle Way Group on government thinking on hunting. A cross-party grouping set up in May 1998 by the Liberal Democrat MP Lembit Opik, Conservative MP Peter Luff, and then Labour MP Llin Golding, the Middle Way Group opposed a ban on hunting, but favoured the introduction of a licensing system in order to tighten regulation and monitoring of hunt activities. Its compromise solution clearly appealed to several senior figures in the Labour government, including the Prime Minister, who had become increasingly nervous about the prospect of banning hunting outright for reasons of both principle and political expediency. Support in parliament more broadly, however, was much more limited. Only 182 MPs backed the Middle Way option when the House of Commons voted on the 'Options Bill' in January 2001 (a majority against of 200), compared with 387 who backed an outright ban. When the Bill passed to the House of Lords in March 2001, the Middle Way option was again rejected, this time by a majority of 80, with the majority of peers backing self-regulation (Clayton, 2004). In March 2002 the government tried again – the first Bill having fallen with the 2001 general election. This time, MPs rejected the Middle Way by 371 to 169, and reaffirmed their support for a total ban by 386 to 175. The House of Lords, however, significantly changed tack and backed the Middle Way option by 366 votes to 59 (Clayton, 2004).

The strategy adopted by the government, though, had anticipated the polarisation of the two Houses. Its hope was that the impasse would eventually force both sides towards accepting the Middle Way option as a compromise. Alastair Campbell, in his diary entries for January 2001, recorded Blair's efforts to find "a way out" on hunting and noted that "one idea now doing the rounds was that it would get blocked in the Lords and we could then put a middle way in the manifesto for the next parliament" (Campbell, 2007, p 488).

The most explicit attempt to engineer a compromise came in September 2002, with a series of televised public hearings organised following the conflicting votes of the House of Commons and House of Lords. Involving a panel comprising representatives of the Campaign for the Hunted Animal, the Middle Way Group and the Countryside Alliance's Campaign for Hunting, the hearings embodied several key New Labour motifs: deliberative policy making, transparency, evidence-based policy making, and a belief in a 'third way'. The purpose of the hearings was described as being to define the principles that could be employed in a Bill that recognised the 'utility' of hunting while limiting its 'cruelty'. Moreover, the panel chair, Defra Minister Alun Michael, reportedly "made it clear from the outset that one of his aims was to look for common ground 'wherever possible'" (Pye-Smith, 2006, p 31). Yet Michael was subsequently accused by hunting supporters of favouring the pro-ban lobby and accepting its evidence more readily than that presented by the Middle Way Group or the Countryside Alliance (Pye-Smith, 2006).

Although the hearings failed to find any substantial common ground, the government nonetheless presented a new Bill in December 2002 that proposed to ban hare-coursing and stag-hunting, but would permit fox-hunting to continue under licence from a government-appointed registrar, supported by a new Hunting Tribunal. The character of the Bill as the first truly New Labour Hunting Bill was recognised, albeit critically, by the Conservative MP David Heathcote-Amory, who described it as "the low point of Labour's Third Way" (Clayton, 2004, p 271). The compromise of the Hunting Bill found favour with neither hunting supporters nor opponents, and the government became caught in a squeeze between the two sides. In an attempt to save the Bill, a government amendment to establish a close season from August to November to protect fox cubs was introduced but quickly withdrawn when it failed to gain support. Instead, a backbench Labour amendment proposed by Tony Banks converting the Bill into a complete ban was passed in the House of Commons with a majority of 208. Yet again the House of Lords adopted a conflicting position by supporting the original proposal for regulated hunting. With another impasse in place, the Bill was allowed to run out of time.

Significantly, in all of these failed efforts to move forward a 'third way' compromise solution on hunting, the government was frustrated not by the pro-hunting lobby, but by its own Members of Parliament. The unwillingness of backbench Labour MPs to toe a 'New Labour' line on hunting had been signalled in May 2000, when Gordon Prentice MP had pre-empted the report of the Burns Inquiry by tabling an amendment to ban hunting to the Countryside and Rights of Way Bill. Anti-hunting Labour MPs were further encouraged in February 2002 when the Scottish Parliament passed a Bill presented by Labour MSP

Mike Watson outlawing fox-hunting and hare-coursing. Moreover, their resolve had been strengthened by the failure of a substantial pro-hunting protest vote to materialise at the 2001 general election. Outside of the handful of most ardent hunting areas, the swing from Labour to Conservative in hunting constituencies was only marginally greater than the national swing, and no Labour MP lost their seat directly due to hunting (Woods, 2002).

The growing confidence of anti-hunting Labour MPs was reflected in a change in the discourses employed to frame opposition to hunting, with some prepared to talk openly of class politics. The veteran left-winger Dennis Skinner reportedly told one Middle Way supporter at the Labour Party conference in September 2004 that "this has nothing to do with animal welfare – this is for the miners" (Pye-Smith, 2006, p 23). More surprisingly, and more notably, the message was repeated by Peter Bradley, Parliamentary Private Secretary to Alun Michael and founder of the Rural Group of Labour MPs, in an article for *The Sunday Telegraph*, in which he stated:

> We ought at last to own up to it: the struggle over the bill was not just about animal welfare and personal freedom, it was class war. But it was not class war as we know it. It was not launched by the tribunes against the toffs – it was the other way round. This was not about the politics of envy, but the politics of power. Ultimately it's about who governs Britain. (Bradley, 2004, p 19)

This re-framing of the hunting debate was significant for a number of reasons. First, it implicitly undermined the rationale behind the Middle Way option by suggesting that constructing the hunting issue as a problem of animal welfare missed the point. Second, it challenged the representation promoted by the Countryside Alliance of the hunting community as an 'oppressed minority', instead, echoing Blair's 'forces of conservatism' speech, it positioned hunting supporters as a privileged elite seeking to cling on to power. Third, it was deliberately calculated to rile the pro-hunting lobby.

Although it might be argued that the government had had more success in persuading pro-hunting figures to support the Middle Way option, many in the hunting community remained deeply suspicious of New Labour and its intentions. In particular, there was a lack of trust in Alun Michael, the Defra Minister charged with overseeing the hunting legislation, who had previously voted for a hunting ban on several occasions and had accepted funding from the LACS during the 1980s (Pye-Smith, 2006). As Pye-Smith records, the pro-hunting Labour peer and former Agriculture Minister Lord Donoughue observed that in asking Michael to find a compromise solution, Blair had "made a mistake appointing someone who'd always been committed to a ban" (Pye-Smith, 2006, p 30).

The Countryside Alliance was also subjected to internal criticism for entering into dialogue with the government over the hunting options and participating in the public hearings in September 2002. Although it successfully overshadowed the hearings with the Liberty and Livelihood March on 22 September, involving 407,791 recorded participants, the march had an edgier feel than the earlier demonstrations, with placards carrying slogans such as 'This is our last peaceful protest'. Radical breakaway groups such as the Countryside Action Network and the Real Countryside Alliance had already engaged in minor direct action protests and media stunts, and the August 2002 issue of *The Field* magazine had carried an article reporting the willingness of hunt supporters to adopt more militant tactics, including road blockades and attacks on reservoirs and electricity pylons (Walton, 2002). Additionally, over 50,000 hunt supporters signed the Hunting Declaration, pledging to carry on hunting in the event of a ban (Woods, 2005).

Thus, in spite of the government's efforts to find a compromise, the militancy of hard-line activists on both sides of the hunting argument increasingly became mutually reinforcing. Staunch hunting supporters rejected any form of negotiation with the government, while for staunch hunting opponents any concession that permitted hunting to continue in any form was tantamount to surrender to the 'forces of conservatism'. Alastair Campbell's diaries again record a conversation with the senior Labour backbench MP Sir Gerald Kaufman before the introduction of the second 'Options Bill' in March 2002, in which Kaufman declared that "If the Tony [Blair] who stood up to Milosevic and bin Laden can't stand up to the Countryside Alliance, I can't support him" (Campbell, 2007, p 610).

Most significant, however, was the shifting wider political context. In November 1997, when the Foster Bill was first debated, hunting was the most prominent and controversial issue before parliament, and the Countryside Alliance looked liked the government's most dangerous opponents. By 2003, however, the government was fighting political battles on several fronts, from foundation hospitals to the war in Iraq. Pacifying discontented backbench MPs and shoring up Labour's majority in parliament became more important than reaching out to Conservative-voting hunt supporters. The hunting ban hence became a bartering chip with rebellious Labour MPs: the Labour Chief Whip Hilary Armstrong, for example, reportedly warned Blair in June 2003 that "if he didn't bring back the Hunting Bill for a third reading soon we would not have a hope in hell of winning the foundation hospital vote" (Campbell, 2007, p 706). The Hunting Bill received its Third Reading two weeks later, with the government capitulating on Tony Banks' amendment supporting a complete ban.

Labour's final Hunting Bill, with the clear intention of banning hunting with hounds, was introduced in September 2004, with a free vote for MPs promised before the end of the parliamentary session that November (Table 6.2). Crucially, it was also announced that the government would use the Parliament Act to force through the legislation if the House of Lords voted against a ban approved by the Commons. However, many hunt sympathisers suspected that the commitment had less to do with a newly re-found resolve on hunting than with wider political calculations. *The Daily Telegraph*, for example, commented that "Tony Blair will make hunting the 'nuclear issue' of the next election by using it to embarrass the Tories and push through fundamental reform of the Lords" (Brogan, 2004, p 1).

Table 6.2: Key dates in the hunting debate, 1997–2005

May 1997	Labour government elected
18 June 1997	Foster Bill First Reading
27 July 1997	Countryside Rally
28 November 1997	Foster Bill Second Reading, passed 411 to 151
1 March 1998	Countryside March
13 March 1998	Foster Bill runs out of time during report stage
3 July 1998	Michael Foster withdraws Bill
8 July 1998	Tony Blair announces on BBC *Question Time* that hunting will be banned
14 November 1999	Burns Inquiry established
12 June 2000	Burns Inquiry reports
December 2000	'Options Bill' published
28 February 2001	House of Commons backs outright ban in Options Bill debate
26 March 2001	House of Lords backs licensing system in Options Bill debate
May 2001	Options Bill falls as general election is called
February 2002	Scottish Parliament passes Watson Bill banning hunting with hounds in Scotland
18 March 2002	House of Commons again backs outright ban in vote on options
19 March 2002	House of Lords backs self-regulation in vote on options
9-11 Sept 2002	Public hearings on hunting
22 September 2002	Liberty and Livelihood March
3 December 2002	New Hunting Bill published proposing licensing system
30 June 2003	Amendment by Tony Banks proposing complete ban passed 362 to 154
10 July 2003	Amended Hunting Bill given Third Reading, passed 317 to 145.
21 October 2003	House of Lords reject ban and reinstate licensing system in Hunting Bill
October 2003	Hunting Bill runs out of time
8 September 2004	Government publishes new Hunting Bill, proposing a ban
16 Sept 2004	Hunting Bill passed by Commons, 356 to 166. Protesters invade House of Commons chamber
18 November 2004	Parliament Act invoked to pass Hunting Bill into law
18 February 2005	Hunting ban comes into force in England and Wales

The Bill received its Second Reading on 16 September by a majority of 356 to 166, against a background of angry and violent demonstrations outside parliament, and the incursion into the House of Commons chamber of five pro-hunting protesters. Yet, the strength of New Labour's ownership of the Bill was brought into question by the absence from the vote of the Prime Minister. According to *The Daily Mail*, Blair's non-appearance indicated his disagreement with a ban, reporting that:

> Asked to explain Mr Blair's abstention, his spokesman made clear that the Bill before the House was not supported by the Prime Minister. He indicated that his preferred option was the compromise deal which would have allowed licensed hunts to continue, rather than the outright ban now being forced through. (Hughes, 2004, p 7)

Up to the last moment, the compromise option continued to be repeatedly floated by senior New Labour figures. With the House of Lords predictably rejecting the outright ban, bringing the two chambers into conflict, Alun Michael again urged the acceptance of a compromise deal on licensed hunting to stave off the use of the Parliament Act. Blair, Home Secretary David Blunkett and Leader of the Commons Peter Hain, all tried to delay the implementation of the ban. A delay until 2006 was backed by MPs in an attempt to reach a deal with the House of Lords, but rejected by the peers. As options became exhausted, the Commons Speaker Michael Martin finally invoked the Parliament Act on 18 November 2004, and the 2004 Hunting Act, banning the hunting of wild mammals with hounds, passed into law.

Conclusion

The hunting ban in England and Wales came into force on 18 February 2005. On Saturday, 19 February, thousands of hunt supporters and sympathisers joined over 270 hunt meets intending to 'hunt within the law'. The Countryside Alliance reported that 91 foxes had been killed legally, although the LACS claimed that this was substantially fewer than would have been killed before the ban. Police investigated four alleged breaches of the ban, but no prosecutions were brought.

Research for the Burns Inquiry in 2000 found that there were 284 hunts in England and Wales (178 fox-hunts, 3 deer-hunts, 83 hare-hunts and 20 mink-hunts), employing 510 full-time employees and 325 part-time employees, involving 27,949 hunt subscribers and 39,159 members of hunt supporters' clubs, and keeping nearly 10,000 hounds (Burns, 2000). Little of this appeared to change in the immediate wake of the ban. The Countryside Alliance claimed that hunting had never been more popular, with subscriptions increasing (Bowcott, 2005). Large numbers of riders and spectators turned out for the traditional Boxing Day hunt meets in 2005 and 2006, and it was claimed that over 100,000 people had taken part in hunts on the first anniversary of the ban in February 2006

(Igguiden, 2006). Privately, however, some hunt officials have suggested that the positive façade hides a deeper problem and that a number of hunts were close to financial collapse by late 2007.

The threatened wave of civil disobedience and militant direct action failed to materialise, as many hunt supporters expressed emotional exhaustion after seven years of protests. Instead, an approach of 'testing' the limits of the ban appeared to be adopted, along with optimism in the prospect of a ban being repealed by a future Conservative government. Hunt supporters organised as constituency workers by the Vote-OK initiative claimed to have helped to defeat 29 anti-hunting MPs at the 2005 general election, but these efforts in themselves were insufficient to overturn the anti-hunting majority in the Commons.

Moreover, the apparent ability of hunts to continue to meet and operate within the parameters of the new law reflected the flexibility of its boundaries and the difficulty of policing the ban on hunting with hounds. In February 2007, the LACS publicly accused 33 hunts of repeated breaches of the law (Bowcott and Meikle, 2007), yet prosecutions under the Hunting Act have been limited, with only 20 convictions achieved by late 2007.

If the visible impact of the Hunting Act in rural areas has been limited, then arguably the hunting debate and its outcome has had more significance in Westminster than in the countryside. Over 700 hours of parliamentary time were devoted to debating hunting between 1997 and 2004 (Pye-Smith, 2006), and as an almost constant issue through Labour's first two terms, hunting can be read as a yardstick of the evolution of the government's sense of authority and its relationship with the Parliamentary Labour Party (PLP). In 1997, the freshly elected government displayed nerves in dealing with its first significant extra-parliamentary challenge from the Countryside Alliance, and wobbled on the Foster Bill. By 2000 it had become confident enough to try to forge its own 'third way' solution. Yet, four years later, the authority of the government over backbenchers had weakened to the point that it was prepared to sacrifice the Prime Minister's own preferred option under pressure from MPs whose support it required on more fundamental issues of policy.

Cowley and Stuart (2005) suggest that the 2004 Hunting Act represented the height of backbench influence during New Labour's first two terms. As they comment:

> The ban on fox-hunting is on the Statute Book precisely because Labour MPs refused to let it go. As one anti-hunting Labour MP remarked after the final vote: 'I'm quite proud of the PLP for getting us here – shows what one can achieve by polite persistence'. Whatever one's views about that policy, and whether one thinks hunting should continue or not, that aspect of the process is striking. The eventually successful struggle by Labour backbenchers to secure a ban on hunting deserves to go down as one of the clearest examples of backbench influence in the post-war period. (Cowley and Stuart, 2005, p 27)

The hunting ban will stand as one of the historic achievements of New Labour. Yet, it is in many ways a distinctly non-New Labour policy. It has some hallmarks of New Labour thinking, notably modernisation and liberal humanitarianism, but these are outweighted by the counts on which it offended New Labour sensibilities on consensus-building, evidence-based policy making and personal choice. Certainly, there is no escaping the fact that in a debate with a century-old history, the distinctive New Labour approach – the 'third way' of licensed hunting – was repeatedly rejected by parliament. Ultimately, however, the hunting ban was perhaps neither a success nor a failure for New Labour, but a muddled unintended outcome, which perhaps is appropriate. As the former BBC political editor Andrew Marr observes, "The fox-hunting story can serve as a symbol for much else in the New Labour years: a long and noisy confrontation at Westminster, which in the end had surprisingly little effect on the ground" (Marr, 2007, p 546).

References

BBC News (1999) 'Tony Blair's speech in full', BBC News website. (Available at news.bbc.co.uk/1/hi/uk_politics/460009.html)

Bradley, P. (2004) 'Yes – this is about class war', *The Sunday Telegraph*, 21 November, p 19.

Brogan, B. (2004) 'Blair to force through Bill to ban hunting', *The Daily Telegraph*, 6 September, p 1.

Bowcott, O. (2005) 'Hunts say ban has brought groundswell of support', *Guardian*, 17 October, p 14.

Bowcott, O. and Meikle, J. (2007) 'Hunts accused of breaching ban', *Guardian*, 17 February, p 3.

Burns, T. (2000) *Report of the Committee of Inquiry into Hunting with Dogs in England and Wales*, London: The Stationery Office.

Campbell, A. (2007) *The Blair years*, London: Hutchinson.

Civil Service Policy Hub (2006) 'How research and evaluation evidence contributes to policy making', Civil Service Policy Hub website. (Available at www.policyhub.gov.uk/evaluating_policy/how_res_eval_evid.asp)

Clayton, M. (2004) *Endangered species: foxhunting – the history, the passion and the fight for survival*, Shrewsbury: Swan Hill.

Clover, C. and Jones, G. (2000) 'Hunt report sets scene for long fight', *The Daily Telegraph*, 13 June, pp 1-2.

Cowley, P. and Stuart, M. (2005) 'Parliament', in A. Seldon and D. Kavanagh (eds) *The Blair effect 2001-5*, Cambridge: Cambridge University Press, pp 20-42.

Defra (Department for Environment, Food and Rural Affairs) (2006) 'Evidence based policy making', Defra website. (Available at www.defra.gov.uk/science/how/evidence.htm)

Flyvbjerg, B. (1998) *Rationality and power: democracy in practice*, Chicago: University of Chicago Press.

George, J. (1999) *A rural uprising? The battle to save hunting with hounds*, London: Allen and Unwin.

Gray, J.A.M. (1997) *Evidence-based health care: How to make health policy and management decisions*, New York and London: Churchill Livingstone.

Hague, W. (1998) 'Marching for freedom', *The Daily Telegraph*, 22 February, p 20.

Hart Davis, D. (1997) *When the country came to town*, Ludlow: Excellent Press.

Hughes, D. (2004) 'Running with the fox and the hounds', *The Daily Mail*, 17 September, p 7.

Iguidden, A. (2006) '100,000 join hunts for ban anniversary', *The Daily Telegraph*, 18 February, p 12.

Labour Party (1997) *New Labour: Because Britain deserves better*, Labour Party manifesto, London: Labour Party.

Marr, A. (2007) *A history of modern Britain*, London: Macmillan.

MORI (1999) 'Eddisbury by-election/hunting of wild mammals with dogs', IPSOS/MORI website. (Available at www.ipsos-mori.com/polls/1999/eddisbur.shtml)

Newby, H. (1987) *Country life: A social history of rural England*, London: Weidenfeld and Nicolson.

Price, L. (2005) *The spin doctor's diary*, London: Hodder and Stoughton.

Pye-Smith, C. (2006) *Rural rites: Hunting and the politics of prejudice*, London: Middle Way Group.

The Observer (2007) *The Blair years, 1997-2007*, Special Supplement, *The Observer*, 6 May.

Thomas, R. H. (1983) *The politics of hunting*, Aldershot: Gower.

Tichelar, M. (2007) '"Putting animals into politics": the Labour party and hunting in the first half of the twentieth century', *Rural History*, vol 17, no 2, pp 213-34.

Walton, E. (2002) 'They can't lock us all up, can they?', *The Field*, August 2002, pp 48-52.

Woods, M. (1997) 'Discourses of power and rurality: local politics in Somerset in the 20th century', *Political Geography*, vol 16, pp 453-78.

Woods, M. (1998) 'Researching rural conflicts: hunting, local politics and actor networks', *Journal of Rural Studies*, vol 14, pp 321-40.

Woods, M. (2000) 'Fantastic Mr Fox? Representing animals in the hunting debate', in C. Philo and C. Wilbert (eds) *Animal spaces, beastly places*, London: Routledge, pp 182-202.

Woods, M. (2002) 'Was there a rural rebellion? Labour and the countryside vote in the 2001 General Election', in L. Bennie, C. Rallings, J. Tonge and P. Webb (eds) *British parties and elections review: Volume 12 – The 2001 general election*, London: Frank Cass, pp 206-28.

Woods, M. (2005) *Contesting rurality: Politics in the British countryside*, Aldershot: Ashgate.

SEVEN

Planning and development in the countryside

Nick Gallent

Introduction

Development in the countryside, and the way the planning system regulates that development, is a hugely contentious issue. This chapter focuses on housing – and related infrastructure – on 'green fields', both at the rural–urban fringe and beyond. It begins by setting out the narrative of planning's 'big debate' regarding housing development, tracing its evolution in the UK through New Labour's time in power since their first general election victory in 1997. But it is impossible to focus on housing *in the countryside* without positioning this issue within a broader examination of house-building, the government's call for 'sustainable communities', the reform of the planning system and the changing structures of local and regional planning, which are being called upon to manage growth in new ways, aligning themselves with a 'market perspective' on house-building.

This chapter is divided into three parts: the first examines the story so far, looking at the changing shape of housing/planning debate since the mid-1990s; this narrative phase ends in 2002/03 when Labour first set out its 'Communities Plan'. The second part picks up where the first left off, focusing on planning reform in the run-up to the 2004 Planning and Compulsory Purchase Act and the Barker Review of Housing Supply (HM Treasury, 2004) and ending with the recent revision of policy guidance dealing with planning for housing (DCLG, 2006). The third section focuses on a particular region – the South East of England – examining the housing growth debate generally and focusing on that component of growth that cannot be accommodated within 'existing' urban areas. Throughout the discussion presented in this chapter, questions of affordability are raised and related to the aspiration of creating a more market-responsive planning system. New connections have been made in the last couple of years between the cost of homes, the efficient operation of housing markets, and the planning system's role in responding to market signals. Most recently, the Treasury (through its 'Barker Review') has focused attention on planning, house-building and the economy, challenging the idea that affordability is a desirable add-on resulting from ad hoc planning intervention (including local plan policies that support the negotiation of a community 'gain' from planning permissions: the "muddling through" approach to procuring affordable homes, according to Hoggart and Henderson, 2005, p 194). The general debate on housing supply in England – and the role of the planning system – has important long-term implications for the countryside. Kate Barker – who undertook the 2004 Review – and others are now arguing that planning has been unresponsive to housing demand (an accusation that rings especially true in rural areas), resulting in a backlog of unmet need and a general crisis in supply. Are we on the brink of concreting over England's countryside? Or are we simply, at long last, going to provide the housing that the nation needs?

Evolving debate – 1997 to 2003

The UK government has been making demographic projections since the 1920s. The Government Actuaries Department – in conjunction with the relevant planning or housing ministry – was set the task of calculating household growth, as a function of base population change, in the 1950s (Gallent, 2007). Hence, the publication of new 1992-based household growth projections by the Department of the Environment in 1995 might have been considered just another low-key event on the housing-planning calendar. How much housing the country needs, and where housing should be put are "amongst the oldest and most basic questions for planners" (Breheny and Hall, 1996, p 4) but the projections published just over a decade ago intensified the housing debate "almost to fever pitch" (Breheny and Hall, 1996, p 4). Things have never been quite the same since, with the housing debate maintaining momentum and becoming increasingly polarised between builders, planners, economists, community groups and the environmental lobby. But why were the 1992 projections the cause of so much initial alarm and subsequent controversy? The answer is one of simple mathematics. They suggested that 4.4 million additional households would be seeking homes in England in the period 1991 to 2016. This represented a 70% increase on the previous 25-year projection (of 2.6 million households), which, at that time, provided the basis of housing allocations set out in Regional Planning Guidance (Breheny and Hall, 1996, p 4). This near-seismic shift in projected growth in households has not been attributed to any significant rise in England's base population, or even to international migration in the era of an expanding Europe. Rather, it is – and will continue to be – a product of falling household size.

The scale of growth projected in the mid-1990s presented a critical challenge: how to promote sustainable residential (and associated) development through the processes of planning for housing. Planning often takes as its starting point an environmental capacity perspective – where can we build? More recently, this perspective has lost ground to a market view – where should we build given housing requirements and market conditions? But in 1995–96 in the run-up to a general election, the environmental perspective remained dominant. This had already been reflected in the Conservative government's last Housing White Paper (HM Government, 1995) which adhered to the fashionable logic 'that by packing more people into existing urban areas, we can both reduce the need to travel – thus reducing fuel consumption and emissions – and minimise the loss of open countryside to development' (Breheny and Hall, 1996, p 4). This logic has never really gone out of vogue. The White Paper of 1995 sought to promote urban compaction by setting a target of securing 50% of future residential development on previously developed land (PDL). When New Labour came to power in 1997, there was soon talk of a 60% target, which was first set out in *Planning for communities of the future* (DETR, 1998), scrutinised by the Urban Task Force (UTF, 1999) and formalised in a revision of Planning Policy Guidance Note 3 (PPG3) in 2000 (DETR, 2000).

The critical housing challenge that the Conservatives grappled with in 1995 and in the run-up to the general election was inherited by a Labour government coming to power after 18 years in opposition. Since 1997, the tension between the environmental capacity and the housing requirement (now a 'market signal') perspective on residential development has been a key focus of planning policy reform. Hooper (1996) perhaps best captured the problem facing the new administration, even before it was elected to power:

> The emerging polarisation between 'housing requirement' and 'environmental capacity'-led approaches to planning for housing is symptomatic of the failure to reconcile policies for the built environment, and to accommodate the rhythms of urban and rural renewal consequent on economic restructuring. Current tensions must raise real concerns about the appropriateness of a planning system based essentially upon the regulation of land-use, with little direct influence upon the social and economic forces determining current patterns of use. (Hooper, 1996, p 30)

Since 1997, Labour has perhaps asked more fundamental questions about the role of planning than any other government for 50 years. Its period in office has been marked, according to its critics, by unprecedented levels of political spin and rhetoric. In response to the challenge it inherited in 1997, it has saturated the planning community with new policy guidance, planning circulars, good-practice guides, official statements, task force reports and so on. The line from *Planning for communities of the future* and revised guidance on planning and affordable housing in 1998, runs through an Urban Task Force Report in 1999, a new PPG3 in 2000, a planning Green Paper in 2001 (DTLR, 2001), instalments of the Communities Plan in 2002 and 2003, a Planning Bill in 2003 and subsequent Act in 2004, and the Barker Review, also in 2004, and has now ended with another Barker Review (HM Treasury, 2006) feeding into a further planning White Paper (DCLG, 2007) and yet another planning Bill, soon to become another Act.

Arguably, there has been a strong urban bias to the housing debate in recent years. But the emphasis on compaction, urban intensification and the use of brownfield land (in preference to greenfield sites) – the essence of a 'sequential approach' to housing land allocation set out in PPG3 (DETR, 2000) – belies a deep-seated concern for planning and development in the countryside, especially the countryside abutting towns and cities. Promotion of these concerns is a central aspect of current debate, and is reflected in the dominance of an 'environmental capacity' perspective since the mid-1990s. This perspective has resulted in something of an impasse, and retrenchment into tightly polarised positions: a view that the countryside cannot and should not absorb additional growth (resulting from inter- and intra-regional migration and from in situ demographic processes) sits in opposition to a view that villages and towns need to grow, and that extensions onto the rural–urban fringe is a viable and sustainable development option.

Locally, proposed housing developments on greenfield sites, either in more open countryside or at the urban edge, face the immediate barrier of nearby opposition expressed through local politics and through the formation of often adversarial pressure groups (see Box 7.1). Nationally, the open countryside has been 'championed' by the Campaign to Protect Rural England (CPRE), an organisation with an agenda now almost entirely dominated by the post-1996 housing debate. CPRE has, over the last 10 years, run campaigns on a number of issues relating to residential development. Green Belts have been celebrated as planning's foremost success story at a time when others have questioned their impact on the promotion of a sustainable urban form, particular in the way they limit urban extension (RTPI, 2002; TCPA, 2002). Any and all development on green fields is viewed as evidence that planning has failed to do enough to promote higher housing densities or land recycling. For instance, the government claimed in 2002 that its 60% recycling target had been exceeded (monitoring figures showed that 61% of new housing had been built on previously developed land), but in the context of a general fall in house-building to its lowest level in more than 70 years. CPRE jumped on the claim, arguing that if 60% could be achieved then so could a higher target. But the price for success is under-supply, with 'brownfield' development becoming a larger component of fewer overall housing completions. A housing requirement perspective – or the need to accommodate economic restructuring – seldom sees the light of day in CPRE campaigning. An urban agenda is floated as the best means of saving the countryside: urban development is viewed as a positive force, promoting regeneration and allowing people to live closer to jobs and services. But housing in the countryside is viewed, nine times out of ten, as inherently negative: as a threat to the supposed qualities of the English countryside.

This debate tends to overshadow the logical questions that need to be asked in the countryside: how much housing is needed, over and above that which can be reasonably accommodated in infill sites within towns and cities? Where should this housing go? And what types of homes are required? These are the 'most basic

Box 7.1: Stevenage West, Hertfordshire

A proposed urban extension onto Green Belt land at Stevenage West in Hertfordshire illustrates the politics and conflicts accompanying housing development. In 1998 the principle for a strategic allocation west of the existing town was established in the County Structure Plan: 5,000 homes with 3,600 to be built before 2011. The site itself (281 hectares) crosses two local planning authorities: Stevenage Borough to the east (1,000 dwellings on 93 hectares in the opening period) and North Hertfordshire to the west (2,600 dwellings on 188 hectares). Following the allocation in the Structure Plan, the two authorities along with the county council and a consortium of developers held a series of public events culminating in a consultation session on a draft master-plan in 1999. In parallel, the local authorities commenced pre-application and scoping discussions involving the developers, statutory consultees and other public agencies in order to establish the technical and detailed aspects for the planning applications. They began translating the Structure Plan allocation into deliverable development frameworks.

It appeared that the structures and procedures were being established to bring forward a coherent development scheme. But the process was already being undermined by a number of unforeseen events alongside political uncertainties and differences. These included, first, a by-election in 1999 after which political power within the county council shifted in favour of those opposed to the Stevenage West allocation. Newly elected conservative elements within the council sought to withdraw the Structure Plan, but were unable to do so because of legal impediments. However, determined to scuttle the development, the county council began an early review of the Structure Plan as a first step to the potential deletion of the allocation. Second, the arrival of a revised PPG3 in March 2000 called into question the appropriateness of larger greenfield housing allocations, and gave the opponents of such allocations the excuse to back away from the Stevenage West development. Third, members of North Hertfordshire District Council had consistently opposed the allocation through the Structure Plan review process. The publication of a new PPG3 in 2000 was jumped upon by the council who, on the basis of legal advice, withdrew their local plan. At the point of withdrawal, North Hertfordshire were already preparing their development plan and were about to insert a chapter on Stevenage West. When PPG3 arrived, it was decided that the planning authority should undertake an urban capacity study before committing itself to a greenfield allocation. It was further decided that the plan should be abandoned and rewritten once the results of the capacity study were known. In neighbouring Stevenage, the District Plan was retained with the council choosing to carry on with their plan review (prior to second deposit) and to undertake a capacity study in tandem with this process. The withdrawal of the North Hertfordshire plan was a turning point for the Stevenage West development.

These events undermined the process in a variety of ways. First, the development consortium no longer had the certainty it needed to commit itself fully to the process. This caused problems later in the planning process because initial technical work on the application had not been as thoroughly undertaken as it might have been had the developers felt more confident that the principle of the development would not be called into question. Second, although joint working continued at an officer level, the relationship between the county and the district authorities became increasingly strained. Officers within North Hertfordshire and the county were obliged to continue the detailed technical work required by the development, but were, at the same time, aware that councillors were entirely opposed to the principle of the development. This in turn meant that working relations between the developers and the county and North Hertfordshire became increasingly difficult.

Public opposition, centring on the Campaign against the Stevenage Expansion (CASE), has been another feature of the Stevenage West story. Its impact on the development has given additional weight to the political opposition at the county level and within North Hertfordshire. Following the close of the public inquiry into the development at Stevenage West (in May 2004) there was a period of silence – lasting a year – from government. During this period, CASE refocused its attention on the East of England Plan (which proposed the development of 478,000 houses in the region), which it bitterly opposed. However, this opposition, arguably, never effectively challenged the principle underpinning the development at Stevenage West or the fact that household growth needs to be accommodated within the district of North Hertfordshire, the county and the region. For this reason, in October, 2005, the Deputy Prime Minister announced that he was "minded to approve" (ODPM, 2005a) the development having scrutinised the results of the previous year's public inquiry into the proposal – from the West Stevenage Consortium – to deliver 5,000 homes west of the A1(M). But he was only minded to approve the first phase (3,600 homes), a decision that surprised the development consortium and that angered North Hertfordshire District Council, which remained committed to blocking the development of housing on its portion of the Stevenage West site.

questions for planners' and need to be answered not only in cities, but also in those areas considered rural. Certainly, there is a case for not shielding rural areas behind the cause of urban compaction. Indeed, Peter Hall (2001) argues that:

> There is a bad reason and a good reason for more compact urban development. The bad one is to save rural land. It is bad because there is no reason to do so, either now or in the foreseeable future. About 10 per cent of the land of South East England, in 1995, was in EU set-aside, growing nothing but weeds. EU farm policies are undergoing

the most fundamental shake-up in their forty-year history, and the outcome is still undecided, but it is certain that agricultural subsidies will be slashed, so if anything the problem of surplus agricultural land will get rapidly worse. (Hall, 2001, p 101)

For Hall, agricultural redundancy poses the challenge of land-use replacement, with urban development able to take over from farming. But this view is balanced against the 'good reason' for urban compaction: travelling less and being generally more sustainable. Set in the context of a need for urban extensions (in many cases, onto agricultural land), and a clear 'housing requirement' in many areas of the countryside, the argument that we are "making a fetish out of land [and especially rural land] without asking why" (Hall and Ward, 1998, pp 107-8) is a powerful one. Planning restraint has brought about a reconfiguration of rural communities in recent years. This assertion has been greatly contested, and debated in the major writings on housing in the countryside for the last 30 years (see, for instance, Shucksmith, 1990; Evans, 1991). The counter-argument is that migration and new forms of housing consumption have been the real drivers of social change and exclusion. More people have retired to the countryside; more people are 'teleworking', buying second homes and investing in rural property: the "greed and carelessness of outside interests" (Gallent et al, 2005, p 1) is depriving local people of a housing resource that is rightfully theirs. If couched in these terms, then society and the housing market becomes divided: between the rural and the urban; the local and the non-local; between legitimate need and conspicuous consumption. Many observers, planners and policy makers think about rural housing markets in these terms: about rights and wrongs and a market that is subject to unnecessary external pressure. But in any market where a good is limited in its production, and exchanged without restriction, there are likely to be relative winners and losers. The difference with housing is that it represents a fundamental human need. In an open market, one answer is to avoid the land fetish and ensure that sufficient land is provided for building and, thereafter, that the conditions are created through the planning system, to ensure that the right types of homes are delivered in the right locations.

Two critical challenges have been identified through the recent planning debate: first, the importance of building greater consensus around the need for new housing, hence breaking the stalemate between the opposing development and environmental lobbies; and, second, to create the conditions within which housing can be delivered more effectively, avoiding the protracted processes and conflicts that have plagued many local schemes in southern England. Labour has responded to the challenge by recasting the housing debate: we are no longer merely building houses, but creating 'sustainable communities' and who, after all, could possibly be opposed to this? But the numbers debate must also be won at a technical and economic level: enter Kate Barker and her Treasury Review of housing supply. In failing to deliver the right homes in the right locations, we have been risking an economic downturn or, worst still, a recession. In the countryside, we have been suppressing the rhythms of 'rural renewal consequent on economic restructuring'. Since 2003–04, the Labour government has fought hard for 'hearts and minds' and it has coupled its efforts with a programme of planning reform that aims to establish the mechanisms needed to deliver new homes. It has moved away from a view of planning as a means simply of controlling the use of land; instead, it has promoted a spatial planning agenda in which it is incumbent on local authorities to develop evidence-based policies, building consensus around these policies within community strategies. But can the planning system deliver sustainable communities through a new development agenda in the countryside?

Sustainable communities and planning reform

The government's 'Communities Plan' (ODPM, 2003) offered a broad statement on the housing and planning challenge facing England: essentially an over-heating market in the south and a steadily weakening market further north (notwithstanding local peculiarities). It represented Labour's first coherent response to the challenge that it inherited from the Conservatives in 1997 – with government highlighting the economic and demographic changes driving housing demand and abandonment – and came midpoint in a sustained assault on what government saw as a failure in the planning system to deliver the housing that the country needed, and to deliver this housing within 'sustainable communities'.

A conflation of the housing debate with sustainable communities and reform of the planning system – which is dealt with in more detail below – is perhaps unfortunate. For many, the idea of sustainable communities is merely a smokescreen behind which to conceal an unprecedented programme of house-building. For others, the phrase itself has been robbed of any meaning: it has come to represent the antidote to everything that is wrong with the planning system and its outcomes since the Second World War. Planning has delivered disjointed answers to development dilemmas; sustainable communities will offer coherent answers: planning has resulted in low-quality housing in ugly developments; sustainable communities will be attractive and well designed; planning has been slow and bureaucratic; and sustainable communities will be born of a visionary process and will be representative of real 'place-making'. The concept itself is often associated with the government's 'Growth Areas' – established initially in Regional Planning Guidance for the South East (GOSE, 2000) – comprising the Thames Gateway, Milton Keynes/South Midlands, Ashford and the London–Stansted–Cambridge corridor. Other 'growth points' have since been added in the context of the South East and East of England Spatial Strategies. The pairing of the Communities Plan with the idea of Growth Areas suggests that new housing is likely to be accommodated within urban extensions on the rural–urban fringe, and might in some cases eat into London's Green Belt. It appears to be an urbanising agenda, extending into the countryside around towns and prompting the current wave of anti-sprawl sentiment sweeping through southern England. But the Plan is about more than 200,000-plus additional homes lumped into Growth Areas in southern England: it is the government's attempt to break the development stalemate. However, it remains wedded to the environmental capacity perspective. It contains a chapter on 'land, countryside and rural communities' that begins, not by setting out the rural development challenge, but with a series of 'key facts' that attempt to demonstrate the government's continued commitment to focusing as much development in towns and cities while protecting the countryside through additional Green Belt designations. Since 1997, an area about 'three times the size of the city of Sheffield' has been added to England's designated Green Belt. There is, of course, a wider debate on the "take and give Green Belt" (Elson, 2003, p 104) with the government accused of adding land at the outer boundary, while allowing incursive development at the urban edge. The Communities Plan also lauds the government's identification of additional previously developed land and its reclamation of 1,100 hectares of brownfield land each year. The challenge that the government sets itself is to tackle housing shortages while protecting the countryside and to 'address the housing needs of rural communities who are often the custodians of the countryside' (ODPM, 2003, p x). How will this be achieved?

A four-pronged approach is set out: English Partnerships (the government's regeneration agency, scheduled to become part of the 'Homes and Communities Agency' in 2009) is leading on land assembly and focusing on strategic housing development; greenfield land will not be used 'wastefully'; the countryside will be protected for the 'benefit of all'; and the supply of affordable housing in small rural settlements will be increased. Over the longer term, this is how the government will address the needs of rural communities: it will increase the amount of land designated as Green Belt; use the 'residential density' direction (and Planning Policy Statement 3 [PPS3] after April 2007 to effectively 'block' developments falling below minimum density standards) to prevent the 'ineffective' use of land; increase investment channelled to English Partnerships; and directly fund brownfield remediation through the Regional Development Agencies (RDAs). Land is a principal concern of the Communities Plan as far as it relates to the countryside and there has been little recent movement away from Hall and Ward's "land fetish" (1998). What happens to communities is, arguably, of secondary importance. The government has committed itself to provide more affordable homes, especially through local plan policies and has also called for new limits on the sale of ex-council housing. It sometimes seems unaware of the small contribution that planning has made to the provision of affordable housing in rural areas in recent years (against absolute need: see Crook et al, 2006), the contradiction of restraining land supply through planning and then intervening, through planning, to procure affordable homes; or the reality of council house sales over the last two decades. With regard to development in the countryside, the message from the government in 2003 appeared to be that it would definitely not be building for the future.

But there have been further shifts in recent years, which may push policy in a new direction. The Communities Plan pre-dates Kate Barker's 2004 Review of Housing Supply in England. This puts rural development in a different light, which is reflected in PPS3's broader emphasis on market signals and market-driven development. The Planning and Compulsory Purchase Act, also appearing in 2004, is not a product of Barker, but can be read in the context of Barker's thinking on the supply issue. Together, these three documents create a changed context for planning and development in the countryside.

The 2004 Planning and Compulsory Purchase Act is the child of New Labour's desire to see a more streamlined system of development planning which concerns itself as much with 'place-shaping'(Lyons, 2007) as with the regulation of land-use. It is also a product of a reawakening, across Europe, of the notion of 'strategic spatial planning': planning as an integrating force in 'spatial governance', bringing together different agendas, reconciling interests and creating visions that these interests can buy into (Friedmann, 2004, p 52). There is a wide literature on the evolution of planning and the departure from a land-use model towards a spatial agenda, which is as much about governance and place-management as the control of land. The 2004 Planning Act – together with Local Government Acts in 1999 and 2000 and more recent legislation – expresses an undercurrent of change. The move to a more strategic brand of spatial planning is reflected in the replacement of regional planning guidance (RPG), which merely set out the targets of central government, with regional spatial strategies (RSSs), which seek to develop regional and sub-regional evidence-based agendas for future development. These strategies provide part of the framework in which to coordinate local development planning. Planning professionals are supposed to *facilitate* the process of planning, working with communities to build visions around which different groups can unite. Since the Local Government Acts of 1999 and 2000 (introducing 'local strategic partnerships' and 'community strategies'), there has been growing enthusiasm for the concept of 'local choice': letting local people decide on the best patterns of development. But how is this objective to be squared with strategic priorities, particularly the priorities identified in the 2004 Review of Housing Supply?

In April 2003, Kate Barker – a member of the Bank of England's Monetary Policy Committee – was asked by the Treasury to "conduct a review of issues underlying the lack of supply and responsiveness of housing in the UK" (HM Treasury, 2004, p 3). The scale of the problem had been brought home in 2001 when housing completions in England fell to a record low. Barker was asked to review the entire system, and to consider the interaction between the house-building industry and planning. A final report appeared in March 2004 (HM Treasury, 2004). This focused on housing (under-)supply and the wider economy, arguing that market volatility – and real-term house price increases of 2.4% per annum over the previous 30 years – is at the root of housing affordability. It was suggested that nationally 120,000 new homes *above current targets* might be required each year to bring UK price inflation in line with the European average (1.1%). The Barker Review has not been without its critics, but it is generally accepted that the supply of new homes has been inadequate over recent years and that the housing market needs to function more efficiently. Barker argued that the government should become more concerned with "improved market affordability" (p 12), setting affordability targets, establishing regional planning executives to advise on the scale and distribution of housing needed to meet these targets, and introducing greater flexibility with extra land releases within local development frameworks triggered by "market signals" (HM Treasury, 2004).

The infusion of 'market principles' into the process of planning for housing was the key message emerging from the Review. After consulting on Barker's recommendations the government published a response in which it signalled its intention to feed some of her recommendations into new planning advice. A broader view of affordability is taking root with planning being called upon to think about affordability in a 'macro-economic' sense: this may mean less emphasis on the 'procurement' of affordable social housing through planning and more attention being paid to controlling house prices through general supply.

This agenda is expressed in the 2006 revision of planning policy relating to housing. PPS3 reflects the greater adherence to market signals advocated by Barker and a need to adopt a "visionary and strategic approach" in the pursuit of 'market responsiveness' (DCLG, 2006, para 11). The stated aim of PPS3 was to "underpin the Government's response to the Barker Review of Housing Supply and the necessary step-change in housing delivery, through a new, more responsive approach to land supply at the local level" (para 2). PPS3 was largely concerned with planning's use of 'strategic housing market' assessments to guide future land allocations, with Annex C of the Statement outlining the form that these assessments should take. Two years earlier, Barker had highlighted the importance of monitoring market signals at a sub-regional level: in PPS3, authorities were instructed to work closely with Regional Planning Bodies, stakeholders (including house-builders) and infrastructure providers in order to identify "broad locations for future growth" (para 55) in addition to immediately "deliverable" sites that were already available, suitable for development and achievable within the next 5 years (para 54). PPS3 could be seen as the government's endorsement of Barker: the monitoring of 'market evidence' figures prominently, as does the identification of 'buffer land' – a Barker phrase expressed as "locations for future growth" (para 55) in PPS3 – to be released, essentially, as the market dictates enabling authorities to roll forward an achievable supply of land for housing (allowing them to respond quickly to market shifts) backed up by a clear implementation strategy. The revised statement provides the government with a vehicle for carrying forward and reflecting changes to the planning system since 2000 and an ambition to achieve wider housing affordability by addressing market disequilibrium. It is impossible at this stage to say what effect this more 'spatial' and market-driven approach to development will have, but it emerges in the context of serious concern over housing supply. In its response to Barker, the ODPM noted that the country faces: *a massive growth challenge*, largely as a result of falling household size; *a crisis of affordability*, with average deposits needed to buy a first home having risen from £5,000 in 1996 to £34,000 in the first half of 2005; *pressure on social housing waiting lists*, viewed as evidence of a wider affordability crisis; and *an economic threat* created by a housing shortage in the South East, producing serious labour shortages (ODPM, 2005, p 2).

The government is pushing hard for a stronger 'housing requirement' perspective on future development, emphasising the importance of general supply. There is a sustained commitment to promoting Growth Areas, and to assisting the development of high demand 'growth points' (ODPM, 2005, p 2). But the agenda of increased market efficiency – viewed primarily as a market supply issue – will have clear implications in the countryside, particularly in the countryside's own 'growth point': the market towns.

The South East of England

The potential impacts of additional house-building in South East England have provoked considerable debate. A draft version of the region's 'spatial strategy' (SEERA, 2005a), offering three levels of growth and two 'spatial options', was at the centre of debate over planned housing growth prior to the 'final selection' of a preferred figure in March 2006 (SEERA, 2006). Proposed growth levels – 25,500, 28,000 or 32,000 additional homes – represented a continuation of recent building rates, the target rate set out in existing RPG, and a higher rate, respectively. The spatial options comprised a "continuation of existing policy" (SEERA, 2005a) rolled forward from RPG, or a "sharper focus" (SEERA, 2005a), with a bigger proportion of growth accommodated in areas deemed to have greater economic potential or to require regeneration. In Table 7.1 the annual growth figures proposed in 2005 are shown next to the Growth Areas (top of the table) and the rest of the counties (bottom of the table). The growth proposed in the top half of Table 7.1 comprised infill and regeneration on larger brownfield sites (for example, the Kent Thames Gateway), or urban extensions onto some areas of greenfield (for example, in the Gatwick Area or onto the London Fringe). The growth proposed in the lower half of Table 7.1 comprised market town infill, smaller extensions or some small developments on greenfield sites. It is, however, difficult to separate potential urban from rural development at this scale of strategic planning.

A sustainability appraisal of these growth levels and options undertaken by the consultants Environmental Resources Management (ERM) in 2005 concluded that the higher growth options were more likely to meet housing demands, but would place new pressure on environmental resources. The lower growth options would place less pressure on these resources, but would not address housing shortages and would restrain economic growth (ERM, 2005, para 4.2.3).

Debate in the South East has continued to focus on this division: between an environmental capacity agenda represented, in 2005, by the lowest rate and a housing requirement agenda thought to be best served by, at the very least, an annual growth level of 32,000 units. The lowest figures were (and continue to be) championed by the CPRE, and have been given more cautious support by Labour's political opponents. Higher figures have been supported by housing

Table 7.1: Spatial options summary table for the South East of England (2005)

Area	Continuation of existing policy			Sharper focus		
	Spatial Option 1			Spatial Option 2		
	25,500	**28,000**	**32,000**	**25,500**	**28,000**	**32,000**
Kent Thames Gateway	2,900	2,900	2,900	2,900	2,900	2,900
Milton Keynes & Aylesbury Vale	3,300	3,300	3,300	3,300	3,300	3,300
East Kent and Ashford	2,400	2,500	2,800	2,600	2,800	3,100
Central Oxfordshire	1,300	1,500	1,700	1,400	1,600	1,900
Gatwick Area	900	1,100	1,300	1,300	1,500	1,800
London Fringe	1,500	1,700	2,100	2,000	2,300	2,800
South Hampshire	2,800	3,200	3,800	2,900	3,300	4,000
Sussex Coast	2,700	3,000	3,600	2,300	2,600	3,100
Western Corridor & Blackwater Valley	3,500	4,000	4,800	4,300	4,900	5,900
Sub total	**21,300**	**23,200**	**26,300**	**23,000**	**25,200**	**28,800**
Rest of Berkshire	100	100	100	100	100	100
Rest of Buckinghamshire	200	200	300	200	300	300
Rest of East Sussex	300	400	500	400	400	500
Rest of Hampshire	1,200	1,400	1,600	700	800	1,000
Rest of Kent	700	800	1,000	200	200	200
Rest of Oxfordshire	700	800	900	300	300	400
Rest of Surrey	200	200	300	200	200	200
Rest of West Sussex	400	400	500	100	100	100
Isle of Wight	400	500	600	400	400	500
Sub total	**4,200**	**4,800**	**5,700**	**2,500**	**2,800**	**3,200**
Grand total	**25,500**	**28,000**	**32,000**	**25,500**	**28,000**	**32,000**

Note: Figures are rounded to the nearest 100, and hence may not sum.

Source: Technical Note 2, Spatial Options (SEERA, 2005b, Table 8).

charities, especially Shelter, and by a powerful economic lobby. The consultants Deloitte (2005) argued that "despite achieving maximum possible improvements in productivity and economic activity, the South East needs around 35,000 dwellings per annum to sustain an annual GVA growth of 3% to 2026" (p 4). In essence, the lower growth levels set out in the 2005 Draft South East Plan (below 32,000) were thought to represent a 'business-as-usual' position: the 25,500 growth figure was the continuation of an old five-year completions average (1999/2000 to 2003/04) that represented a failure to deliver on the RPG9 target; the 28,000 figure was the actual RPG9 target (achieved for the first time in 2003/04). None reflected Barker's thinking on market signals or housing affordability, and none was concerned with the migration patterns that are a key driver of the South East's housing market. The higher level of 32,000 units was, however, concerned with reflecting long-term migration trends. In 2005, SEERA explained that:

> If long-term trends in migration were to continue over the period 2001 to 2026, the South East would see the number of households increase by 723,800 (or 22 per cent). This is equivalent to an average 29,000 households per annum. The total number of net additional homes implied by such growth would be 746,200, equivalent to an annual average of 29,800. The twenty year period 2006 to 2026 would see a higher rate of growth, equivalent to an annual average of 31,300 homes per annum. (SEERA, 2005c, p 4)

However, more recent trends in migration suggest a different pattern of demographic growth:

> If short-term trends in migration were to continue over the period 2002 to 2027, the South East would see the number of households increase by 847,300 (or 26 per cent). This is equivalent to an average 33,900 households per annum. The total number of net additional homes implied by such growth would be 874,300, equivalent to an annual average of 35,000. The twenty year period 2006 to 2026 would see a higher rate of growth, equivalent to an annual average of 35,500 homes per annum. (SEERA, 2005c, p 4)

SEERA committed to its preferred growth level (28,900 dwellings per annum) in a draft plan submitted for an "examination in public" (SEERA, 2006, p 5) due to conclude in 2007. At the time of writing an approved plan is expected to appear late in 2008. The figure reflects neither the long- nor the short-term migration trends affecting the region.

Indeed, 'market signals' – which are in part a product of underlying demographic growth – suggest a need for additional homes in the region. Furthermore, the risk of exacerbating existing labour supply shortfalls in the region also seems to support the case for a higher building rate (Gallent and Tewdwr-Jones, 2005, p 34). But perhaps nowhere else at the present time is the environmental perspective on growth more at odds with this housing requirement/economic growth agenda. The CPRE (2005) contends that "there is not a long-term undersupply of market homes" (p 4) and any move to raise house-building levels will result in over-supply with severe environmental consequences. For the CPRE, demand reflected in house prices should not be a driving force in housing supply: "we strongly disagree with the Barker Review recommendation that house prices should play a leading role in the planning of new homes, with more land being released when prices are high" (CPRE, 2005, p 6). A resistance to 'demand' and a more limited focus on the measures of need is the standard 'environmental perspective' response to the 'threat' of house-building in the countryside. The arguments are all very simple: demand is generated by house-building, and without house-building, there is no new demand; villages can therefore remain as they are, with planning simply meeting local need (through planning agreements with landowners) when this need arises; all migration can and should be resisted. A lack of any bigger picture is accompanied by a general suspicion of the strategic view presented by the government, the regional assemblies and now by Barker. But there are also legitimate concerns. Additional land release should, according to Barker, be triggered by market signals and one such signal is house price inflation (set against wage levels, see Meen, 2005, p 970). But the South East is a region of significant contrasts in terms of such market signals. Work by WSP Consultants for the Regional Assembly (WSP, 2005) has revealed that, in 2001, the South East Region was a "net exporter of 175,000 commuters – 5 per cent of its resident labour force" (p ii). An exodus of home-buyers from London into the South East – with subsequent return commuting – is a key feature of the region's housing market. Some villages and towns within easy reach of rail links have become housing demand hot spots with prices rising well beyond the reach of local buyers. This was reflected in affordability figures published by the Commission for Rural Communities (CRC) in 2005. In all regions, including the South East, housing is less affordable – relative to local wages – in rural compared to urban areas (CRC, 2005, p 44). What the CPRE does not want is house price rises in these settlements to be used as a trigger for speculative building, which it believes will only fuel additional commuter in-migration; rather, the only reasonable course of action in such situations is to focus on local need through a provision of affordable homes.

Excessive reliance on market signals might well cause an intensification of demand. The question, therefore is how might planning reconcile the regional and sub-regional view of market efficiency (emphasised in the new PPS3) with the local demand pressures that might result in a concentration of development in and around some rural hot spots? Planning's adoption of a more strategic market rationale suggests an erosion of local power; but this is contradicted by a coupling of development planning – in the form of local development frameworks – with community strategies. There is now an increased danger of Barker's market philosophy finding itself at loggerheads with local interests. It is not at all clear how the new system will work in practice. Will communities live under the shadow of 'locations for future growth' and the threat of unprecedented speculative building, or will market information be used to release more land exclusively for local needs? Local conflicts are likely to become more commonplace if local authorities use 'a requirement and market argument' to impose new house-building on communities expressing contrary local choices. The key concern is that a strategic view will take precedence and run contrary to local interests: this is the age-old fear – that planning will be locally unresponsive. Therefore, such agendas, whether market-driven or not, tend to be opposed.

Conclusions

Housing development outside urban areas is a multilayered issue. It is possible to focus on the detail of local markets and the conflicts which regularly envelop planning decisions, or to examine the bigger picture: to position greenfield development and local planning in the broader context of a shifting demographic base and a new rationale for planning that is only slowly being defined. Environmental groups have recognised that this is the new arena for debating planning and development in the countryside. In the future, local development planning will continue to determine the location of new homes on settlement fringes or in more open countryside; it will certainly have the power to face down the threat of inappropriate development that contravenes planning guidance. But if the principles that guide development are predominantly market-led and if urban capacity declines, then housing will still need to be accommodated *somewhere* in the countryside. The government has tried to rally support behind its growth agenda: it talks about the need to deliver 'sustainable communities', a term designed to tug at a collective social conscience. But behind the Communities Plan is a technical case for moving to a higher rate of house-building: this is grounded in the periodic household projections, and Barker's view that market volatility in house-building is the root cause of unaffordable housing, and subsequent volatilities in the wider national economy.

Hence, the government creates a planning system – linked to new forms of 'spatial governance' emerging from local government reform – with the outward appearance of empowering communities; but behind the scenes, the case is made for an almost unprecedented national programme of house-building. There is a great deal of reconciling to be done: between national aspirations and regional planning, and between strategic necessity and local choice. However, environmental groups have never been more vociferous in their opposition to housing development, attacking the fundamental principles on which the case for growth is made. In contrast, some housing groups and the national government appear intent on forging ahead with the current agenda. In 2005 the housing charity Shelter came out in favour of the government's house-building programme, much to the annoyance of the CPRE and Friends of the Earth (O'Hara, 2005), arguing that the housing agenda should be about the availability of decent homes for all, rather than a narrower focus on social provision. Shelter has also intervened in the South East, arguing for higher growth rates and aligning itself to the house-building lobby.

The current house-building debate is generating new conflicts, not merely focused on specific developments, but on the rationale for, and direction of, national policy. New Labour and its critics are locked in a struggle for 'hearts and minds': what the first presents as an essential and sustainable programme of development, the latter view as reckless environmental vandalism. The new planning system, and the agenda for housing, has emerged from two competing policy streams. The first – a statutory planning stream – emphasises strategic priority; the second – a local government stream – is promoting local choice. How will the two be reconciled? Barker and PPS3 suggest a potential acceleration of house-building in the countryside, but this may be resisted by communities empowered by recent local government reforms. The acid test for 'spatial planning' will be whether it can balance these competing interests, achieving the compromise between business and communities and between the strategic and the local that long eluded the previous system.

References

Breheny, M. and Hall, P. (eds) (1996) *The people – where will they go?*, London: Town and Country Planning Association.

CRC (Commission for Rural Communities) (2005) *State of the countryside 2005*, Cheltenham: CRC.

CPRE (Campaign to Protect Rural England) (2005) *Building on Barker*, London: CPRE.

Crook, A., Monk, S., Rowley, S. and Whitehead, C. (2006) 'Planning gain and the supply of new affordable housing in England: understanding the numbers', *Town Planning Review*, vol 77, no 3, pp 353-73.

DCLG (Department for Communities and Local Government) (2006) *Planning policy statement 3 (PPS3): Housing*, London: DCLG.

DCLG (2007) *Planning for a sustainable future*, London: DCLG.

Deloitte (2005) *Sustaining success in a prosperous region: Economic implications of the South East Plan*, report for South East England Development Agency, Guildford: SEEDA.

DETR (Department of the Environment, Transport and the Regions) (1998) *Planning for communities of the future*, London: DETR.

DETR (2000) *Planning policy guidance note 3: Housing*, London: DETR.

DTLR (Department for Transport, Local Government and the Regions) (2001) *Planning: Delivering a fundamental change*, London: DTLR.

Elson, M. J. (2003) "A 'take and give" green belt?', *Town and Country Planning*, vol 72, no 3, pp 104-5.

ERM (Environmental Resources Management) (2005) *Draft sustainability appraisal report on the consultation draft of the South East Plan*, London: ERM.

Evans, A. W. (1991) '"Rabbit hutches on postage stamps": planning, development and political economy', *Urban Studies*, vol 28, no 6, pp 853-70.

Friedmann, J. (2004), 'Strategic spatial planning and the longer range', with an introduction by P. Healey and comments by L. Albrechts et al, *Planning Theory and Practice*, vol 5, no 1, pp 49-67.

Gallent, N. (2007) 'Regional household protections and strategic housing allocations', in H. T. Dimitrou and R. Thompson (eds) *Strategic planning for regional development in the UK*, London: Routledge, pp 198-219.

Gallent, N. and Tewdwr-Jones, M. (2005) *Impacts of regional growth in South East England: A review of the evidence base*, Guildford: South East England Regional Assembly.

Gallent, N., Mace, A. and Tewdwr-Jones, M. (2005) *Second homes: European perspectives and UK policies*, Aldershot: Ashgate.

GOSE (Government Office for the South East) (2000) *Regional planning guidance 9 for the South East of England,* Guildford: GOSE.

Hall, P. (2001) 'Sustainable cities or town cramming?', in A. Layard, S. Davoudi and S. Batty (eds) *Planning for a sustainable future*, London: Spon Press.

Hall, P. and Ward, C. (1998) *Sociable cities: The legacy of Ebenezer Howard*, London: John Wiley & Sons.

HM Government (1995) *Our future homes: Opportunity, choice, responsibility*, London: Department of the Environment/Welsh Office. (Also available at www.archive. official-documents.co.uk/documents/doe/our homes/our future.htm)

HM Government (1999) *Local Government Act 1999*, chapter 27, London: The Stationery Office. (Also available at www.opsi.gov.uk/Acts/acts1999/ukpga_ 19990027_en_1)

HM Government (2000) *Local Government Act 2000*, chapter 22, London: The Stationery Office. (Also available at www.opsi.gov.uk/ACTS/acts2000/ukpga_ 20000022_en_1)

HM Government (2004) *Planning and Compulsory Purchase Act 2004*, c 5, London: The Stationery Office. (Also available at www.opsi.gov.uk/acts/acts2004/ ukpga_20040005_en_1)

HM Treasury (2004) *Review of housing supply – delivering stability: Securing our future housing needs*, London: HM Treasury.

HM Treasury (2006) *Barker review of land use planning*, London: HM Treasury.

Hoggart, K. and Henderson, S. (2005) 'Excluding exceptions: housing non-affordability and the oppression of environmental sustainability?', *Journal of Rural Studies*, vol 21, pp 181-96.

Hooper, A. (1996) 'Housing requirements and housing provision: the strategic issues', in M. Breheny and P. Hall (eds) (1996) *The people – where will they go?* London: Town and Country Planning Association.

Lyons, M. (2007) *Place-shaping: A shared ambition for the future of local government* (Report of the Lyons Inquiry into Local Government), London: The Stationery Office.

Meen, G. (2005) 'On the economics of the Barker review of housing supply', *Housing Studies*, vol 20, no 6, pp 949-71.

ODPM (Office of the Deputy Prime Minister) (2003) *Sustainable communities – Building for the future*, London: ODPM.

ODPM (2005a) Letter from the First Secretary of State (Town and Country Planning Act 1990 – Section 77: Applications by the Stevenage West Consortium at Land West of A1(M) at Stevenage, Hertfordshire) to Barton Willmore Planning acting for the Consortium, 20 October.

ODPM (2005b) *Planning for housing provision – Consultation paper*, London: ODPM.

O'Hara, M. (2005) 'Method man' (Interview with Adam Sampson, Director, Shelter), *Guardian*, 19 January.

RTPI (Royal Town Planning Institute) (2002) *Modernising green belts: Discussion paper, May 2002*, London: RTPI.

Shucksmith, M. (1990) *House building in Britain's countryside*, London: Routledge.

SEERA (South East England Regional Assembly) (2005a) *A clear vision for the South East: The South East Plan core document*, Guildford: SEERA.

SEERA (2005b) *Consultation draft South East Plan: Technical note 2: Spatial options*, Guildford: SEERA.

SEERA (2005c) *Consultation draft South East Plan: Technical note 5 (revised): Demography*, Guildford: SEERA.

SEERA (2006) *A clear vision for the South East: The South East Plan executive summary (draft plan for submission to government)*, Guildford: SEERA.

TCPA (Town and Country Planning Association) (2002) *'Green belts' policy statement*, London: TCPA.

UTF (Urban Task Force) (1999) *Towards an urban renaissance*, London: Taylor and Francis and the UTF.

WSP (2005) *Journey to work analysis: Part 1 regional*, London: WSP.

EIGHT

Countryside access and the 'right to roam' under New Labour: nothing to CRoW about?

Gavin Parker

Introduction

Over the past ten years or so, since the May 1997 general election, the Labour Party in government under Tony Blair has taken a number of controversial decisions and implemented, or otherwise avoided, measures that impact on the countryside directly and indirectly. The Blair administrations had styled themselves as a great reforming government with change, review, iteration and reorientation unfolding on many policy fronts. However, it appears that the New Labour project was as much an opportunist and pragmatic politics (Powell, 2000) as a coherent 'third way', as some might argue (see, for example, Giddens, 1998, 2001). If anything the New Labour project is an example of emergent 'practice without theory'. In terms of rural policy and politics one detects that this lack of coherence may be due to a lack of confidence in addressing rural affairs and the unforeseen and often forced circumstances surrounding a number of the rural political issues that have arisen in the past decade. It also has to do with the history of, and background to, prior political projects, and in this sense reviewing Blairism necessarily entails a degree of juxtaposing with predecessor administrations that is not possible in this chapter (see Andersen and Mann, 1997; Powell, 2000). However, the focus on countryside access as a rural political issue is given some historical consideration here as well as reflecting on how the issue throws into relief (dis)continuities and motives of previous Labour governments.

The way that New Labour has moved to address rural issues and develop new institutional arrangements across the policy spectrum is perhaps notable for the level of activity and noise generated, if not necessarily for the degree of change brought about by policy or the radical nature of those policies. Labour legislative programmes over the past decade result largely from policy developed in the early 1990s, that is prior to coming to power, while others were subsequently lighted upon as iterations of existing ideas or practices implemented or suggested by other parties or interests. A further set of decisions and outcomes have been forced upon the government as the result of emerging and unforeseen circumstances, some of which are detailed in other chapters in this volume. All three sources and implementations have been played out in and upon rural areas. The delivery of a manifesto pledge to extend public access to the countryside for recreation features as a pre-designed idea, but it has a long and tangled history. This commitment was addressed via the passing of the 2000 Countryside and Rights of Way Act (the CRoW Act). On the face of it the CRoW Act does deliver on a contentious and radical policy pledge, and the background and subsequent implementation of this policy forms the basis of the chapter. First, a brief commentary and policy history on the issue of countryside access in terms of rural politics is provided in order to situate it within the New Labour project.

The significance of countryside access and rurality in national politics

The context of the 2000 CRoW Act and the approach to countryside access is briefly rehearsed by outlining how the 'access issue' has developed over time and how this has served a much wider political lobby over the past hundred or so years. Debate over public access to the countryside has been a long-running feature of rural politics and at certain key points it has been used to depict a particular urban–rural dynamic as well as a class issue. The rehearsals of the arguments over the needs, rights and impacts of competing groups has reflected the tensions apparent in changing social and economic circumstances, as well as being a symbol of class relations and class power both in and over rural space. As a result the conflicts have not always been concerned with the practice of recreation; they have concerned and indicated a deeper preoccupation with the distribution and ownership of land and property in Britain (Cox, 1984; Shoard, 1996; Darby, 2000; Cahill, 2001). This dynamic also reflected a period where party politics were played out on clearer class lines. As outlined below, part of the New Labour project has been to break or avoid such polarisations and the access issue as inherited in 1997 represented somewhat of an uncomfortable historical legacy because it was viewed as a class issue.

In terms of the changing countryside Murdoch et al (2003, p 8) explain that: "the hierarchy of activities that has long dominated rural space has been challenged by alternative demands on rural land". In recent decades the challenges and practice of leisure use and tourism potential have altered perceptions of rural space and the function and control of the idea of rurality has become contested: in particular who, where and when certain groups and activities may be deemed appropriate in rural space (Sibley, 1995, 2006; Parker, 2007). Furthermore, there are questions about what regulatory techniques and practices should be permissible across rural space/activity. Thus a changing countryside precipitates multiple changing and discursive interplays; with changing conditions presenting opportunities to advance certain claims over others.

When features of post-consumer society, such as the relationship between cultural consumption and citizenship rights (Eder, 1993; Isin and Wood, 1999; Urry,

2000), are considered with the foregoing points, and given widespread concern over the impacts of modern farming and the tax subsidies used to maintain farming and the rural landscape, then attitudinal shift is likely to be reflected politically. It is hardly surprising that pressure to open up the countryside for recreation has persisted and an NOP poll taken in 1998 demonstrated 85% popular support for increased public access to open land (also known as 'the right to roam'). The argument has developed into one about the scope of property rights in a civil society versus proto-market-based consumer/citizenship rights to the countryside as recreational space. There is also a deeper contestation reflected in the access issue: about the authorship of the entire trajectory and 'project' of rurality.

Political attitudes and policy trajectories promoted by New Labour have raised a question about which interest group rural policy is *for* as well as highlighting the notion and control of rurality. This reorientation is in part related to a concern with claims to the 'cultural ownership' (Eder, 1993) or stewardship of rurality (CLA, 1998; Parker, 2002), and indeed the competency to steward the rural, as opposed to contests over legal ownership of rural space. The struggle over such control is reflected in a question posed by Lord Mancroft in the House of Lords in response to the 2002 Curry Report on farming and food:

> Do the government see their role as that of producing a countryside that suits the government and the urban electorate, or is that role one of enabling those that live and work in the countryside, and who are largely responsible for how it has developed up until now, to continue to manage and develop it in the way they think best, in the way their instincts lead them? (*Hansard*, HL Deb, 30 April 2002, col 668)

This kind of dichotomy has been used often in the past decade in the press (see Woods, 2005, pp 113-14). The implication is obvious – that the government and the urban majority have effectively wrested control of rurality from traditional interests. Woods (2005) has argued that such a shift towards rural managerialism or the urbanisation of rural affairs is part of the transformation of the politics of the countryside to 'a politics of rurality' and a politics *over* rurality: "there has been an unexpected political awakening of rural Britain, articulated by a new 'politics of the rural' in which the very meaning and character of the countryside lies at the heart of the struggle" (Woods, 2005, p 21). This has stemmed in part from changes that have taken place in rural dynamics, a restructuring rural economy and the weakening of certain policy communities but, importantly, is also due to wider changes in information, perception and the shift towards cultural and consumption economies. As part of this the countryside has become increasingly viewed as a shared cultural good (Featherstone, 1991; Valentine, 2001) and as a 'threatened environment' (Shoard, 1987; Clark et al, 1998). Indeed this shift has been developing gradually, and the access issue is one reflection of such a change, where cultural dispositions and challenges have affected the (rural) political field (Parker, 1999, 2007).

Meanwhile the media have portrayed rural politics in adversarial terms, typically as urban versus rural. The press have caricatured the access issue in these terms since at least the 1930s and it has been a favourite byline story for local and national newspapers which regularly report on incidents and misdemeanours relating to walkers, landowners and others in the countryside. This reportage typically features a cast that includes the 'ignorant townee', the 'feudal landowner', the 'Bolshevik rambler' and the 'intemperate farmer' (see Blunden and Curry, 1989; Merriman, 2005; Parker, 2006). Yet while the focus of the political argument has centred around a claim to extend access rights over open land the motives have arguably shifted over time, with early efforts reflecting a romantic and preservationist ethic based on a wish to conserve the landscape, as much as a claim for healthy and free recreational space for the working classes (as it became in the inter-war period) (see Sheail, 1981; Shoard, 1987; Blunden and Curry, 1989). Latterly, since the inter-war period, the issue has been framed as an assault on liberty by landowning interests, while others, including successive Labour governments, have viewed the extension of access as a fair and equitable trade that latterly reflects a shift to a post-feudal countryside and which "affords a greater freedom for people to explore the countryside" (DETR, 2000, p 1). Blair's line about providing more access to land is encapsulated in a response he gave in 2004 as the CRoW Act was being implemented: "I hope and believe that matters can be resolved sensibly, so that people have access to more of our countryside, which they have wanted for many years, without interfering with the proper use of the land by its owners" (*Hansard*, HC Deb, 15 September 2004, col 1267).

Land-use conflicts often centre on the exclusive use of land (Williams, 1973; Cox, 1984). Over time different uses have become more or less important or more or less supported or monopolised by powerful interests. As a result the way that (property) rights accrue and are shared by different interests reflect social and cultural priorities as well as economic ones – the political equilibrium is arrived at and stabilised by a continual flow of, and adjustments to, rights and responsibilities. This ebb and flow of property rights allocations and challenges to their distribution reflect iterations to socio-spatial orderings and custom and practice (Parker, 2002, 2006; Whatmore, 2002). In essence the gaining of rights of access represents wider socio-political gains: rights of access to the countryside can be read as symbolic of changing power relations between competing groups in society and of a 'politics of rurality', whereby the legitimate character and control over the countryside is being contested. Access can be regarded as an example of a 'boundary issue', not only given its spatial implications, but clearly as an issue that impacts on numerous interests and elements and involves different justifications and multiple rights claims for change and continuity in practice and law. In short the consideration of countryside access highlights numerous long-running yet changing factors that characterise and preoccupy both rural studies and also the interests of key actors in a wider rural politics.

Access becomes an issue

English rural history is characterised by numerous and ongoing disputes and protests over the governance and rights to land (see, for example, Mingay, 1989;Thompson, 1993), and these struggles have significantly shaped rural politics. Early conflicts in the English countryside notable here relate to the effects of enclosure that stretch back to at least the 16th century (Wordie, 1983). Enclosure was effectively a piecemeal land-reform process which reorganised and modernised the land ownership structure and expanded the idea and reach of private land ownership.This process effectively curtailed the accessibility of rural space (Malcolmson, 1973; Shoard, 1987). By the early 19th century the effects of enclosure, particularly around towns and cities, along with industrialisation and urbanisation were prompting concerns over the 'loss' of rural land and landscape. The emerging preservationist movement and the associated and influential Romantic Movement were establishing the notion of the countryside aesthetic and expressing a wish to retain 'wild' or open areas for their own sake as well as for public enjoyment. Indeed it is possible to trace the origins of a politics of rurality here.This period saw the establishment of the Commons and Open Spaces Preservation Society in 1865 and the National Trust in 1895, and the slowing down and closer regulation of enclosure. Political reforms in the late 19th century and into the 20th century provided increasing opportunity for political voice regarding claims and counter-claims over appropriate regulation and use of land. The first Bill presented to parliament that attempted to provide extended access to the countryside was in 1886. After this time numerous attempts were made to legislate on the issue – all failed to make the statute book or did not deliver new access rights (see Blunden and Curry, 1989, for a fuller account of legislative attempts prior to 1939). Much of the frustration of these parliamentary challenges was due to the House of Lords, which was the interest group most likely to lose out, given that so many of its members were landowners. In retrospect the flurry of activity in the period during the Second World War set up the conditions for the politics of countryside access up until the CRoW Act.

Old Labour/New Labour: the 1949 National Parks and Access to the Countryside Act

By the inter-war period the first minority Labour administrations had been elected and the Left was growing stronger. In Marshallian terms (Marshall and Bottomore, 1992) the welfare state was being constructed and associated social rights were being accumulated.Trade unions, the provision of paid holidays and five-day working weeks were all helping to establish leisure time for the working class (Clarke and Critcher, 1985).There was a concomitant increasing political sensibility and sensitivity over the supply and restrictions on leisure and recreational space.The countryside access issue became a cause for the Left through which to highlight social inequality and the role of landowners in society: beyond the practical use lay another political utility. The claims for a general right of access over open land, led by the Ramblers' Association (founded in 1935), were quickly cast by the press and traditional interests as 'Bolshevik' and an 'urban attack on the rural' in their implication and source (Blunden and Curry, 1989; Stephenson, 1989). This period was notable for a series of direct actions (known as the 'mass trespasses') to highlight the access issue, where organised groups of ramblers occupied areas of open land not available for access by right (see Rothman, 1982).

The intervening war years were witness to an unprecedented level of activity aimed at understanding and assessing capacity, needs and planning for the post-war future – to create 'a land fit for heroes'. Many Labour politicians in the 1930s and 1940s were strong supporters of the access lobby, seeing class inequality and the Labour class struggle reflected in the arguments concerning private property rights and public access rights. The access issue was considered by several studies, including the Dower report in 1945 and the Hobhouse report in 1947 (Cherry, 1977). The post-war Labour government promised a resolution to those struggles by undertaking to deliver a general public right of access to open land (see Shoard, 1999). As a result the period culminated in the passage of the National Parks and Access to the Countryside Bill, which originally included such a right of access to open land (to include 'mountain, moor, heath and common').

After a lengthy struggle through the parliamentary process the Bill was passed, but *without* the general right of access over open land – the 'right to roam' had been controversially dropped in favour of a voluntary approach (for an account of this, see Cherry, 1977; Blunden and Curry, 1989; Parker and Ravenscroft, 1999). Unaccountably the Secretary of State responsible, Lewis Silkin, had softened his stance and accepted a voluntary approach during the passage of the Bill. As a result the 1949 Act was a great disappointment to the Ramblers' Association and the socialist lobby – in many ways it represented a triumph of containment for the landed interests. Despite such a right to roam failing to materialise, other measures relating to countryside access were included in the Act, for example the enablement of Access Agreements and Orders (see Shoard, 1987; Curry, 1994), whereby each separate agreement had to be negotiated and paid for over parcels of land. While some limited areas of land were entered into access agreements, notably in the new National Parks (see Shoard, 1987), efforts to negotiate wider access to the countryside proved generally unsuccessful.

A period of several decades of rumbling discontent over access was set in train, and prior to 1997 the provisions of the 1949 Act were viewed as incomplete and unsatisfactory by the Ramblers' Association and many wondered if a right to roam would ever be enabled: "it could be argued that a mistake was made, and it is one we are now very unlikely to ever put right" (Blunden and Curry, 1989, p 131). Instead numerous tweaks and minor policy provisions were brokered to provide access opportunities, although none was controversial or radical in reception or intent. The access issue was addressed piecemeal (Curry, 1994). Despite many changes to national political attitudes a kernel of activists and politicians on the Left maintained hope, and a degree of pressure, to see exclusive use of private open land challenged. Fifty years later this was the position from which New Labour approached the access issue – as a long-standing unresolved argument that, to many, appeared to be an anachronistic sideshow, much perhaps as with the hunting issue (see Chapter 6 in this volume). Yet in both cases there were principles and moral arguments that appealed to a general population looking for social reform from New Labour. Both a hunting ban and a right to roam had significant public support and would appeal to the Left of the Labour Party.

During the 1980s and early 1990s the Ramblers' Association had pressed their case for a 'right to roam', pointing to public opinion, growing leisure use (in their view) of the countryside and the failure of landowners to provide access voluntarily as justification for the original 1949 Bill provisions to be applied. By 1994 the arguments were seemingly accepted by the Labour Party and a policy to extend access rights was formally adopted as a manifesto commitment. The wording in the 1997 election manifesto was deliberately vague, however, with a rather telling balancing clause included at the end: "Our policies include greater freedom for people to explore our open countryside. We will not, however, permit any abuse of a right to greater access" (Labour Party, 1997).

Despite scepticism about the likelihood and resolve of Blair to act radically the legislation that was eventually passed in 2000 delivered a belated and somewhat limited 'right to roam', among other wide-ranging rural policy provisions (see Parker and Ravenscroft, 2001; Payne, 2001). This policy was to be strongly contested by sections of the rural population and the Conservative opposition in the Commons and the Lords. Indeed in the late 1990s several rural issues were linked or bundled together by traditional rural interests and cast as an 'urban attack' on the rural way of life. Such protests culminated in several demonstrations and marches across the country and notably in central London (see Parker, 2002; Woods, 2003, 2005).

The 2000 Countryside and Rights of Way (CRoW) Act

When the Labour Party returned to government after 18 years away from office it embarked on implementing a broad-ranging policy agenda with a focus on reforming the welfare state. It also devised a highly effective communications and marketing strategy to mediate its ideas and achievements. It was acutely aware of the priority of various policy innovations that were to be pursued – most of which had been outlined in the party election manifesto. In 1997 it appeared that the manifesto pledge to extend countryside access provision would be fulfilled, although it might have to be shelved while more pressing matters were tackled. This in part explains Blair's politically astute offer to land managers in late 1997 of the opportunity to make voluntary arrangements, essentially designed to enable landowners to gift access to the nation without government resorting to passing a new law and using precious parliamentary time. This approach – by now a standard tactic of New Labour – was one that was strangely reminiscent of the 1949 Act and the failed access agreements contained therein. However, it was also made clear that if such arrangements were not forthcoming the government would press ahead with legislation – tantamount to a fist in a velvet glove. The strategy towards policy reform developed by New Labour involved a process of negotiation, compromise and then stronger action if required. However the first stages of this strategy did not result in any substantial amounts of land being dedicated. The Country Landowners' Association (CLA) was seen as the focal point for landowner opinion. This last opportunity to avoid legislation on the matter was not embraced by landowners, and led George Monbiot to observe that:

> So reluctant have landlords been to share their good fortune with the great unwashed that the £70,000 the government gave to the Country Landowners Association in 1997 to fund voluntary access agreements have secured just twenty acres for public enjoyment, all of them on the CLA president's land. (Monbiot, 1999, p 1)

By 1999, just as Blair appeared to be wavering in the face of determined opposition, legislation was again urged by the then Environment Minister, Michael Meacher, and the Ramblers' Association. Despite concerns amongst some of Blair's advisors New Labour had effectively cleared the way for a populist, and now apparently 'reasonable', law to extend access as of right to England and Wales. Other arrangements have subsequently been made for Scotland through Part I of the 2003 Land Reform (Scotland) Act (see Sellar, 2006), where arguably the third way has been refracted through a rather different political and historical context and with different provisions being implemented.

The long-running debate about open access and the 'right to roam', left unresolved by the 1949 Act, was eventually brought to a degree of resolution with the passing of Part I of the Countryside and Rights of Way (CRoW) Act in late 2000. This part of the Act concerns the new countryside access provisions and contains the definition and management approach for the 'right to roam' access lands (see Ellison, 2001; Ewins, 2001; Parker and Ravenscroft, 2001; Riddall and Trevelyan, 2001). Other parts include rights of way provisions, Areas of Outstanding Natural Beauty (AONBs) management changes and nature conservation stipulations. The enactment of the CRoW Bill and the subsequent inclusion of provisions to define, map and dedicate new 'access land' over particular categories of open and common land was met with a degree of surprise in many quarters. It appeared, on the face of it, to be an 'old' Labour anachronism: a tokenistic nod perhaps to the 'Clause Four' generations. CRoW provides access 'rights' to just under 700,000 hectares of land, something like 8% of the land area of England. However, these provisions are hedged with numerous conditions and managerialist regulations (see the English countryside access website at www. countrysideaccess.gov.uk and the website of the Countryside Council for Wales at www.ccw.gov.uk).

As a result the new access areas required a four- to five-year period whereby the 'new' access land was identified, defined, confirmed and mapped with areas being opened in regional phases as the finalised maps were produced. The last region in England completed this process in October 2005. There is little evidence as yet about the levels of use of the newly mapped access lands. Any clear inference about current or future use levels is difficult to draw when these lands have been legally accessible for only a short time. However, the overall trends of access use have not clearly shown increased demand for a number of years (see Curry, 2001; Curry and Ravenscroft, 2001; GB Leisure Day Visits, 2004).

The new access provisions are tempered with various exceptions and restrictions. Landowners or managers are able to restrict use for land management or on safety grounds for limited periods, and these exclusions may be made without recourse to another authority (that is, the relevant access authority) for up to 28 days. Longer restrictions have also been negotiated, for example for shooting or for other livestock management reasons (Ewins, 2001; Cowburn, 2006). These are expressed by Natural England (formerly the Countryside Agency) as 'common sense' restrictions, and such rules and regulations can be viewed on the countryside access websites as detailed above. However, as Parker (2006) argues, the depiction of regulations of this type as 'common sense' underplays the potential for obfuscation by dint of their complexity and the mutability of such rules. They effectively become constraining factors for users and another method of dissuading the public from using the countryside. They are also further examples of the kind of conditional welfarism or conditional citizenship identified in other policy arenas (Dwyer, 1998; Parker, 2002) and which indicate the kind of pragmatic policy evolution that is by now a hallmark of the past ten years of New Labour.

The new 'rights' are still questionable therefore in terms of clarity and their practical accessibility – the lands are fragmented and often poorly connected to other access routes and areas. The symbolic gains and the practical gains are not equal and CRoW, as the New Labour response to the access issue, is significant but insubstantial. It is a compromise representing a primarily political achievement rather than a practical one, delivering far less than it may first appear. Indeed, as is arguably the case with the New Labour project in general, it flatters to deceive. However, this outcome, as it stands, is not likely to overly trouble the landed or traditional rural interests.

Discussion

A constant theme since at least the 1940s surrounding discussions about countryside access has been a generalised defence of 'rurality' against the urban 'trespasser' on the part of landed interests. This type of approach has been a feature of the CLA (Country Land & Business Association) and the Countryside Alliance in the past decade, which have sought to wrap specific and interest-based defences up into wider rural concerns (see, for example, Anderson, 2006). Such arguments found implied governmental endorsement in the 1940s with, for example, the Hobhouse report (1947) including the following assertion: "much of the ill feeling which has existed in the past has been due to ignorance or thoughtless behaviour on the part of some townsmen" (MTCP, 1947, p 44). The arguments over the effects of access then centred on perceived social and cultural impacts on rurality as much as any likely economic impact on the countryside. Subsequently the anticipated rise in rural recreational use prompted mediating tools such as the Country Code to be devised to buffer rural space and rural interests from 'untutored' users (Merriman, 2005; Parker, 2006). During the 1960s the introduction of country parks under the 1968 Countryside Act served a similar function in channelling urban populations into managed urban fringe locations (Patmore, 1971; Curry, 1994).

The factors that came together to influence New Labour should be carefully reflected upon, given that the above claims were still being used in the 1990s, and yet the action taken to resolve the issue was different and on the face of it a class action – out of time with the new politics (Eder, 1993). In respect of countryside access policy the sentimental version has it that the 'right to roam' pledge reflected an earnest desire to memorialise John Smith, the popular party leader and keen walker who died in May 1994 and who appeared sure to win the election for Labour. However, on closer inspection the practical politics surrounding the CRoW Act meant that such a move needed a large majority in parliament, and the wording of the manifesto pledge was sufficiently vague to justify almost any policy iteration.

After the May 1997 election Labour held 419 seats, with a parliamentary majority of 179. In terms of the rural vote Labour laid claim to something like 180 rural seats after the count, although that number is somewhat debatable (see Ward, 2002). Regardless of exact numbers the shift in representation provided some legitimacy for Labour to implement its rural policies. The overall majority and the large number of new rural seats also indicated that Labour needed to consider the rural vote for the first time in its history. A new consideration was the preservation of at least some of the votes in its newly conquered rural constituencies. This must have played a part in the political calculations over the access issue, with the two factors – the overall majority and the capture and significance of rural votes – providing for contrary arguments about the likely political fallout of a right to roam policy.

The New Labour response to certain rural issues has been surprising. Its eventual banning of hunting in 2005 (Anderson, 2006) and introduction of a form of right to roam provide headlines that appear rather radical. However, the detail illustrates a rather different picture: how the pragmatic politics identified by commentators such as Powell (2000) is clearly operating even through these *managed processes* of change. It is also clear that the populist nature of both access and hunting has proved a significant factor in persuading the government of the political viability of the steps taken.

The political recalculation involved in pursuing the CRoW provisions was also affected by trends in economic activity in rural areas. Future new (Labour) policy is likely to cohere around a post hoc 'making sense' of recreational supply in order to provide a useable integration of sites and routes that may be of benefit to rural economic interests as well as to users. Meanwhile the politics of the rural appears to centre on changes in terms of the way that the countryside is viewed and reified as space that requires political defence and intervention. Under New Labour the primary concern has been to ensure socially efficient (read pragmatic) allocations without a clear or consistent political philosophy – if conditions allow then policy is created and implemented or redesigned to placate opposition.

As such the CRoW Act policy development is the primary New Labour response to the access issue and a result of a pragmatic assessment of self-interest and the strategic interplay of rural interest groups, which had bitterly contested the principles and practical implications of public rights on 'private' land. The CRoW Act is a significant and symbolic iteration but it masks a complex situation where groups and activities are implicated in a choreography of access that involves a continual manoeuvring and contestation at different levels and in different ways. While the national political debate over access has all but died away, local level decisions about exclusions and rights of way preoccupy the local access forums set up under CRoW (see Ravenscroft et al, 2002). For New Labour it seems the Act is a convenient tool to direct criticism away from the socialist wing of the party and also enough of a compromise to mollify landed interests and please the crucial middle ground, the middle class.

Conclusion

The long-running conflict in England over access to land for recreation masks a deeper issue that is experienced by most societies: that is the relationship between groups which hold critical control over resources and those which seek to wrest control away from those groups or at least in some way to undermine the significance of that control. This symbolic struggle over access, as a reflection of status, power and prestige, is one that is situated as a rural political issue but is also a reflection of wider tensions in society. Debates and possibilities concerning the legitimate distribution of rights that confer privilege are somewhat limited (see Cox, 1984). Property rights have become so entrenched and symbolic of personal freedom in many societies that efforts to reorganise or affect these, and the value that attaches to them, are typically met with fierce opposition. This makes many different policies that relate to land use incredibly politicised and potentially damaging for governments. Such rights are often entangled with historical and cultural attachments and meanings. Access debates, as with hunting, have been sources of contention when powers to exclude or participate in particular activities on land are altered.

The introduction of the CRoW Act, in common with the hunting ban, has surprised many political commentators. The determination to implement these pieces of legislation is seemingly out of kilter with the way that the Blair governments have behaved. In line with so many New Labour policies, whether intentionally or not, these appear as much symbolic and aimed at political gain with urban voters (and to maintain Labour Party cohesion) rather than possessing a functional utility, meeting 'demand' or otherwise withstanding scrutiny in terms of consistency in philosophical or ideological terms. The legacy now of New Labour has been to effect a compromise and instigate a set of rather complicated, managerial legislative provisions for open access. Looking to the future the general population will arguably be the net losers if accessibility is not addressed in the coming years (see Mulder et al, 2006). The handling of this dimension of rurality is likely to continue to be a source of conflict, yet the pragmatic politics at the heart of New Labour, for better or worse, appears well suited to manage it.

References

Andersen, P. and Mann, N. (1997) *Safety first: The making of New Labour*, London: Granta Books.

Anderson, A. (2006) 'Spinning the rural agenda: the Countryside Alliance, fox hunting and social policy', *Social Policy and Administration*, vol 40, no 6, pp 722-38.

Blunden, J. and Curry, N. (eds) (1989) *A peoples' charter?* London: HMSO.

Cahill, K. (2001) *Who owns Britain?*, Edinburgh: Canongate.

Cherry, G. (1977) *The history of environmental planning, Vol II: The 1949 National Parks and Access to the Countryside Act*, London: HMSO.

Clark, J., Ward, N., Seymour, S. and Lowe, P. (1998) *Moralizing the environment: Countryside change, farming and pollution*, London: Routledge

Clarke, J. and Critcher, C. (1985) *The devil makes work*, Basingstoke: Macmillan.

CLA (Country Landowners' Association) (1998) *CLA response to the government consultation paper on access to the countryside*, June, London: CLA.

Cowburn, L. (2006) *The Countryside and Rights of Way Act 2000: Exclusions or restrictions of access*, Unpublished MSc thesis, University of Reading, UK.

Cox, A. (1984) *Adversary politics and the land*, Cambridge: Cambridge University Press.

Curry, N. (1994) *Countryside recreation, access and land use planning*, London: Spon.

Curry, N. (2001) 'Access for outdoor recreation in England and Wales: production, consumption and markets', *Journal of Sustainable Tourism*, vol 9, no 5, pp 400-16.

Curry, N. and Ravenscroft, N. (2001) 'Countryside recreation provision in England: exploring a demand-led approach', *Land Use Policy*, vol 18, no 3, pp 281-91.

Darby, W. J. (2000) *Landscape and identity: Geographies of nation and class in England*, Oxford: Berg.

DETR (Department of the Environment, Transport and the Regions) (2000) *Countryside and Rights of Way Act (2000): Explanatory notes*, London: DETR.

Dwyer, P. (1998) 'Conditional citizens? Welfare rights and responsibilities in the late 1990s', *Critical Social Policy*, vol 18, pp 493-517.

Eder, K. (1993) *The new politics of class*, London: Sage.

Ellison, M. (2001) 'A new role for recreation?' *Countryside Recreation*, vol 9, no 3-4, pp 26-30.

Ewins, A. (2001) 'Countryside and Rights of Way Act: Part 1 Access to the countryside', *Countryside Recreation*, vol 9, no 1, pp 2-5.

Featherstone, M. (1991) *Consumer culture and postmodernism*, London: Sage.

GB Leisure Day Visits (2004) *Report of the 2002-03 Great Britain day visits survey*, London: ONS.

Giddens, A. 1998) *The third way*, Cambridge: Polity Press.

Giddens, A. (2001) *The third way and its critics*, Cambridge: Polity Press.

Isin, E. and Wood, P. (1999) *Citizenship and identity*, London: Sage.

Labour Party (1997) *New Labour because Britain deserves better*, Labour Party election manifesto 1997. (Available at www.bbc.co.uk/election97/background/parties/manlab/8labmanhertrans.html)

Malcolmson, R. (1973) *Popular recreations in English society 1700-1850*. Cambridge: Cambridge University Press.

Marshall, T. and Bottomore, T. (1992) *Citizenship and social class*, London: Pluto Press.

Merriman, P. (2005) '"Respect the life of the countryside": the Country Code, government and the conduct of visitors to the countryside in post-war England and Wales', *Transactions of the Institute of British Geographers* NS, vol 30, no 3, pp 336-50.

Mingay, G. (ed) (1989) *The unquiet countryside*, London: Routledge.

Monbiot, G. (1999) *New Labour, old feudalism*, posted 11 February 1999. (Available at www.monbiot.com/archives/1999/02/11/new-labour-old-feudalism)

MTCP (Ministry of Town and Country Planning) (1947) *Report of the Special Committee on Footpaths and Access to the Countryside* (the Hobhouse Report), Cmd 7207, London: HMSO.

Mulder, C., Shibli, S. and Hale, J. (2006) 'Rights of way improvement plans and increased access to the countryside in England: some key issues concerning supply', *Managing Leisure*, vol 11, no 2, pp 96-115.

Murdoch, J., Lowe, P., Ward, N. and Marsden, T. (2003) *The differentiated countryside*, London: Routledge.

Parker, G. (1999) 'Rights, symbolic violence and the micro-politics of the rural. The case of the Parish Paths Partnership scheme', *Environment and Planning:A*, vol 31, pp 1207-22.

Parker, G. (2002) *Citizenships contingency and the countryside*, London: Routledge.

Parker, G. (2006) 'The Country Code and the ordering of countryside citizenship', *Journal of Rural Studies*, vol 22, no 1, pp 1-16.

Parker, G. (2007) 'The negotiation of leisure citizenship: leisure constraints, moral regulation and the mediation of rural place', *Leisure Studies*, vol 26, no 1, pp 1-22.

Parker, G. and Ravenscroft, N. (1999) 'Citizenship, nationalism and hegemony: fifty years of the 1949 National Parks and Access to the Countryside Act', *Leisure Studies*, vol 21, pp 297-313.

Parker, G. and Ravenscroft, N. (2001) 'Land, rights and the gift: CRoW 2000 and the negotiation of citizenship', *Sociologia Ruralis*, vol 41, no 4, pp 381-98.

Patmore, J. (1971) *Land and leisure in England and Wales*, London: Fairleigh Dickinson University Press.

Payne, S. (2001) 'From carrots to sticks. Natural habitat protection after the Countryside and Rights of Way Act 2000', *Environmental Law and Management*, vol 13, no 5, pp 239-48.

Powell, M. (2000) 'New labour and the third way in the British welfare state: a new and distinctive approach?' *Critical Social Policy*, vol 20, no 1, pp 39-60.

Ravenscroft, N., Curry, N. and Markwell, S. (2002) 'Outdoor recreation and participative democracy in England and Wales', *Journal of Environmental Planning and Management*, vol 45, no 5, pp 715-34.

Riddall, J. and Trevelyan, J. (2001) *Rights of way. A guide to law and practice* (3rd edn), London: Ramblers' Association and Open Spaces Society.

Rothman, B. (1982) *The 1932 Kinder Trespass*, Altrincham: Willow Press.

Sellar, W. (2006) 'The great land debate and the Land Reform (Scotland) Act 2003', *Norsk Geografisk Tidsskrift*, vol 60, no 1, pp 100-9.

Sheail, J. (1981) *A history of conservation in interwar Britain*, Oxford: Oxford University Press.

Shoard, M. (1987) *This land is our land*, London: Grafton.

Shoard, M. (1996) 'Robbers vs revolutionaries: what the battle for access is really all about', in C. Watkins (ed) *Rights of way: Policy, culture and management*, London: Pinter, pp 11-23.

Shoard, M. (1999) *A right to roam*, London: Grafton.

Sibley, D. (1995) *Geographies of exclusion*, London: Routledge.

Sibley, D. (2006) 'Inclusions/exclusions in rural space', in P. Cloke, T. Marsden and P. Mooney (eds) *Handbook of rural studies*, London: Sage.

Stephenson, T. (1989) *Forbidden land*, Manchester: Manchester University Press.

Thompson, E. P. (1993) *Customs in common*, Harmondsworth: Penguin.

Urry, J. (2000) *Sociology beyond societies*, London: Routledge.

Valentine, G. (2001) *Social geographies*, Harlow: Pearson.

Ward, N. (2002) 'Representing rurality? New Labour and the electoral geography of rural Britain', *Area*, vol 34, pp 171-81.

Whatmore, S. (2002) *Hybrid geographies*, London: Sage.

Williams, R. (1973) *The country and the city*, London: Chatto and Windus.

Woods, M. (2003) 'Deconstructing rural protest: the emergence of a new social movement', *Journal of Rural Studies*, vol 19, no 4, pp 309-25.

Woods, M (2005) *Contesting rurality: Politics in the British countryside*, Aldershot: Ashgate.

Wordie, J. (1983) 'The chronology of English enclosure, 1500-1914', *The Economic History Review*, New Series, vol 36, no 4, pp 483-505.

NINE

Agricultural policy

Alan Greer

Introduction

The agricultural policy of the New Labour governments has been central in their approach to governing the countryside. This is highlighted in the rhetoric of multifunctional agriculture, which stresses the contribution that farmers make to the delivery of a wide range of policy objectives – not only in food production but also in rural development, environmental sustainability, animal welfare and food quality. Thus in a speech to the Royal Agricultural Society in July 2006, David Miliband, the newly appointed Secretary of State for Environment, Food and Rural Affairs, commented that "farming is at the heart of our society, our economy and our cultural heritage. It's about people, food, landscape and the environment. It touches every member of society every day.... It is important not just for the countryside but for the whole country" (Miliband, 2006).

This chapter discusses the main issues that have structured the agricultural policy agenda since 1997. This has involved a combination of old and new problems, for example: bovine spongiform encephalopathy (BSE), bovine TB and avian influenza; recurring issues – the stagnation of agricultural incomes; the pursuit of long-standing policy commitments at the international level – radical reform of the Common Agricultural Policy (CAP) and greater liberalisation of world trade; and organisational reform – the creation of the Department for Environment, Food and Rural Affairs (Defra) and the impact of devolution. The chapter also links agricultural policy to New Labour's approach to the modernisation of the policy process, especially the emphasis on joined-up governance, evidence-based policy, learning from experience and other countries, and consultation with stakeholders (Cabinet Office, 1999).

Agricultural crisis and policy development

In 2004 the agri-food sector accounted for 7.6% of the total value of the UK economy and 14% of employment (nearly 3.8 million jobs). However, the agricultural industry now accounts for less than 1% of the economy and just 1.8% of total employment, although there are important variations between territories and between production sectors (Defra/SEERAD/DECP/DARD, 2005). Crucially for New Labour, its election coincided with the onset of a severe recession in the agricultural economy that led to a substantial reduction in farming incomes, which reached their lowest level in real terms for 75 years. Total income from farming in the UK in 2005 was estimated at £2.5 billion and while this was 40% above the nadir reached in 2000, it was still 60% below the 1995 high point for farming profitability. Such fluctuations reflect the volatility of the euro/sterling exchange rate, world commodity and oil prices, and the impact of market shocks caused by BSE and foot and mouth disease (FMD). The dramatic fall in farm incomes contributed to a perception, certainly among the agricultural community, that the countryside was in crisis (Greer, 2003) and concern about the state of agriculture was a central driver in periodic protests by farmers from the winter of 1997/98 onwards. This general discontent fed into the fuel blockades of 2000 and the countryside marches in 1997, 1998 and 2002.

In this context, government policy combined emergency measures with long-term strategic planning that involved the search for a 'new vision' for farming. The approach was encapsulated in a series of documents such as *A new direction for agriculture* (December 1999), the *Action plan for farming* (March 2000) and *The strategy for sustainable farming and food* (Defra, 2002). Emergency packages of support measures were also provided. As noted by the House of Commons Environment Committee (2002, p 48), much domestic agricultural policy had been formulated "in response to the need to 'fire-fight' farming crises. The result has been a welter of ad hoc packages intended to support the industry". In September 1999, for example, the government announced emergency aid for livestock producers worth £537 million, followed six months later by another £200 million in the *Action plan for farming*.

Long-term policy development has been underpinned by the basic belief that agriculture needs to become more competitive, diverse, modern and sustainable, with the state working in partnership with the industry to help farmers make their businesses more efficient and more responsive to the market. In the farming chapter of its five-year departmental strategy published in 2004 Defra noted progress in areas such as CAP reform and the approach to animal health. Targets for the future included further trade liberalisation and CAP reform, promoting environmental stewardship, ending the ban on beef exports, implementing the Single Payment Scheme and delivering a new strategy for farming regulation (Defra, 2004).

Defra presented much of its work as a continuation of existing interventions, especially the 2002 *Strategy for sustainable farming and food*, which became the central driver of policy after the FMD crisis. The Strategy incorporated many of the 105 recommendations made in the Curry Report (report of the Policy Commission on the Future of Farming and Food, appointed in August 2001 as part of the response to the FMD outbreak). Its central themes were sustainable development and 'reconnection'. So the key objective for public policy should be to "reconnect our food and farming industry: to reconnect farming with its market and the rest of the food chain; to reconnect the food chain and the countryside; and to reconnect consumers with what they eat and how it is produced" (Policy Commission on the Future of Farming and Food, 2002, p 6). Drawing on this approach, the overarching aim was "to promote a competitive and efficient farming and food sector which protects and enhances our countryside and wider environment, and contributes to the health and prosperity of all our communities" (Defra, 2002, p 49).

To carry forward the strategy, the 2002 Spending Review allocated £500 million over a three-year period for a range of measures in agriculture and rural development including those to promote environmental sustainability, tackle animal disease, improve marketing and training, and develop speciality foods. Funded under 'pillar II' of the CAP, the England Rural Development Plan for 2000 to 2006 (RDP) was also a key element in delivering the multifunctional strategy, supporting agri-environment schemes, the organic sector and diversification into areas such as energy crops and tourism (Greer, 2005, pp 153-61). The Environmental Stewardship scheme introduced in 2005, and intended to provide the heart of the new RDP for 2007 to 2013, was based in a recommendation in the Curry Report for a basic 'broad but shallow' scheme that would bring more farmers into the remit of agri-environment measures. This was structured on two levels: Entry Level for new entrants and Higher Level for more advanced management of high-priority landscapes and habitats.

Other important 'daughter' strategies included new frameworks such as the Food Industry Sustainability Strategy, the Animal Health and Welfare Strategy, and the Farm Regulation and Charging Strategy (Defra, 2006). Regulation has been a constant theme, partly in response to complaints from farmers about form filling, inspections and what they term 'gold-plating' (imposing standards higher than the minimum set down at the EU level). Policy documents such as the *Action plan for farming* have included commitments to root out 'unnecessary' regulation. For David Miliband the approach was simple: "if the NFU or anyone else makes a serious and well-founded complaint about a regulation, we will justify it, reform it, or ditch it" (Miliband, 2006). This reflected Defra's commitment to use non-regulatory instruments wherever possible, improve the efficiency and effectiveness of regulation where it was needed, and to make it more 'customer focused'. A key target was for a 25% reduction in red tape by 2009, and a new 'whole-farm' approach was intended to provide more integrated regulation and advice, reducing burdens from form filling and overlapping inspections. A central theme was 'burden-sharing' – collaboration between the state and the farmers to find new ways to share the responsibilities and costs of intervention, for example in tackling animal diseases such as bovine tuberculosis (bTB) (Defra/SE/WAG, 2005, p 15). The introduction of the CAP Single Payment Scheme (to be discussed later) was also designed to reduce substantially the administrative burden on farmers.

Following a review of its approach, in July 2006 the government published its *Sustainable farming and food: Forward look* document (Defra, 2006), which concluded that the existing strategy remained a "robust vehicle for change". Although the policy context had changed, especially with CAP reform, "both the broad direction of the strategy, and the need for an effective partnership between Government and industry to drive forward delivery remain as valid today as when the Strategy was first published"(Defra, 2006, p 10). Five closely interrelated priority themes – said to reflect the interdependence of the economic, social and environmental pillars of sustainability – were identified: 'succeeding in the market', 'improving the environmental performance of farming', 'sustainable consumption and production', 'animal health and welfare' and 'climate change and agriculture'.

A crucial shift was the much greater emphasis on the importance of climate change. Therefore, because farmers are in the front line of climate change (with the potential for more frequent storms, heat stress and increased risk of pests and disease), they must play their full part in addressing it, for example through better land management to lower greenhouse gas emissions, the reduction of food miles, and increased production of bioenergy and other non-food crops. Based on estimates that the farming sector contributes 7% of national greenhouse gases, Defra increasingly referred to the need to reduce the "significant environmental footprint of the farming and food sector" (Defra, 2006, p 7). In the official rhetoric, the idea that agriculture must not take out more from the planet than it gives back has been dubbed 'one planet farming'. As elaborated by Miliband, this presents a vision of a "farming that reflects the need for us to live within the means of the planet, and farming which helps us live within the needs of the planet". To cut the ecological footprint we need "one planet farming as well as one planet living – one planet farming which minimises the impact on the environment of patterns of food production and consumption, and farming which maximises its contribution to renewal of the natural environment" (Miliband, 2006).

CAP reform and the liberalisation of world trade

The major policy objectives of Labour governments after 1997 exhibited a high degree of continuity from previous administrations, especially the fundamental commitment to CAP reform and the liberalisation of world trade. Here the self-perception of the government is that it has "been in the vanguard of those pressing for ambitious liberalisation in both CAP and WTO negotiations" (House of Commons Environment, Food and Rural Affairs Committee, 2003, p 5). A joint Treasury/Defra paper, *A vision for the Common Agricultural Policy*, published in December 2005, set out a long-term vision for agricultural policies that:

> better protect the environment, more effectively support those most in need, and promote more broad-based sustainable economic development in rural areas. They seek to reduce the costs of protectionism on developing countries and promote the expansion of world trade. And in so doing, they help ensure Europe can meet the challenges of globalisation in the decades ahead. (HM Treasury/Defra, 2005, p 3)

Although the government was particularly vocal in its support for trade liberalisation, progress in the Doha Development Agenda trade round launched in November 2001 has been described, perhaps generously, as "intermittent and limited" (House of Commons International Development Committee, 2006a, p 7). The Doha Round has been characterised by stalemate and a series of missed 'deadlines', with the original target for the completion of negotiations by January 2005 extended several times. Last-ditch efforts to resuscitate the process in July 2006 also failed, leaving the Doha Round on the verge of final collapse, and attention turned increasingly to the development of alternative regional and bilateral trade agreements.

Agreement on agriculture, especially between the EU and the US, was widely regarded as the key to progress on the Doha Round. However, core disagreements about export subsidies, market access and trade-distorting agricultural support measures could not be easily resolved. The EU approach was basically conservative, emphasising market liberalisation within the framework of the multifunctional 'European model of agriculture'. Leading up to the World Trade Organization (WTO) Ministerial Conference in Hong Kong in December 2005, the EU Trade Commissioner, Peter Mandelson, tried to unblock the impasse by offering more concessions – which he described as at the "outer limits" (*Guardian*, 2005) of his mandate. This caused considerable controversy among member states, many of which did not share the British preference for substantial liberalisation. Indeed, France argued that his offer went beyond the limits of his mandate, and President Chirac threatened to veto any deal that undermined the 2003 CAP reforms.

For many in the UK policy and political elites, the solution to the problem was simple: the EU should "improve its offer in agriculture. Greater market access is the key to unlocking the round for developing countries" (House of Commons International Development Committee, 2006a, p 3). However, while the government was willing to support more concessions on agriculture, it noted that a balance had to be struck between the views of all member states (then 25), the majority of which were unwilling to move until other WTO members made improved offers on agricultural domestic support and industrial goods (House of Commons International Development Committee, 2006b, p 6).

The difficulties in the Doha Round were closely linked to debates about the reform of the CAP – another long-standing policy preference of British governments and a core priority for New Labour. Ambitions for the medium term set out in the *Sustainable farming and food: Forward look* document included further reform of the CAP, full decoupling of subsidies from production, phasing out of market price support, more funding for rural development and the removal of export subsidies. These objectives envisaged building further on the existing lines of CAP reform, and were partly embodied in the EU offer in the Doha Round, for example an end to export subsidies by 2013. More crucially the 2003 Luxembourg Agreement on the CAP, building on incremental changes agreed at the Berlin summit in March 1999 under the rubric of Agenda 2000, arguably presaged the most radical changes since the MacSharry reform in 1992.

The central elements were the 'decoupling' of subsidies from production and the introduction of a Single Payment Scheme (SPS) that replaced most of the plethora of direct payments under different commodity regimes and was linked directly to cross-compliance with basic mandatory environmental, food safety and animal welfare standards. Within an overall expenditure ceiling for the agricultural budget up to 2013 increased funds would be made available for rural development, environmental, animal welfare and other programmes under the second pillar (achieved through reductions in direct payments, or *modulation*).

For the British government the 2003 reforms embodied many of its long-standing preferences in both policy objectives and mechanisms. Indeed decoupling subsidies from production to encourage the farming industry to move closer to the market was a core recommendation of the Curry Report. On the other hand the government regarded CAP reform as a 'work in progress', progress that was heavily constrained by intergovernmental bargaining. For example, the European summits at either end of the UK's presidency of the EU in the second half of 2005 were beset by severe disputes over the EU budget, the British rebate and the future of the CAP. After much heated discussion at the December Council the 'red-line' British demand for a 'meaningful' review of farm expenditure before 2013 was watered down to allow agreement on the budget, although the government insisted that the extra money provided through a reduction in the rebate would not fund expenditure on agriculture. It also took solace in an agreement that the Commission should undertake a full, wide-ranging review of all aspects of EU spending, including the CAP, in 2008.

A core feature of the Luxembourg Agreement was the considerable scope for national discretion in a wide range of areas, for example on the extent of decoupling (full or partial) and the application of the single payment. In the UK, a 'national' decision was taken to implement full decoupling from the earliest possible date (an option was to delay implementation for up to two years), and in January 2005 the Single Payment Scheme replaced 11 separate production subsidies. For the application of the scheme in England Defra adopted a 'dynamic hybrid' model in which flat-rate area-based payments will be phased in by 2012. Although most farmers preferred the alternative 'historic payments' approach (in which receipts are based on subsidies received during 2000-02), the government justified its decision as best suited to giving farmers greater freedom to respond to market demands and as better able to reward environmentally friendly farming practices.

The introduction of the single payment in England became one of the most publicly visible policy failures of the New Labour government in the agricultural sector, producing loud public and parliamentary criticism that led to the removal of the Chief Executive of the Rural Payments Agency (RPA) in March 2006. The root of the fiasco was the inability of the RPA to pay farmers their money on time. At the end of March 2006 it had disbursed only 15% of funds to just 27% of claimants, set against a target for 96% of payments to be made by this date. By invoking a partial payments contingency plan, the RPA managed to disburse

95% of funding by the end of June 2006 (against an EU requirement for 96.14%), although over 8,000 farmers (7%) still had not received any money (NAO, 2006). In the face of the criticism, Defra resorted to sticking plasters, announcing that it would reimburse lost interest and give the farming help charities additional money to help farmers cope with stress.

A report by the National Audit Office (NAO) concluded that the implementation shambles had caused distress and anxiety to a "significant minority" of farmers, cost them money in additional interest and bank charges, and undermined the farming industry's confidence in the RPA. The problems with the scheme had emanated from a combination of several factors: the high risk nature of the project, the complexity of the scheme, the development of a new IT system, and a relatively short delivery timescale. Moreover matters were made worse by the concurrent reorganisation of the RPA that aimed to reduce staff by 1,800 and make efficiency savings of £164 million by 2008/09. Far from making the savings envisaged, the mess over the single payment actually increased costs, for example through the recruitment of extra agency staff without the experience and knowledge of those who had left (NAO, 2006).

It was not as if the government had not been forewarned. In a report in May 2004 the Environment Committee expressed concern about the administrative capacity of the RPA, noting its ongoing reorganisation, past problems with IT systems and data management, and previous delays in making payments. While Defra acknowledged the size of the task, ministers argued that the new system was actually less complex than those it replaced and expressed cautious confidence in the ability of the RPA to deliver (House of Commons Environment, Food and Rural Affairs Committee, 2004). In a subsequent report in January 2006, the Committee complained that the government had taken little notice of its previous warnings and pronounced itself "dismayed at the complacency of the Minister, who refused to admit that any mistakes had been made or that anything could have been done differently to avoid the problems" (House of Commons Environment, Food and Rural Affairs Committee, 2006b, p 7) The Committee also was "deeply unimpressed" by the failure to plan properly for the implementation of the scheme, and concluded that Defra gave "insufficient consideration to the administrative complexity of the chosen model" and should have considered delaying its application until 2006 to allow more time for preparation (2006b, p 4). Neither could Defra fall back on the complexity of the system as an excuse because the implementation of a similar system in Germany, although also not without problems, had allowed a higher proportion of payments to be made (NAO, 2006).

Animal disease and risk management

The foot and mouth epidemic may have crystallised the weaknesses at the heart of the approach of British governments to tackling animal diseases but New Labour was initially preoccupied by an earlier disease policy fiasco – BSE. In

December 1997 one of its first acts in the agricultural sector was to announce the creation of a committee of inquiry on the approach to BSE in the decade since its discovery in 1986 (Greer, 1999). The Phillips Inquiry began its work in January 1998 and its findings, published in a massive report in October 2000, provide a comprehensive account of the episode, including the lessons to be learned for public administration and policy making (BSE Inquiry, 2000).

Governments after 1997 also continued to work towards key reforms in several thorny aspects of BSE policy. A crucial priority was to remove the EU ban on beef and cattle exports introduced in March 1996. Progress was largely incremental and the result of continuous intensive negotiation with the EU Commission and other member countries. In March 1998 export of beef from Northern Ireland under the Export Certified Herd Scheme was approved. In August 1999 the introduction of a Date Based Export Scheme allowed limited exports of UK beef subject to stringent conditions, although the French government continued to maintain a ban until legal action taken against it by the European Court of Justice in 2001 eventually secured compliance. A harmonised approach to BSE throughout the EU was formalised in the 2001 EU regulation on transmissible spongiform encephalopathies (TSEs). Implemented in the UK during 2002, this laid down rules for the prevention, control and eradication of TSEs and incorporated principles of traceability, inspection and surveillance.

More important were the efforts to secure the complete removal of the EU export ban. Two key preconditions set by the EU Commission in its TSE Road Map were recognition that the British cattle herd was 'moderate' risk status for BSE (confirmed in an opinion of the European Food Safety Authority in March 2005) and a satisfactory report on the UK's BSE controls by the EU Food and Veterinary Office (delivered in September 2005). With both major preconditions met the government introduced a new BSE testing regime in autumn 2005 to replace the 'Over Thirty Month' scheme (introduced in 1996 to prevent older cattle from entering the food or feed chains). This was accompanied in January 2006 by the introduction of a transitional Older Cattle Disposal Scheme for cattle born before August 1996, officially described as "an exceptional market support measure" that would last until the end of 2008. Finally, in March 2006, EU member states in the Standing Committee for the Food Chain and Animal Health unanimously approved a Commission proposal to lift the ten-year ban on the export of cattle and bovine products from the UK, applicable from 2 May 2006 (excluding those born before August 1996). Accordingly, the Date Based Export Scheme and the Export Approved Scheme were wound up and controls were harmonised with other EU countries.

As an overarching framework, the Animal Health and Welfare Strategy for Great Britain was launched in 2003. (A separate strategy for Northern Ireland was prepared in the context of the development of an all-Ireland animal welfare plan.) This covered a variety of risks including bovine tuberculosis in cattle (bTB) and avian influenza, both of which had (potentially) serious economic consequences for farmers and the agricultural industry. For example bTB was estimated to have cost the taxpayer £90.5 million in 2004 and was officially regarded as one of the most difficult animal health issues faced by farmers. A five-point plan introduced in 1998, following the report of an independent scientific review group chaired by Sir John Krebs, recommended improved research, regular testing and a scientific trial on the effects of culling badgers (the Randomised Badger Culling Trial, conducted between 1998 and 2006). In the light of emerging evidence from the trial, and the failure of the five-point plan to halt the spread of the disease, a review of strategy was announced at the annual general meeting of the National Farmers' Union (NFU) in 2003. This was followed by separate consultation exercises in England, Scotland and Wales (2004), with a new jointly agreed ten-year strategy document published in March 2005 (Defra/SE/WAG, 2005). In December 2005 the government announced further measures to tackle bTB in England, including a testing system for cattle and the creation of a new independent stakeholder advisory group. The most controversial element, which saw farmers at loggerheads with the animal welfare lobby, was the unresolved issue of the culling of badgers, which was to be the subject of an extensive public consultation (to be discussed later).

Avian influenza (especially the highly pathogenic sub-type H5N1 – or 'bird flu' in the media jargon) emerged as a major issue on the government's policy agenda from late 2003, when cases were confirmed in several Asian countries. Particular concern centred on the potential disaster for the British poultry industry should 'bird flu' reach the UK. As avian influenza gradually spread into Europe policy focused both on prevention and on how to tackle any outbreak. For example Defra did not regard the introduction of a general ban on keeping poultry outdoors as justified by its risk assessment or as a proportionate response, because bringing large numbers of free-range birds indoors would itself create a significant welfare problem. Action focused on the need for intensified surveillance, maintenance of effective control of imports and national biosecurity measures, including guidance to farmers. Increasing concern at the highest levels of government was highlighted in October 2005 when the Prime Minister joined with the NFU to launch a central register of commercial poultry keepers, coordinated by Defra, the Scottish Executive and the Welsh Assembly Government. Any outbreaks would be tackled through early detection and slaughter of infected birds, and the imposition of movement controls. As a result of a review of existing contingency plans in July 2006 Defra also decided, on the advice of the Chief Veterinary Officer, to stockpile ten million doses of vaccine as a precautionary measure. In April 2006 the efforts put into contingency planning had their first test when strains of avian influenza were detected in a swan found dead in Scotland, and subsequently in a poultry farm in Norfolk. However, although they caused much excitement in the media, these were isolated outbreaks and had minimal impact on both the agricultural sector and public health.

Modernisation, policy delivery and stakeholder interaction

The agriculture sector highlights central themes in New Labour's approach to the modernisation of the policy process, especially ideas about the 'principles of good policy making' such as joined-up governance, evidence-based policy, learning from experience and from other countries (policy transfer), and consultation with stakeholders (Cabinet Office, 1999).

Joined-up governance

Institutional innovation and reorganisation was heavily influenced by considerations about joined-up governance and more effective policy implementation. Most obviously the creation of Defra to replace the Ministry of Agriculture, Fisheries and Food was designed to produce 'joined-up' thinking and actions rather than perpetuate "traditional 'silos' of policy and practice" (Defra, 2001, p 4). The search for effective and efficient policy delivery also underpinned the formation of the Food Standards Agency in 2000 and the reorganisation of Defra's agencies into a smaller number of bodies with clearer and more accountable roles (Defra, 2003 – the Haskins Report), including the launch of Natural England in October 2006 as an integrated countryside and land management agency.

Devolution also placed increased importance on policy coordination and joined-up governance, given that Defra effectively became responsible for England alone on broad swathes of policy. The new realities were reflected in the formulation of separate 'visions' and strategic plans in Scotland, Wales and Northern Ireland as counterparts to that of the Policy Commission in England: *A forward strategy for Scottish agriculture*, the Welsh Assembly's *Farming for the future* and the Northern Ireland *Vision* exercise (Greer, 2005). Four separate Rural Development Plans were also drawn up and there was considerable variation in the application of the single payment with each territory opting for a different approach (historic payments in Scotland and Wales, a 'static hybrid' in Northern Ireland). Also important is increasing emphasis on regional flexibility within England itself. Effective regional and local delivery through partnership working was viewed as essential to the success of interventions such as the bTB strategy, the Rural Development Plan and the Strategy for Sustainable Farming, which involved the Government Offices and Regional Development Agencies in the development of action plans (Defra, 2006, p 44).

Consultation and partnership

Another central theme of the policy approach of New Labour has been the emphasis on consultation and partnership with a wide range of stakeholders. As noted in a report by the House of Commons Science and Technology Committee (2006, p 66), formal consultations "are now an established part of the policy making process and have been widely welcomed as a means of promoting public engagement in the political process and in producing more informed and better policy". In a broad sense, the commitment to multifunctionality requires going beyond the traditionally narrow corporatist relationship with producer organisations (such as the NFU) to develop cooperation with a much wider range of interests including retailers, environmentalists and consumers. The government's response to the BSE Inquiry also emphasised that consultation and openness, especially on issues of risk, should be a first step towards the greater involvement of stakeholders and the wider public in policy development and decisionmaking (Defra/HM Government, 2001).

In its approach to bTB, especially with regard to the highly emotive issue of badger culling, Defra tried to manage a difficult issue through a transparent and open consultation process. A consultation exercise conducted between December 2005 and March 2006 was designed to involve the wider public in the decision process on both the principle of badger culling and the delivery options. Moreover, although the policy agenda was heavily influenced by farmers' campaigns for urgent action, the government believed it essential that "appropriate weight and balance" be given to contending stakeholder views and pointed to the "important role" of animal welfare and wildlife groups in developing bTB policies (Defra/SE/WAG, 2005, p 29).

This preference for more open consultation on policy formulation is closely linked to the belief that collaboration and constructive 'partnership' between stakeholders and the state is central to effective policy implementation. At the root of this is a recognition that successful policy delivery often depends on voluntary behavioural change, especially in a sector where there is significant resistance to new ways of doing things. For the government this places a high premium on developing collaborative working that is based on a shared understanding and ownership of objectives. So a new relationship between industry and government was envisaged by the Policy Commission and formed the basis of the Strategy for Sustainable Farming and Food. In a sector "made up of many thousands of small and medium-sized businesses" the government and industry "need to work together in partnership, at a national and regional level, to deliver the leadership and the policy framework required to enable change to be realised" (Defra, 2006, p 10). Similarly the bTB strategy aimed to "improve stakeholder buy-in, encourage a shared vision and ownership of the problems, and develop clear governance arrangements" (Defra/SE/WAG, 2005, p 15).

Central to this approach is the understanding that while continuing regulation is inevitable, of equal importance is the promotion of capacity building, strategic oversight, leadership, benchmarking and "the spread of good practice up and down the food chain as ways of raising performance" (Defra, 2006, p 9). Established forms of interaction such as advisory and stakeholder groups play a key role. Between 2002 and 2006, for example, Sir Don Curry chaired a ten-member independent Implementation Group to drive forward the Strategy for Sustainable Farming and Food. This body viewed its role as "a combination of challenge and facilitation", providing strategic oversight and stakeholder perspectives, and acting as an external 'champion' (SFSS, 2006, p 3). Defra can even envisage such groups taking potentially important decisions. For example, in 2006 a small bTB stakeholder group was established to advise on policy development and delivery, but in the longer term Defra also saw this group becoming a forum "where shared decisions or those not requiring Ministerial involvement can properly be taken" (Defra/SE/WAG, 2005, p 33).

However, consultation is not without its problems, and cannot replace the need for governments to take difficult political decisions. The consultation on badger culling, for example, generated nearly 50,000 responses of which 70% were received from public campaigns run by wildlife and farming groups. In numerical terms the vast majority of responses opposed badger culling, but opinion among stakeholders and in lengthy 'substantive' public responses was more evenly divided (Defra/PKF Accountants, 2006). There also was some strong criticism of the quality of the consultation document, for example that it did not identify all of the relevant questions and also that Defra had not conducted adequate pre-consultation soundings of scientific experts (House of Commons Environment, Food and Rural Affairs Committee, 2006a). This reflected unease that government was biased in favour of a particular outcome, using the consultation to manage acceptance of its preferred decision. For some it also illustrated the dangers involved in using consultations as an indicator of public opinion, not least because respondents are self-selecting and the approach favours well-organised campaigns by pressure groups (House of Commons Science and Technology Committee, 2006, p 68).

In general terms the Science and Technology Committee noted that consultations play a very useful role "in improving not only transparency but the quality of policy making". However, it voiced several concerns about "consultation fatigue" and "growing doubts surrounding the link between consultation and the content of policy". Indeed "early engagement with the right stakeholders may be more important on occasion than full-blooded public consultation" (2006, p 72). So, while public consultations are good practice and often valuable, they are not always essential, especially in policy areas where the "options are reasonably clear, the arguments have been well rehearsed in public, and both scientific views and public opinion are well documented" (2006, pp 69-70).

Evidence-based policy and policy learning

Such criticisms highlight the tension between democratic considerations, based on wide consultation to gauge opinions, and narrow technocratic approaches to policy making that focus on scientific evidence and the advice of experts. As well as open consultation, New Labour has grounded its policy approach in the assumption that better policy making involves a rational assessment of evidence, and learning from experience and other countries. Crucially for New Labour, 'evidence-based' policy making has its roots in its modernising agenda and its "commitment to 'what works' over ideologically driven policy" (House of Commons Science and Technology Committee, 2006, p 10).

Evidence-based policy has been viewed as especially crucial in the handling of animal disease and welfare issues such as BSE and avian influenza, where scientific expertise is vital to the effective management of risk. Influenced by the recommendations of the BSE Inquiry, the government reformed the arrangements for embedding scientific advice into the policy process. Within Defra, for example, a Science Advisory Council (SAC) was created in February 2004 to give expert and independent advice on the science underpinning policy development. Indeed Defra is "frequently cited as an exemplar of good practice in terms of its scientific advisory system" (House of Commons Science and Technology Committee, 2006, p 35).

Much of the approach to bTB also has been based on a commitment to obtaining the best available scientific evidence, using for example the Independent Scientific Group established in 1998 and a sub-group of the SAC. This approach also involves the use of scientific trials and pilot schemes, such as the badger culling trial and those conducted on genetically modified (GM) crops. In an example of lesson drawing from other countries the government also paid close attention to the progress of scientific trials on badger culling conducted in Ireland, as well as those it sponsored itself. On the other hand the Environment Committee criticised Defra and the RPA for a failure to pilot elements of its approach to the Single Payment Scheme, notably the land registration system (House of Commons Environment, Food and Rural Affairs Committee, 2006b).

The problem with evidence-based policy is that a rational-technocratic approach is not value-free, and cannot remove political considerations from decision making. On badger culling, for example, the government clearly recognised that scientific certainty and consensus "are not always achievable" and that it is necessary to "find the means of interpreting science where there is conflicting advice" (Defra/SE/WAG, 2005, p 29). Therefore, in considering the evidence it was necessary to take account of costs, practicality of delivery, conservation implications and wider public opinion as well as assessing the scientific merits of options. As Miliband made clear, any decision on badger culling "needs the backing of scientific, practical, financial and organisational logic that has the confidence of farmers and animal welfare organisations. They may not agree on the outcome, but there has to be shared understanding of the facts" (Miliband, 2006).

There has also been some criticism of 'evidence-based policy', indicating an unease that the concept has been used by New Labour as an ideological construct to help justify essentially political decisions. The Environment Committee noted that while Defra "prides itself" on its commitment to evidence-based policy making, the decision about the Single Payment Scheme "was based on pragmatism and political expediency" (House of Commons Environment, Food and Rural Affairs Committee, 2004, p 9). In the Science and Technology Committee's inquiry, several witnesses questioned the very notion of evidence-based policy making, and in its report the Committee argued that government "should not overplay this mantra, but should acknowledge more openly the many drivers of policy making, as well as any gaps in the relevant research base" (House of Commons Science and Technology Committee, 2006, p 3).

What is 'new' about New Labour?

The agricultural policy of 'New' Labour governments since 1997 has been characterised by consistency in major policy objectives from previous governments, especially on the reform of the CAP and the preference for substantial trade liberalisation. Other core priorities such as the development of the Strategy for Sustainable Farming and Food and the approach to animal disease also do not generate much political controversy in terms of general aims and objectives. There is broad consensus on the basic aim to encourage the development of a viable agricultural industry that can compete on the world market without production support that is also consumer-friendly and environmentally and socially sustainable. There have been changes in emphasis, however. The rhetoric of 'one planet farming' in particular perhaps highlights ever-increasing concern for environmental sustainability rather than the unbridled primacy of the market.

What New Labour really wanted to establish was a reputation for efficient and effective delivery of services – summed up in the Blairite mantras 'delivery, delivery, delivery', and 'what is best is what works'. This critically placed the core focus on the modernisation of the policy *process* to deliver better services rather than any major political differentiation on objectives and outcomes. For example, the government portrayed the work of the BSE Inquiry, and its response to it, as a notable instance of lesson drawing and policy learning, contrasting favourably its preference for joined-up government and evidence-based policy with the muddle of the previous Conservative administrations (Defra/HM Government, 2001). So it is unfortunate for New Labour that major advances in some crucial policy areas – notably the 2003 reforms of the CAP – have been overshadowed by disasters in implementation, especially on FMD and the single payment. In the joint Foreword to Defra's five-year strategy, Tony Blair and Margaret Beckett claimed that the government had "achieved what has eluded all previous Governments" – delivering radical reform of the CAP. Yet they also boldly asserted that the government would "deliver on a fundamentally new relationship with farming – replacing the complexities of the CAP with a new streamlined approach summed up as 'one form, one date, one payment and one face from Government'" (Defra, 2004, pp 7-8).

Despite the rhetoric, however, the government has been unable to implement this approach successfully, summed up in the disaster of the single payment. More crucially this has a wider impact on other policies, especially in the context of the attempt to build a new partnership between the state and stakeholders in both policy formulation and implementation. Commenting on budget cuts imposed by Defra, an editorial in the *Guardian* noted for example that "the economic consequences of the single farm payment disaster may do visible damage to the

British countryside and undermine projects designed to make a vital contribution to the restoration of natural environments in the cities" (*Guardian*, 21 October 2006). The NAO also detected a feeling among stakeholders and representative bodies that the 'breakdown in trust' on the single payment had deterred farmers from participating in other government initiatives, such as the environmental stewardship schemes. Indeed as David Miliband acknowledged in his speech to the Royal Agricultural Society, the delivery of the basic services such as the single farm payment was crucial because farmers "will not be confident partners of us in ambitious projects if we do not deliver on the day-to-day necessities" (Miliband, 2006).

In the end, moreover, the ability of New Labour to deliver on its pledges in agricultural policy was not substantially helped by its efforts to modernise the policy process. As one commentator noted, the single payment issue was a "monumental mess that bears all the hallmarks of New Labour's style of government: over-centralisation, inflated expectations of IT, ruthless job cuts, overpaid senior executives", added to an "impatient ambition and a refusal to listen to anything they didn't want to hear" (Madeleine Bunting, *Guardian*, 8 May 2006). What is unfortunate, at least in the short term, is that the New Labour governments actually have made substantial progress on the major long-standing policy objectives, notably on CAP reform, but that this has been eclipsed by failures in policy implementation. The solace for New Labour may be that when the delivery problems are eventually sorted out, its policy successes will then be fully appreciated.

References

BSE Inquiry (2000) *Report, evidence and supporting papers of the inquiry into the emergence and identification of bovine spongiform encephalopathy (BSE) and variant Creutzfeldt-Jakob disease (vCJD) and the action taken in response to it up to 20 March 1996* (the Phillips Report), London: The Stationery Office.

Bunting, M. (2006) 'The Yorkshire Moors is the place to learn about our new Foreign Secretary', *Guardian*, 8 May.

Cabinet Office (1999) *Professional policy making for the 21st century*, London: Cabinet Office. (Also available at www.policyhub.gov.uk/docs/profpolicymaking.pdf)

Defra (Department for Environment, Food and Rural Affairs) (2001) *A new department, a new agenda: Aim and objectives – have your say*, consultation document, August 2001, London: Defra.

Defra (2002) *The strategy for sustainable farming and food: Facing the future*, London: The Stationery Office.

Defra (2003) *Rural delivery review: A report on the delivery of government policies in rural England* (the Haskins Report), London: The Stationery Office. (Also available at www.defra.gov.uk/rural/pdfs/ruraldelivery/haskins_full_report.pdf)

Defra (2004) *Delivering the essentials of life: Defra's five year strategy*, Cm 6411, December, London: The Stationery Office.

Defra (2006) *Sustainable farming and food strategy: Forward look*, London: The Stationery Office.

Defra/HM Government (2001) *The government response to the BSE Inquiry*, Cm 5263, London: The Stationery Office.

Defra/PKF Accountants (2006) *Public consultation on controlling the spread of bovine tuberculosis in cattle in high incidence areas in England: Badger culling. Summary of responses*, London: The Stationery Office. (Also available at http://www.defra.gov.uk/corporate/consult/badgers-tbcontrols/responses-summary.pdf)

Defra/SE/WAG (Department for Environment, Food and Rural Affairs/Scottish Executive/Welsh Assembly Government) (2005) *Government strategic framework for the sustainable control of bovine tuberculosis (bTB) in Great Britain: A sub-strategy of the Animal Health and Welfare Strategy for Great Britain*, London: The Stationery Office.

Defra/SEERAD/DEPC/DARD (Department for Environment, Food and Rural Affairs/Scottish Executive Environment and Rural Affairs Department/Welsh Assembly Government Department for Environment, Planning and Countryside/Department of Agriculture and Rural Development [Northern Ireland]) (2005) *Agriculture in the United Kingdom 2005*, London: The Stationery Office.

Greer, A. (1999) 'Policy coordination and the British Administrative System: evidence from the BSE Inquiry', *Parliamentary Affairs*, vol 52, no 4, pp 523-42.

Greer, A. (2003) 'Countryside issues: a creeping crisis', *Parliamentary Affairs*, vol 56, no 3, pp 598-615.

Greer, A. (2005) *Agricultural policy in Europe*, Manchester: Manchester University Press.

Guardian (2006) 'Wrong note for nature', Leader article, 21 October.

HM Treasury/Defra (Department for Environment, Food and Rural Affairs) (2005) *A vision for the Common Agricultural Policy*, London: The Stationery Office.

House of Commons Environment, Food and Rural Affairs Committee (2003) *The mid-term review of the Common Agricultural Policy: Government reply to the Third Report of Session 2002-03,* Fourth Special Report, Session 2002–03, HC 615, London: The Stationery Office.

House of Commons Environment, Food and Rural Affairs Committee (2004) *Implementation of CAP reform in the UK*, Seventh Report, Session 2003–04, HC 226-I, London: The Stationery Office.

House of Commons Environment, Food and Rural Affairs Committee (2006a) *Bovine TB: Badger culling*, Sixth Report, Session 2005–06, HC 905-I, London: The Stationery Office.

House of Commons Environment, Food and Rural Affairs Committee (2006b) *Rural Payments Agency: Interim report*, Fifth Report, Session 2005–06, HC 840, January 2006, London: The Stationery Office.

House of Commons International Development Committee (2006a) *The WTO Hong Kong Ministerial and the Doha Development Agenda*, Third Report, Session 2005–06, HC 730-I, London: The Stationery Office.

House of Commons International Development Committee (2006b) *The WTO Hong Kong Ministerial and the Doha Development Agenda: Government response to the Committee's Third Report of Session 2005–06,* Third Special Report, Session 2005–06, HC 1425, London: The Stationery Office.

House of Commons Science and Technology Committee (2006) *Scientific advice, risk and evidence based policy making,* Seventh Report, Session 2005–06, HC 900-I, November 2006, London: The Stationery Office.

Miliband, D. (2006) 'One planet farming', Speech given at the Royal Agricultural Show, 3 July 2006. (Available at www.defra.gov.uk/corporate/ministers/speeches/david-miliband/dm060703.htm)

NAO (National Audit Office) (2006) *Department for Environment, Food and Rural Affairs, and Rural Payments Agency. The delays in administering the 2005 Single Payment Scheme in England.* Report by the Comptroller and Auditor General, Session 2005-06, HC 1631, October 2006, London: The Stationery Office.

Policy Commission on the Future of Farming and Food (2002) *Farming and food: A sustainable future* (the Curry Report), London: The Stationery Office. (Available at http://archive.cabinetoffice.gov.uk/farming/pdf/PCReport2.pdf)

SFSS Implementation Group (2006) *The sustainable farming and food strategy, three years on: Reflections on progress.* (Available at www.defra.gov.uk/farm/policy/sustain/implement/pdf/ig-finalreport-060718.pdf)

Part Three
Policies for the rural economy, society and environment

TEN

Rural community development and governance

Graham Gardner

Introduction

New Labour has made the development and governance of local communities a key focus of rural policy. This chapter sets that focus in the context of wider strategies of government and considers its implications for rural society in Britain. The first part argues that New Labour's concern with making rural communities more active in their own governance and development reflects an ongoing transition in the 'governmentality' of Western liberal democracies. In the course of this shift, communities are becoming key instruments of government. The second part discusses the mechanisms through which New Labour has sought to make rural communities more active in their own development and governance. Towns and villages have become key targets of regeneration strategies based on partnership working, community-based service provision and local collective planning. At the same time, the government has held back from radical reform of parish and town councils while emphasising the importance of local government in community leadership. The third part considers the impact of New Labour's policy on rural community development and governance. In particular, it argues that it is likely to have helped reinforce an uneven geography of development and governance.

Community development and governance in New Labour's rural policy

Towards 'active' rural communities

Community development and governance is a core focus of New Labour's rural policy. Arguing that 'active communities' are vital to the social, economic and democratic well-being of the British countryside, New Labour has made it clear that it wants to make people living in rural areas play a greater part in local decision making and voluntary action.

The importance of community in New Labour's rural policy is made clear in its White Paper for rural England, published in 2000. On the one hand, the White

Paper acknowledges that local community self-governance is a long-standing feature of many rural areas: "The community strength of rural England is an important part of the character of the countryside. Many communities are strong, remoteness often fostering self-reliance" (DETR/MAFF, 2000, p 9). On the other hand, the White Paper suggests that community action is to some considerable extent out of line with government objectives. This is most clearly evident in a chapter entitled "Local power for country towns and villages", which outlines four key concerns, including community involvement in the targeting of services, levels of partnership working and attitudes to change:

- Rural communities could play a much bigger role in running their own affairs, influencing and shaping their future development, but they often lack opportunities and support.
- Lack of involvement can result in an adversarial approach to change and less well-targeted services.
- There is a need for better partnership between all types of authorities, a greater willingness to work together and deliver locally managed services.
- Rural areas often have a strong sense of community and a valuable network of voluntary groups, but these are under threat as ways of life, people and attitudes change. (DETR/MAFF, 2000, p 145)

On the basis that "a healthy and active voluntary and community sector is essential to the effective functioning of society – urban and rural" (DETR/MAFF, 2000, p 155), the White Paper sets out four key objectives regarding the transfer of responsibilities for community development and governance from the state to local 'communities':

- People living in rural areas being fully involved in developing their community, safeguarding its valued features, and shaping the decisions that affect them.
- Flourishing local councils acting as the voice of the local community.
- Strong partnerships between county, district and town and parish councils, supporting and encouraging rural communities on matters which local councils can manage themselves, and working in partnership on wider local services.
- Support for established voluntary networks in rural areas. (DETR/ MAFF, 2000, p 145)

Rural policy in wider context

New Labour's enthusiasm for greater community involvement in the development and governance of rural areas continues and advances a wider trend. The theme of New Labour's Rural White Paper echoes the theme of the Rural White Papers published by the previous Conservative government. The Conservative White Papers, published separately for England, Scotland and Wales, argued that responsibility for rural governance and development was a shared responsibility that began "with individuals, families and local communities" (DoE/MAFF, 1995, p 16). In turn, the Conservative White Papers helped to cement a principle that had already become apparent in public policy both in Britain and across Western liberal democracies over the preceding decade. Since the late 1980s, policy at national and international scales has increasingly sought to encourage people living in both rural and urban areas to take more responsibility for their own welfare (Edwards, 1998; Ward and McNicholas, 1998; Herbert-Cheshire, 2000; Taylor, 2003). On the one hand, this has meant the state creating opportunities for greater participation in decision making over local services and planning through initiatives such as Neighbourhood Watch, Parent–Teacher Associations and the European LEADER programmes. On the other hand, it has meant the state withdrawing or deciding not to provide particular services and encouraging local residents to fill the resulting gaps in provision. In 1996, the Cork Declaration agreed by the member states of the European Union enshrined the principle that community involvement should be at the heart of rural development initiatives.

The election of New Labour marked, among other things, the continuation of this trend. New Labour repeatedly made clear its commitment to the principle of community involvement in local development and governance; Prime Minister Tony Blair said, "I want it to become as natural to be involved in the community as it is to watch television or go to the cinema" (Blair, 2000). In 1998, the government established the Active Communities Unit within the Home Office to develop strategies for involving local communities in both development and regeneration. New Labour's Urban White Paper, published in 2000, places community involvement at the heart of its plans for an "urban renaissance", as does its linked strategy for "neighbourhood renewal" (Imrie and Raco, 2003; Whitehead, 2004; ODPM/Home Office, 2005). In 2003, the Home Office launched a 'civil renewal agenda', since rebranded as 'Together We Can', in which it emphasised the government's commitment to building "a society in which citizens are inspired to make a positive difference to their communities, and are able to influence the policies and services that affect their lives" (Civil Renewal Unit, 2003, p 1). The government sees community involvement as vital to tackling a host of problems, from social exclusion to urban renewal to lack of trust in public institutions.

'Government through community'

For some commentators, New Labour's enthusiasm for greater community involvement in local development and governance reflects little more than a pragmatic response to the challenge of governing a society characterised by increasing differentiation and autonomy (for a prime example of this argument see Temple, 2000). This is certainly one of the influences cited in the White Paper, and the rhetoric of 'pragmatism' is a key element of third way politics (see Giddens, 2001). However, while there are undoubtedly objective social, economic and cultural conditions to which the state must respond, claims that any policy response is merely 'pragmatic' must be treated with some scepticism. Public policy is never determined simply by the objective reality confronting it. Rather, policy responses are also shaped by ideologies and values, which in turn are contingent on the wider political economy (Fischer, 2003). Any evaluation of policy that seeks to go beyond a 'thin' or 'shallow' analysis, approaching policy as "a narrow, technical concern to be tackled within the confines of state(d) aims and objectives" (Peck, 1999, p 132), must seek to situate policy within wider topographies of power.

In the present context, an obvious 'driver' of public policy is the neoliberal impulse to make market exchange and free enterprise the dominant method of resource distribution. Since the late 1970s, neoliberal ideology has increasingly shaped the domestic statecraft of Western liberal democracies, resulting in states increasingly seeking to place responsibility for social welfare on individuals and communities (Peck and Tickell, 2002; Harvey, 2005). Under the previous Conservative administration, the UK state underwent neoliberalisation to a greater extent than any other European liberal democracy, and many neoliberal impulses, including the liberalisation or 'deregulation' of markets, the privatisation and 'marketisation' of the public sector and the 'flexibilisation' of the labour force, have been actively embraced and propagated by New Labour (Jessop, 2003).

However, the New Labour project also represents a distinct modification of the neoliberal project manifested under the Conservatives. According to Jessop (2003, p 4), New Labour has "moved towards a more socially inclusive hegemonic project. This addresses the limitations of the possessive individualism favoured by neo-liberalism and recognizes the need to re-embed market forces into a broader, more cohesive social order." Consequently, New Labour has embraced the ideology of communitarianism, arguing that the 'rights-based' culture of neoliberalism needs to be tempered by the renewal of a form of community in which individuals recognise their responsibilities to a common good (Rose, 2000).

In turn, New Labour's move to communitarianism reflects a wider shift in the governmentality of Western liberal democracies. 'Governmentality', a concept drawn from the work of Foucault, refers to the ways in which governmental authorities, which include but are not limited to the state, reflect on and practise government (Dean, 1999). This involves the continual *problematisation* of both the objects of government and the techniques of government. Those who seek to govern are constantly questioning the world and their power over it. Such questions include: What is our capacity to act? To what ends should we act? What is the nature of the world within the borders of our authority? How can we best know it? How can we best govern it? In answering these questions, governmental authorities construe the world in ways that give rise to governmental ambitions. Such ambitions are both embodied in and in part driven by the various administrative techniques or 'technologies' through which government is practised.

The last 30 years have seen a governmentality of 'advanced liberalism' increasingly supplant a previous governmentality of 'managed liberalism' (Rose, 1996a, 1996b, 1999; Dean, 1999). This shift entails Western states increasingly abandoning their previous attempts to intervene directly in the regulation of the economy and society. Instead, states seek to promote 'free markets' and 'civil society', the former characterised by minimal demand management by the state (Harvey, 2005), the latter characterised by spontaneous, self-organising non-governmental institutions and forms of voluntary collective action (Keane, 1998). Advanced liberalism is thus characterised by an emphasis on *freedom* and *responsibility*. No longer will the state take direct responsibility for the welfare of its citizens. Instead, its task is to provide individuals with sufficient freedom that they can take responsibility for themselves.

In this ongoing shift from managed liberalism to advanced liberalism, 'community' has become a key territory of government. As Rose puts it, individuals "are to be governed through their freedom, but neither as [the] isolated atoms [envisioned by] classical political economy, nor as citizens of society [as under managed liberalism], but as members of heterogeneous communities of allegiance" (Rose, 1996a, p 41). The challenges of government are identified and made amenable to action "*in terms of* features of communities ... their strengths, cultures and pathologies" (Rose, 1996b, p 331; original emphasis). The increasing importance of community as a territory of government has been charted by Taylor, who notes that:

> as the globalisation of the economy has advanced through the 1990s, so has a new language of community, participation and civil society, a nexus of ideas which also includes 'communitarianism', 'social capital', 'networks', 'networking', 'community empowerment', the 'social economy', 'mutuality', 'partnership' and 'civic engagement'. (Taylor, 2003, p 1)

This growing significance of community as a means of understanding and responding to the challenges of government became clear in the set of Rural White Papers published by the last Conservative government (Murdoch, 1997). The White Papers employed the language of community to problematise a series of issues that included service provision, crime and disorder, conservation and the rural economy. According to the White Papers, it was *communities* which were affected by these issues and *communities* that had to respond to them. The same line of thinking is evident in the Rural White Paper published by New Labour (DETR/MAFF, 2000), which envisions the countryside as a space characterised by "diversity and local distinctiveness" (p 11) in which "for most country people, the town or village is the defining measure of local identity" (p 146). In the course of its 176 pages, the White Paper mentions the word 'community' 292 times (Edwards and Woods, 2004).

Government through community does not simply involve the 'rolling back' of the state. Rather it represents a qualitative shift in the nature of state intervention, in which the state seeks to harness and guide communities in the manner of a shepherd guiding a flock or a minister guiding a congregation (cf Foucault, 1981). Thus, New Labour's Rural White Paper positions the state as a partner of rural communities, helping them to become more active in their own development and governance:

> We will empower local communities so that decisions are taken with their active participation and ownership. We want to enable rural communities to improve their quality of life and opportunity. We want to give them a bigger say in managing their own affairs and the chance to give everyone in the community a say in how it develops. (DETR/MAFF, 2000, p 146)

The ongoing instrumentalisation of community signifies what Kim (2000) calls a 'softening', if not a total abandonment, of the classic liberal doctrine of non-intervention into the realm of civil society. Historically, since its emergence as a distinct realm of associations and relations in the mid-18th century, civil society in liberal democracies has served as a counterweight to the state; its adherents and defenders have positioned it as a bulwark against state despotism, whether of the 'hard' or 'soft' kind (Galston, 1991; Keane, 1998; Prochaska, 2002). From this perspective, the absence of civil society has often been equated with totalitarian, or at least strongly statist, regimes, such as the former Soviet Union and Eastern Bloc, and contemporary China and North Korea. Indeed, the (re)discovery of community and civil society in the late 1980s and early 1990s was associated with the collapse of the Berlin Wall and the rise of popular protest movements in one-party states (Keane, 1998).

To serve as a counterpoint to the state, civil society must be independent of government. While in practice this independence has tended to be relative – there is a long-standing tradition of state intervention into civil society, whether in terms of sponsorship or a more active enrolment of voluntary organisations into state projects (Rose and Miller, 1992) – the principle of independence has been maintained. However, the position adopted by adherents of the third way and its associated ideologies such as communitarianism, do not adhere to the principle of civil society acting as a counterpoint to state despotism. Rather, they see it as an adjunct to state power (Kendall, 2003; Taylor, 2003). The brief but telling reference in the Rural White Paper to lack of involvement in partnership working resulting in "an adversarial approach to change" (DETR, MAFF, 2000, p 145) is indicative of New Labour's wider indifference or active hostility to forms of civil society and models of collective action that work against the state rather than with it (Rose, 2000). While some commentators identify the impulse towards government through community as neoliberal, it is perhaps better characterised as *illiberal* (cf Kim, 2000) or, from a historical perspective, *post-liberal* (cf Gray, 1993).

No longer are communities envisioned as passive recipients or targets of governmental action. Instead, they are envisioned as active citizens that should take responsibility for their own welfare (Rose, 2000). As a consequence, community has increasingly become an instrument of public policy, to be defined and mobilised in the interests of specific government objectives.

Mobilising community involvement in development and governance

In seeking to mobilise community involvement in the development and governance of rural areas, New Labour has particularly directed its attention towards two key scales: the town and the village. The Rural White Paper identifies the town or village as the defining measure of local identity, and policy on community development and governance has been geared accordingly. This section outlines the four key initiatives targeted at these scales: a funding programme to encourage partnership working in small towns; support for local village services; a voluntary benchmarking scheme for parish and town councils; and support for the production of town and village plans. In addition, it considers the significance of local government reform, particularly the new duty for principal local authorities to produce 'community strategies'.

Partnership working in small towns

The Rural White Paper identified small towns with populations of between 2,000 and 20,000 as critical sites for regeneration strategies that would mobilise local actors in the interests of wider social and economic development (DETR/MAFF, 2000, pp 73-88). In part, this focus reflects New Labour's recognition that many small towns – more specifically, market towns – are vital nodes in the wider rural economy and rural society, providing employment and services not only to the immediate population but also to the residents of their hinterlands. It also reflects an assumption that the populations of small towns and their hinterlands constitute relatively unified communities of interest that can effectively and efficiently engage with development and regeneration initiatives.

The White Paper set out a strategy for small town development and regeneration that included funding of £37 million over three years for market towns in or near deprived 'priority' areas. In part, the strategy drew together existing initiatives that were being administered by the Countryside Agency and Regional Development Agencies. In turn, these had replaced the Rural Challenge initiative, launched by the previous Conservative government; although in principle this had been open to all rural communities, in practice it benefited only market towns. The strategy has provided funding and other forms of practical support for 120 towns to undertake what the Countryside Agency called 'health checks'. These health checks involve principal local authorities, local businesses, voluntary organisations and other 'partners' working together to identify the strengths and weaknesses of their town, decide on priorities for change, construct an 'action plan', and subsequently seek funding from outside sources. Since April 2005, following the demise of the Countryside Agency, responsibility for administering the scheme has rested solely with Regional Development Agencies (RDAs).

Village-based services

In addition to the focus on small towns, the Rural White Paper also identified villages as important sites for local community-based enterprise and service provision. This reflected the government's recognition that the steady loss of village services, particularly in terms of retail provision, over the last 30 years, had resulted in many rural residents living in smaller settlements experiencing difficulty accessing services, jobs, housing and transport. As in the case of small towns, it also reflected an assumption that village settlements were natural, or at least self-evident, scales of community.

The focus on community-based services at the scale of the village led to the Countryside Agency developing its Vital Villages programme. Vital Villages consisted of four limited-life funding programmes, two of which built on programmes set up by the former Rural Development Commission under the previous Conservative administration, and two of which were wholly new, having been announced in the Rural White Paper (see Box 10.1). The Countryside Agency envisioned Vital Villages as a strategic 'branding exercise' with which it could build on the successes of earlier schemes and fully establish its official credentials as Rural Champion in the eyes of rural communities (Countryside Agency, 2000). Its focus on settlements of under 3,000 people meant that to some extent it overlapped the Market Towns Initiative, which included settlements of between 2,000 and 10,000 people. This overlap was deliberate, to ensure that no settlements would be in principle ineligible for either programme. Between April 2001 and April 2004, Vital Villages provided total funding of £35 million.

Modernising parish and town councils

The focus on small towns and villages in the Rural White Paper and subsequent policy statements placed parish and town councils at the heart of its new localism agenda (see DETR/MAFF, 2000). As the White Paper made clear, parish and town councils are the statutory third tier of local government in rural areas, serving all but the smallest rural communities and having a wide range of powers and responsibilities. However, the actual stance of New Labour on parish and town councils has been somewhat confused and uncertain. On the one hand, it has been keen to build the capacity of the sector, on the basis that its performance is geographically uneven (DETR/MAFF, 2000, p 146). On the other hand, political nervousness has made it reluctant to engage in the wholesale reform of the sector that many within the Labour Party think is long overdue. Concerns that moribund and undemocratic parish councils could significantly hinder the implementation

Box 10.1: Vital Villages (2001–04)

The Community Services Grant Scheme encompassed the established Village Shops Development Scheme and Public Houses Scheme, both of which had been running since 1994. It provided £11.5 million over three years, along with practical advice and other support, to assist both the development of existing locally owned services and the establishment of new services where basic needs were not being met. Eligible services included independent and collectively owned shops, garages and post offices, with grant support funding capital and first-year revenue costs only.

The Parish Transport Grants Scheme provided £13.0 million over three years to support small-scale local transport initiatives meeting specific needs, such as car and moped pools for households otherwise without access to private transport, and vouchers for public transport. Grants were for a maximum of £10,000, and community groups had to demonstrate that their initiative would not undermine existing services and activity.

The Rural Partnership Grants Scheme, which succeeded the Rural Transport Partnership Scheme and Rural Transport Development Fund, supported larger-scale local transport initiatives. The scheme focused on integrating existing local transport provision, and provided support for commercial schemes in addition to the community transport sector.

Vital Villages also included funding for **parish and town plans** (discussed in following text).

of the civil renewal agenda in rural England led the Rural Group of Labour MPs to propose a review of their current effectiveness with a view to offering the best councils enhanced powers and responsibilities and restricting the role of the remainder (RGLMP, 2000). At one point there were rumours that New Labour was considering bypassing or replacing the worst councils with alternative local arrangements (Bevan, 1999). However, fearing a backlash even greater than that provoked by making parish councillors subject to the new Code of Conduct for local government officers, the government restricted itself to creating a voluntary benchmarking programme in the form of the Quality Parish and Town Council Scheme (ODPM, 2003).

To qualify for Quality status, councils must fulfil a range of criteria intended to demonstrate that they are representative of their communities, accountable, properly managed, in touch with their electorate and that their councillors observe good standards of conduct. Council clerks must possess one of two qualifications specified by government, at least 80% of councillors must have stood for election rather than been co-opted, the council must meet at least six times a year, all councillors must attend all meetings or provide good reasons for their absence, council accounts must be formally audited, and all councillors must have formally agreed to the new Code of Conduct for local government. Councils must also be communicating with the electorate through a regular newsletter, annual report and a range of other means. In return for meeting these standards, the scheme suggests, Quality councils will be offered greater opportunities for partnership working by principal local authorities and have a higher status in the local community. The government also envisions that Quality status will be its own reward, in that Quality councils can be sure that they are meeting "the standards of the best" (ODPM, 2003, p 5).

Parish and town planning

Reflecting its belief – or assertion – that the town or village is often the defining measure of local identity, New Labour's programme of reform for community development and governance also targets local planning. As with parish and town councils, however, its stance is somewhat ambiguous. On the one hand, the White Paper and the accompanying policy statement on rural planning policy (Countryside Agency, 2000) suggest that the government was committed to fully involving local communities in decision making over future development; on the other hand, the government has not given local communities any further power over the local planning process. Rather, New Labour's strategy, in its own words, is to "reduce the adversarial nature of new proposals and reduce costs for all" (DETR/MAFF, 2000, p 150). To this end the government has encouraged all rural communities to develop town and village plans. These plans give local communities the opportunity to "indicate how they would like their town or village to develop, to identify key facilities and services, to set out the problems that need to be tackled and demonstrate how its distinctive character and features can be preserved" (DETR/MAFF, 2000, p 146). Government guidance suggests that plans should be developed by a steering group or working committee representing the entire local community, with the assistance of the principal local authority and the local Rural Community Council. Between March 2001 and March 2004 the Countryside Agency ran a 'demonstration project', as part of its Vital Villages scheme. Since the demise of Vital Villages, the scheme has been incorporated into Defra's Rural Social and Community Programme, planned to run until April 2008. Funding is administered by local agencies, primarily the network of 38 Rural Community Councils, and usually covers up to 75% of costs.

Local government and community leadership

The reform or 'modernisation' of local government has been a major goal of New Labour since its election in 1997. Although the modernisation agenda is not specific to rural areas, it is a key element of policy on rural community development and governance. As well as introducing new performance management systems, notably in the form of BestValue and the Comprehensive Performance Assessment (CPA), based on the principles set out in 'new public management theory', and giving councils a choice of constitution, New Labour has sought to give local government a greater role in leading, guiding and directing local communities.

In this respect, the most significant reforms regarding the relationship between local government and local communities were introduced by the 2000 Local Government Act. The Act gave local authorities a new power to promote 'community well-being' beyond the provision of statutory services and amenities. In tandem with this power to promote community well-being, the Act also gave local government a duty to prepare and maintain a 'community strategy' for "promoting or improving the economic, social and environmental well-being of their area" (s 4(1), 2000 Local Government Act) (and also "contributing to the achievement of sustainable development in the United Kingdom"). Community strategies should be prepared and maintained in consultation with local communities, although it is up to individual local authorities to decide what methods of consultation they use.

The role of local government in community leadership was reiterated and strengthened by the recent local government White Paper (DCLG, 2006). As well as confirming the principle of community involvement in local service delivery and other aspects of local governance, the White Paper established ward councillors as 'champions', 'leaders' and 'advocates' of local communities. Only a backlash by parish councils and their representative body prevented the White Paper proposing that ward councillors should be represented on all parish and town councils.

Evaluating the impacts of government through community

This section considers the impacts of New Labour's policy on rural community development and governance for rural society. Its arguments are based on evidence drawn from a range of empirical studies, including evaluations of specific initiatives and wider surveys. First, it considers the implications for levels of community action in towns and villages. Second, it considers the implications for the geography of community development and governance. Third, it considers the implications for inclusion and exclusion in rural community governance. Fourth and finally, it considers the implications for the relative power of state and society in rural community development and governance.

Levels of community action in towns and villages

In the short term, the key policy initiatives targeted at rural community development and governance have certainly resulted in more community action of the type encouraged by New Labour. In particular, this has included increased levels of partnership working and community-based service provision and significant enthusiasm for parish and town planning. Evaluations of the

Market Towns Initiative scheme suggest that its outcomes have included projects to regenerate the built environment, address the needs of marginalised groups, increase community cohesion and promote economic development (Countryside Agency, 2002; Countryside Agency/Defra, 2004). More generally, it has "brought coherence and structure to the complex process of regeneration" (Countryside Agency, 2002). Although many market town 'health checks' were undertaken by existing partnerships, the scheme also led to the creation of new partnerships in at least a third of the 220 towns that received funding. Between April 2001 and April 2005, the Vital Villages initiative helped community groups, parish councils, local transport partnerships and small businesses to undertake a total of just over 5,000 small-scale projects that have enhanced service provision in small rural communities. At the time of writing (April 2008), over 2,000 communities have produced parish or town plans, and a further 1,000 are in the process of producing a plan. The Quality Parish and Town Council Scheme has also generated significant levels of interest. At least 16% of the rural population is now served by a parish council with Quality status.

In the long term, however, it is not at all certain that the sort of activity favoured by New Labour can or will be sustained. The Market Towns Initiative provided funding for only three years; Vital Villages provided funding for four years. Both initiatives now focus on the development of 'best practice'. The withdrawal of funding is likely to have had a significant impact on partnership working and community-based provision of services. An evaluation of partnership working in rural areas, which included the Welsh Market Towns Initiative on which the Countryside Agency modelled its small town 'health checks', showed that once funding ended, the majority of partnerships either dissolved or went into dormancy (Edwards et al, 2000). Indeed, the post hoc evaluation of the Market Towns Initiative in England (Countryside Agency/Defra, 2004) has raised serious concerns about the sustainability of many town partnerships. Few local regeneration partnerships in rural areas have a life of more than five years, irrespective of whether or not they achieve their aims, and smaller-scale partnerships – those constituted beneath the scale of the county – tend to be the most short-lived. Similarly, community-based service provision is often heavily dependent on state sponsorship. The idea that initiatives will become self-sustaining once funding is withdrawn may be more aspiration than reality. Historically, the end of external funding has forced many community groups to restrict or even end their activities.

Out of the initiatives targeted at rural community development and governance, the Quality Parish and Town Council Scheme is perhaps most likely to sustain activity over the long term. The scheme is still being promoted, and (at the time of writing) is in the process of being revised to take account of lessons learned from its first four years of operation. Although many Quality councils have been disappointed that the realities of Quality status have fallen short of the expectations raised by government, the majority intend to seek re-accreditation when their first four-year period of accreditation expires (Woods and Gardner, 2007).

Geographies of rural community development and governance

Whether or not the rural community action encouraged by New Labour is sustainable over the long term, it has undoubtedly been spatially uneven. The policy of community empowerment has targeted some communities while neglecting others, helping to reproduce the uneven geography of community development and governance that has long been characteristic of the English countryside.

To some extent, this has been due to the geographical selectivity of particular policy initiatives. This is particularly the case regarding regeneration and development activity in small towns. The geographical selectivity of the Market Towns Initiative meant that inevitably it left many communities out in the cold. It provided funding for only a quarter of all market towns (the eventual number was 220) and included only towns that were close to what the government had designated as 'priority areas' and that could demonstrate they could serve as foci for economic growth and act as service centres for the local population (Countryside Agency/Defra, 2004). In comparison, the Vital Villages programme was far more geographically inclusive both in principle and in practice, covering more than 5,000 smaller rural communities.

The geographical unevenness of community development and governance has also been fostered by the uniform expectations placed on rural communities regardless of their capacity or willingness to either engage with specific policy initiatives or respond to the demands of the wider policy agenda. On the one hand, lack of resources means that many communities are limited in their ability to become more active in their own development and governance. Many small towns were ineligible for funding through the Market Towns Initiative because they lacked local businesses and voluntary sector organisations able and willing to commit resources to partnerships (Edwards et al, 2003). Parish councils representing small populations in remote locations or in economically disadvantaged areas often lack the resources necessary to develop their capacity to the point where they can obtain Quality status (Woods and Gardner, 2007). Consequently, government programmes have tended to funnel resources towards relatively more prosperous communities, often characterised by concentrations of middle-class residents with high levels of economic, social and organisational capital, and left less prosperous communities to fend for themselves.

On the other hand, there is evidence that community elites in some towns have actively chosen not to engage with government programmes, on the basis that they do not wish to submit to the accompanying regulation. While in some cases this may reflect a collective local spirit of autonomy and independence, in other cases it has not reflected the interests of the wider community that community elites claim to represent. In this respect, the refusal of some parish and town councils to participate in the Quality Parish and Town Council Scheme is a case in point. The voluntary basis of the benchmarking scheme means that those councils that wish to maintain a low profile within their communities can continue doing so (Defra, 2004; Woods and Gardner, 2007).

Democracy and inclusion in rural community development and governance

Under New Labour, community development and governance in rural areas has been characterised by participatory and deliberative modes of democracy (cf Bell et al, 2005). Partnership working and consultation have increasingly supplemented the representation of local interests through parish and town councils. While to some degree this has made communities more inclusive and democratic, in other cases it has tended to reflect and reproduce established patterns of inclusion and exclusion.

Traditionally, parish and town councils have been the cornerstones of local democracy in rural areas. However, participation in council elections has long been in decline, bringing their democratic credentials under question. Contested elections are now the exception rather than the rule, and many councils have vacant seats (see Table 10.1). While the Quality Parish and Town Council Scheme includes a requirement for participating councils to have filled at least 80% of its seats with members who stood for election, it has had little or no impact on overall participation rates (Woods and Gardner, 2007).

The government has set great store on the ability of partnerships and consultation to ensure a relatively equitable representation of community interests in development and regeneration strategies. However, it is difficult for partnerships to be truly representative. Evaluations of the Market Towns Initiative (Countryside Agency, 2002; Countryside Agency/Defra, 2004) were broadly positive regarding the extent to which local partnerships had sought to be inclusive, but identified significant problems regarding the actual representativeness of the partnership organisations and the extent to which consultation by partnerships had adequately engaged the entire community. Close to a third of partnerships had not "actively involved individual members of the public" (Countryside Agency, 2002, p 2; cf Countryside Agency/Defra, 2004) and a quarter had not involved the voluntary

Table 10.1: Candidates nominated in elections to local tier councils (% of council wards)

	1964–67[1]	1987–90[2]	1998-2000[3]
More candidates than seats	32	44	28
Same number of candidates as seats	46	38	32
Fewer candidates than seats	22	18	36
Uncontested (nk)[4]	n/a	n/a	4

Notes: [1] 1964–67 = Royal Commission on Local Government survey; parish councils in England only; n = 6538

[2] 1987–90 = Aston Business School survey; town and parish councils in England only; n = 810

[3] 1998-2000 = University of Wales Aberystwyth survey; town, parish and community councils in England and Wales; n = 8573

[4] Uncontested (nk) = Election uncontested where number of candidates or seats not known

sector. In some cases, partnerships included a broadly representative range of local stakeholders. In most cases, however, they simply represented an established community elite. The evaluation also raised particular concerns that many consultations had not adequately engaged with the populations living in the hinterlands of small towns or with hard-to-reach groups "less used to promoting their interests" (Countryside Agency, 2002, p 2; cf Countryside Agency/Defra, 2004).

The requirements of the 2000 Local Government Act have led local authorities to experiment with a variety of participatory and deliberative methods of consultation. However, while exercises of this type have been broadly welcomed by those who participate, they engage only a small proportion of the rural population, raising questions about the representativeness of the interests represented. The extent to which consultation exercises actually give communities substantial influence over community strategies is also open to question (as discussed below).

Power and influence in rural community development and governance

New Labour has undoubtedly increased the opportunities for rural communities to become more active in their own development and governance. However, the rhetoric of community empowerment belies a reality in which communities continue to be subordinate to the power of the state and private interests.

This subordination of community interests to wider scales of power is perhaps most evident regarding the planning process. Although a handful of local authorities have experimented with devolving particular aspects of development control to parish councils, there is no duty on them to do so and no evidence that this is likely to become widespread practice. In principle, parish and town plans, identifying actions which can be undertaken "by the parish council, by other individuals and groups within the community or by other service providers and statutory bodies" (Countryside Agency, 2004, p 7), provide communities with "a real opportunity to influence the nature and quality of future development" (DETR/MAFF, 2000, p 150). However, parish and town plans have no statutory power in the formal planning process. Rather, local authorities have the option – not a duty – to endorse parish and town plans as supplementary planning guidance and to incorporate them into the 'folder' that accompanies the Local Development Plan, as long as a plan "is consistent with the local Development Plan, and the relevant national planning guidance" (DETR/MAFF, 2000, p 150). While some local authorities have actively sought to engage with parish and town plans, others have largely ignored them. Parish and town plans must also be set in the context of subsequent reforms to local planning introduced by the 2004 Planning and Compulsory Purchase Act. According to the government, the principles behind these reforms included "Strengthening community and stakeholder involvement in the development of local communities, especially early in the process" (ODPM, 2004, p 2), but in practice the reforms give priority to regional plans on which local communities have no input.

In principle, the requirement for local authorities to produce community strategies provides a route for communities to influence development. In practice, however, this strategy of engagement is more to do with the local state building an evidence base on which it can base its 'strategic thinking' than with genuine participatory or deliberative democracy, while the scales at which consultation occurs are frequently out of step with the community boundaries recognised by local residents. The role of the state as the strategic actor has been reinforced by the creation of Local Strategic Partnerships, coterminous with local government boundaries, which give a greater steering and coordinating role to principal local authorities alongside other public sector actors and private interests.

Local development partnerships, such as those established by the Market Towns Initiative, do provide a channel for more equitable relationships between the state and communities. However, these partnerships tend to militate against the genuine involvement of community members. Their styles of operation resemble the bureaucratic and highly professionalised worlds of local government. Community members are often unfamiliar and uncomfortable with this style of business, lacking the time, training and expertise to fully participate (Edwards et al, 2003). The 'house style' of partnerships is more than a technical problem requiring a technical solution. Rather, it reflects the institutionalised hierarchies of power between local communities and public and private sector elites.

Even where relatively equitable relationships are established, it is the state that determines the parameters and trajectories of rural community development and governance. As Woods et al note:

> Top-down direction and intervention have been replaced by arms-length regulation and self-regulation.... Funding programmes distribute resources according to criteria set by the state and award grants that come with lengthy conditions and regulations; development plans and policy documents set priorities and objectives that favour certain projects and outcomes over others; professional consultants and agency workers guide local actors towards particular solutions and problems; and the representatives of state institutions and funding bodies sitting on partnership boards use their resource power and professional expertise to steer the operation of rural governance. (Woods et al, 2006, p 211)

Moreover, the embeddedness of local communities in wider, national and global topographies of power, constituted not only by the state but also by corporations, interest groups and the media, limits the capacity of local actors to address many of the challenges to society, the economy, environment and culture that have a significant impact on their lives.

Conclusion

This chapter has examined the growing significance of rural communities as instruments of public policy. Over the course of its decade in office, New Labour has sought to make people living in the countryside perform a more active role in local development and governance. This strategy reflects a wider shift in the governmentality of Western liberal democracies. Under a regime of 'advanced liberalism', in which states increasingly focus on securing economic and social 'freedoms' rather than more directly providing for the well-being of their populations, communities are no longer envisioned as passive objects of government. Rather, states seek to harness and guide the capacities of communities in the interest of making their populations take responsibility for their own welfare. This shift reflects not a 'rolling back' of the state but rather a changing mode of state intervention.

Under New Labour, small towns and villages have become the key sites through which the strategy of 'government through community' has been manifest. Major policy initiatives include limited-life funding programmes to encourage partnership working in small towns, support for community-based services, attempts to raise the profile of parish and town councils, and emphasis on community planning. At the same time, a strategy of local modernisation has increasingly positioned principal local authorities as community leaders.

New Labour's focus on the local scale reflects an assumption that the populations of small towns and villages constitute unified communities of interest that are both willing and able to effectively and efficiently engage with development and regeneration initiatives. However, evidence suggests that some communities are more able and willing to participate than others, and policy initiatives have been spatially selective. The result is increased levels of community action but also the reinforcing of an uneven geography of development and governance.

While in principle the partnerships and consultation associated with local regeneration and rural governance should make communities more inclusive and democratic, in practice they have a tendency to reflect and reproduce established patterns of inclusion and exclusion. Local partnerships tend to be dominated by community elites who do not necessarily represent the wider community, and consultation frequently fails to engage marginalised groups. It is also evident that despite moves to make local government more accountable to communities, policy shifts have left intact the scalar hierarchies of power already institutionalised in rural governance.

On the one hand, the evidence and argument presented in this chapter might point to the need for rural policy to be more sensitive to the differentiated nature of rural areas. On the other hand, it perhaps questions the entire wisdom of a strategy of government that seeks to tackle inequality while largely ignoring the connections between the development and governance of communities in rural areas, the structure of rural society, and the wider forces helping to reshape the economic and social landscape of 21st-century rural Britain.

References

Bell, D., Thompson, N., Deckers, J., Brennan, M. and Gray, T. (2005) *Deliberating the environment*, Newcastle: Centre for Rural Economy.

Bevan, S. (1999) 'Labour threatens to abolish parish councils', *Sunday Times*, 3 October, p 12.

Blair, T. (2000) 'The new givers', *Guardian*, 1 March, p 3.

Civil Renewal Unit (2003) *Building civil renewal: A review of government support for community capacity building and proposals for change*, London: The Stationery Office.

Countryside Agency (2000) *Planning tomorrow's countryside*, Cheltenham: Countryside Agency.

Countryside Agency (2002) *Research note*, CRN60, Cheltenham: Countryside Agency.

Countryside Agency (2004) *Parish plans: Guidance for parish and town councils*, Cheltenham: Countryside Agency.

Countryside Agency/Defra (Department for Environment, Food and Rural Affairs) (2004) *Assessment of the market towns initiative: A summary*, Cheltenham: Countryside Agency.

DCLG (Department for Communities and Local Government) (2006) *Strong and prosperous communities*, London: The Stationery Office.

Dean, M. (1999) *Governmentality: Power and rule in modern society,* London: Sage.

Defra (Department for Environment, Food and Rural Affairs) (2004) *Review of the Rural White Paper*, London: The Stationery Office.

DETR/MAFF (Department of the Environment, Transport and the Regions/Ministry of Agriculture, Fisheries and Food) (2000) *Our countryside: The future – a fair deal for rural England*, (the Rural White Paper), Cm 4909, London: The Stationery Office.

DoE/MAFF (Department of the Environment/Ministry of Agriculture, Fisheries and Food) (1995) *Rural England: A nation committed to a living countryside*, London: The Stationery Office.

Edwards, B. (1998) 'Charting the discourse of community action: perspectives from practice in rural Wales', *Journal of Rural Studies*, vol 14, no 1, pp 63–78.

Edwards, B. and Woods, M. (2004) 'Mobilising the local: community, participation and governance, in L. Holloway and M. Kneafsey (eds) *Geographies of rural cultures and societies*, Aldershot: Ashgate, pp 173–196.

Edwards, B., Goodwin, M., Pemberton, S. and Woods, M. (2000) *Partnership working in rural regeneration*, Bristol: The Policy Press.

Edwards, B., Goodwin, M. and Woods, M. (2003) 'Citizenship, community and participation in small towns: a case study of regeneration partnerships', in R. Imrie and M. Raco (eds) *Urban renaissance? New Labour, community and urban policy*, Bristol: The Policy Press, pp 181–204.

Fischer, F. (2003) *Reframing public policy: Discursive politics and deliberative practices*, New York: Oxford University Press.

Foucault, M. (1981) 'Omnes et singulatim: towards a criticism of "Political Reason"', in S. McMurrin (ed) *The Tanner Lectures on Human Values: Volume two*, Utah: Utah University Press, pp 223-54.

Galston, W. (1991) *Liberal purposes: Goods, virtues and diversity in the liberal state*, Cambridge: Cambridge University Press.

Giddens, A. (2001) *The global third way debate*, Cambridge: Polity Press.

Gray, J. (1993) *Post-liberalism: Studies in political thought*, London: Routledge.

Harvey, D. (2005) *A brief history of neo-liberalism*, New York: Oxford University Press.

Herbert-Cheshire, L. (2000) 'Contemporary strategies for rural community development in Australia: a governmentality perspective', *Journal of Rural Studies*, vol 16, no 2, pp 203-15.

Imrie, R. and Raco, M. (2003) 'Community and the changing nature of urban policy', in R. Imrie and M. Raco (eds) *Urban renaissance? New Labour, community and urban policy*, Bristol: The Policy Press, pp 3-36.

Jessop, B. (2003) *From Thatcherism to New Labour: Neo-liberalism, workfarism, and labour market regulation'*, Working Paper, published by the Department of Sociology, Lancaster University. (Available at www.comp.lancs.ac.uk/sociology/soc131rj.pdf)

Keane, D. (1998) *Civil society: old images, new visions*, Cambridge: Polity Press.

Kendall, J. (2003) *The voluntary sector: comparative perspectives in the UK*, London: Routledge.

Kim, S. (2000) '"In affirming them, he affirms himself": Max Weber's politics of civil society', *Political Theory*, vol 28, no 2, pp 197-229.

Murdoch, J. (1997) 'The shifting territory of government: some insights from the Rural White Paper', *Area*, vol 29, no 2, pp 109-18.

ODPM (Office of the Deputy Prime Minister) (2003) *The Quality Parish and Town Council Scheme: The Quality scheme explained*, London: The Stationery Office.

ODPM (2004) Explanatory memorandum to the Town and Country Planning (Local Development) (England) Regulations 2004, SI 2004/2204.

ODPM/Home Office (2005) *Citizen engagement and public services: Why neighbourhoods matter*, London: The Stationery Office.

Peck, J. (1999) 'Editorial: grey geography', *Transactions of the Institute of British Geographers*, vol 24, pp 131-35.

Peck, J. and Tickell, A. (2002) 'Neo-liberalising space', *Antipode*, vol 34, pp 380-404.

Prochaska, F. (2002) *Schools of citizenship: Charity and civic virtue*, London: Civitas.

RGLMP (Rural Group of Labour MPs) (2000) *A manifesto for rural Britain*, London: RGLMP.

Rose, N. (1996a) 'Governing "advanced" liberal democracies', in A. Barry, T. Osbourne and N. Rose (eds) *Foucault and political reason*, London: UCL Press, pp 37-64.

Rose, N. (1996b) 'The death of the social? Re-figuring the territory of government', *Economy and Society*, vol 25, pp 327-65.

Rose, N. (1999) *Powers of freedom: Reframing political thought*, Cambridge: Cambridge University Press.

Rose, N. (2000) 'Community, citizenship and the third way', *American Behavioral Scientist*, vol 43, no 9, pp 1395-1411.

Rose, N. and Miller, P. (1992) 'Problematics of government: political power beyond the state', *British Journal of Sociology*, vol 43, pp 173-205.

Taylor, M. (2003) *Public policy in the community*, London: Palgrave Macmillan.

Temple, M. (2000) 'New Labour's third way: pragmatism and governance', *The British Journal of Politics and International Relations*, vol 2, no 3, pp 302-25.

Ward, N. and McNicholas, K. (1998) 'Reconfiguring rural development in the UK: objective 5b and the new rural governance', *Journal of Rural Studies*, vol 14, no 1, pp 27-40.

Whitehead, M. (2004) 'The urban neighbourhood and the moral geographies of British urban policy', in C. Johnstone and M. Whitehead (eds) *New horizons in British urban policy: Perspectives on New Labour's urban renaissance*, Aldershot: Ashgate, pp 59-76.

Woods, M. and Gardner, G. (2007) *Evaluation of the Quality Parish and Town Council Scheme*, London: Defra. (Available at www.defra.gov.uk)

Woods, J., Edwards, B., Anderson, J. and Gardner, G. (2006) 'Elites, institutions and agency in British rural community governance', in L. Cheshire, V. Higgins and G. Lawrence (eds) *Rural governance: international perspectives*, London: Routledge, pp 211-26.

ELEVEN

New Labour, poverty and welfare in rural England

Paul Milbourne

Introduction

> Our economy and society are changing fast. Our welfare state must help us respond to these changes. It must focus its energy on tackling poverty and social exclusion. Society has a responsibility to support those unable to support themselves. It should help support people in acquiring the new skills they need for the jobs of the future. It must help UK companies succeed in the new global economy. (Hutton, 2006, p i)

> ... the lack of information about rural disadvantage in government research programmes and in assessments of how policy is working in tackling rural disadvantage suggests that consideration is not being given to rural issues (and particularly rural disadvantage) at all stages of policy processes. (CRC, 2006a, p 19)

In the first extract, taken from the Foreword to the 2006 Green Paper on welfare reform in the UK, John Hutton, Secretary of State for Work and Pensions, sets out the government's general approach to welfare provision. On the one hand, he suggests that the welfare state should continue to provide support for vulnerable and needy groups within society. On the other, Hutton argues that the welfare system should play a role in bringing excluded groups into the labour market, strengthening Britain's position within the increasingly competitive global economy. In the first part of this chapter I want to discuss the development of New Labour's reforms of the welfare state since it came to power in 1997, highlighting the main elements of these reforms and positioning them within a broader historical context. This provides the introduction to the main part of the chapter, which examines New Labour's approach to poverty and welfare in rural areas.

As is apparent from the second extract above, little research or analysis has been undertaken on the rural impacts of New Labour's welfare policies. While government has claimed that its welfare policies are aimed at disadvantaged groups in all parts of the country and that it is aware of the distinctive dimensions of poverty in rural areas, there exists little evidence of the impacts of welfare reform in rural (and urban) spaces. This evidence gap, together with the government's initial prioritisation of urban forms of poverty and social exclusion, has led to claims that New Labour's anti-poverty and welfare agendas have been insensitive towards the rural dimensions of disadvantage (see CRC, 2006b). A key aim of the chapter is to provide a comprehensive account of the government's approach to tackling poverty and social exclusion in rural England. In addition, it examines the rural impacts of welfare reform, first in terms of how levels of low income and benefit receipt in rural areas have changed since New Labour was first elected and then by considering the performance of selected national welfare programmes in rural spaces.

New Labour and welfare reform

> Social security alone, as it has been traditionally perceived, is no longer a sufficient goal for UK welfare policy. (Alcock, 2005, p 87)

There has been much discussion over recent decades about the shifting states of welfare in the UK (see Rodger, 2000; Clarke et al, 2001; Lund, 2002). Established in the late 1940s by a reforming Labour government, the welfare state was designed to provide a 'national minimum' for its citizens through the provision of new national systems of healthcare, education and social security. This approach to the welfare state sat within a broader Keynesian macro-economic policy framework based on the principles of full employment and the active regulation of the economy by the state (Powell, 2000). The essential components of this welfare system remained relatively untouched by successive UK governments in the post-war period. By the 1970s, though, things began to change as national economic and fiscal crises led to discussions about the future of the welfare state. The election of the first of four Conservative governments in 1979 initiated a significant programme of welfare restructuring. While it is not possible to review this programme in any detail here, these New Right governments sought to 'roll back the welfare state': efforts were made to reduce levels of welfare spending, choice was introduced into the welfare system and mechanisms for delivering welfare assistance were altered, with the role of local government diminished, the powers of non-state agencies enhanced and internal markets created. Important changes were also introduced to the benefits system, with universal rights to state assistance replaced by a more selective benefit entitlement system.

It was this changed landscape of welfare policy that the New Labour government inherited when it was swept to power in 1997. Welfare reform constituted a significant component of Labour's campaign for election. New Labour proposed a new approach to welfare based on the political philosophy of the 'third way' (Giddens, 1998). It was claimed that the third way approach – involving a fusion of old Left and New Right political ideas and policies – could combine wealth promotion and entrepreneurial economic policies with a commitment to tackling poverty (Deacon, 2002). In addition, New Labour argued that issues of work and welfare needed to be combined within a new type of welfare system: one that could meet the needs of the national economy faced by increasing global competition. As Page (2005) suggests:

> New Labour's belief that properly regulated markets provide the best means of securing future prosperity has led them to favour those welfare policies that work *with* rather than *against* the grain of such an economic strategy. (p 120)

While there has been considerable discussion of the third way approach to welfare and work, particularly in relation to neoliberalism, citizenship and equality (see Levitas, 1998; Lister, 1999; Peck, 1999; Giddens, 2000; Glover, 2003), the most appropriate reading of New Labour's approach to welfare is one that is based on the pragmatic practice of policy adoption and adaption. For Deacon (2002), New Labour has sought "to respond to Conservative ideas about [benefit] dependency without abandoning altogether the goal of greater equality" (p 105). Similarly, Powell (2000) suggests that New Labour's pragmatic response to the welfare landscape that it inherited was "to accept or modify the reforms that appeared to work, and to reject those that did not" (p 57).

At the core of the New Labour programme of welfare reform is the belief that paid employment is the best route out of poverty for those people able to work. As is stressed in the most recent Green Paper on welfare restructuring, "[work] strengthens independence and dignity. It builds family aspirations, fosters greater social inclusion and can improve an individual's health and well-being" (DWP, 2006a, p 2). New Labour has recognised, however, that for those groups unable to participate in the formal labour market, 'dignity and security' will need to be provided by the welfare state. The main facets of the government's welfare reform programme have been the introduction of a national minimum wage, the fusing of the benefit and tax systems to make paid employment financially more attractive for those moving from welfare to work, and the encouragement of those people who are able to work to take advantage of new opportunities in the labour market (see Powell, 2000). In other words, the New Labour approach to welfare has addressed the structural *and* the cultural elements of poverty and exclusion, resulting in "a package of measures, some of which are designed to level the playing field and some of which are designed to activate the players" (Deacon, 2002, p 117).

Significant within the government's welfare-to-work programme has been a series of New Deals aimed at different out-of-work groups. The first and largest of these New Deals, introduced in 1997 and financed by a windfall tax on the privatised utility companies, focused on young unemployed people. Other New Deals followed for lone parents, the long-term unemployed, the older unemployed, disabled people and the partners of unemployed people (see Finn, 2005). These New Deals have striven to develop more proactive and individualised systems of advice to unemployed groups in an effort to meet their particular needs and problems. As Finn (2005) explains, "the key innovation was the role of front line New Deal Personal Advisers who individualised employment assistance and worked with claimants to tackle employment barriers" (p 94).

In addition to these initiatives, Prime Minister Tony Blair announced in March 1999 that the government would work towards the eradication of child poverty by 2010, and measures have been introduced by government to provide extra financial assistance to working families. New Labour also established the Social Exclusion Unit in 1997 to develop new cross-departmental governmental approaches to tackling poverty and other forms of exclusion. While space prevents any comprehensive review of its work here, the Social Exclusion Unit has developed a series of new initiatives to tackle different aspects of exclusion, including ones addressing rough sleeping, school exclusions, teenage pregnancies and service provision for socially excluded groups.

New Labour's approach to poverty and welfare in rural areas

> While rural areas are on average less deprived than their urban counterparts, there are still significant numbers of disadvantaged rural residents. The broad features of disadvantage are similar wherever you live – financial exclusion, lack of skills, lack of affordable housing and limited social mobility. But the spatial characteristics that define rurality can create particular challenges and often imaginative, innovative and tailored delivery systems. (DWP, 2006a, p 24)

Rural forms of poverty and disadvantage first became recognised in the UK in the late 1970s (Walker, 1978; Shaw, 1979) through policy-based discussions of the allocation of funding to local government rural areas. The first significant research on rural poverty and deprivation was commissioned by the Labour government in the late 1970s. Undertaken by Bradley and McLaughlin in five areas of the English countryside, the research highlighted that an average of 25% of households were living in, or on the margins of, poverty in 1980/81 and that significant proportions of the rural population were deprived of essential services. While the research report was never published, its key findings were used in the 1980s to demonstrate that poverty and deprivation in rural areas required increased recognition by central government. With the possible exception of problems relating to the supply of social and affordable housing in rural areas, the Conservative governments of the 1980s and early 1990s remained largely reluctant to acknowledge, let alone address, issues of rural poverty. The publication of further evidence on the scale of rural poverty that emerged in the mid-1990s (Cloke et al, 1994) from government-funded research[1] did little to raise the problem up the government's policy agenda, with poverty and related issues of disadvantage conspicuous only by their absence from the first English Rural White Paper, which appeared in 1995 (DoE/MAFF, 1995).

The election of the first New Labour government in 1997 was welcomed by many anti-poverty organisations. The fear among those active in rural areas was that Labour's traditional urban focus and power base would lead to its neglect of the rural forms of poverty and disadvantage. While some of the government's early policy announcements on poverty reflected these fears, as they addressed spatial concentrations of poverty in inner-city areas, rural issues soon began to rise up New Labour's political and policy agendas. There were two reasons for this growing importance of 'the rural' within government. First, the scale of the election victory in 1997 meant that New Labour had a much larger number of MPs representing rural areas than it had anticipated and been accustomed to. In its first term of office (1997-2001), there were 180 New Labour MPs representing rural or semi-rural constituencies in parliament, making up about 40% of the parliamentary Labour Party. This meant that New Labour had become the main party of rural Britain, with more rural MPs than the Conservatives and Liberal Democrats combined. Within six months of the election, the Rural Group of Labour MPs (RGLMP) was established to promote rural issues within the party and government. In the Foreword to its 2000 manifesto document, Peter Bradley MP, the then chair of the RGLMP, argued that New Labour's agenda was also relevant to the electorate in rural areas:

> Rural Britain is not a foreign country. People in rural communities do not speak a different language. They do not have a separate agenda. They want just as much as their urban neighbours to see investment and improvement in the schools their children attend. They are just as anxious to see the National Health Service restored and extended. They want secure jobs with a decent day's pay for a decent day's work. They worry about crime. They want affordable homes for their sons and daughters. They demand better public transport. These are rural priorities no less than they are urban. (RGLMP, 2000, p 3)

What was required, Bradley suggested, was recognition within government of some of the distinctive elements of disadvantage in rural areas. Referring to problems associated with remoteness and sparsity, limited public transport provision, additional pressures on housing markets and the rigidity of the planning system, he claimed that "these are national issues with distinct rural features and it is clear that the Government policies which seek to address them must have their rural dimension too" (RGMLP, 2000, p 2).

The second reason that New Labour began to embrace the rural agenda relates to political debates about the future of hunting with dogs in Britain. The campaign by the Countryside Alliance to save hunting involved a broader assault on the New Labour government's approach to addressing rural issues. In a shrewd political move, the Alliance reconfigured the government's willingness to allow parliamentary time to discuss the hunting issue as not just an attack on hunting as a countryside activity but also on the rural way of life more generally, pointing to the lack of government intervention in relation to the closure of sub-post offices and schools in rural areas as examples of government neglect of the countryside. While this move initially placed New Labour on the back foot, it responded by providing a comprehensive assessment of the state of rural Britain, highlighting its relative advantages as well as its problems, and by stressing how its national economic and welfare policies were benefiting disadvantaged groups in urban *and* rural areas. In an important policy document, published in 2000, the Cabinet Office concluded that while rural areas are generally less disadvantaged than other parts of the country, the government would ensure that its national (welfare) policies took account of rural circumstances:

> The vast majority of government expenditure is through national programmes that have an impact on rural and urban areas – e.g. schools, health care, transport and welfare payments. An important aspect of policy development and monitoring is checking that these mainstream programmes take proper account of the needs of those living and working in the countryside. (Cabinet Office, 2000, p 77)

The year 2000 also witnessed the publication of the New Labour government's first Rural White Paper (DETR/MAFF, 2000). This was preceded by a national consultation on a broad range of rural themes, with social exclusion forming one of these themes. In the consultation document (DETR, 1999), the government asked whether more action was required to sensitise national programmes to rural needs and to develop specific policies to tackle rural forms of social exclusion. Interestingly, the social exclusion questions received by far the lowest number of responses of all the questions included within the consultation. The topics of poverty and social exclusion also received relatively little attention within the Rural White Paper. While much more attention was given to providing better quality services in rural areas – including housing, health, education and transport services – than in the previous Rural White Paper, there was very little explicit reference to how government proposed to tackle poverty and other social welfare issues in the countryside.

The 2000 Rural White Paper did commit government to consider the rural impacts of all new domestic policies. Promoted by the Rural Development Commission during the late 1990s, this process of 'rural-proofing' requires that government departments and agencies evaluate whether any new policy is likely to impact differently in rural areas, undertake a thorough evaluation of these impacts and, if appropriate, adjust the policy to ensure that it meets rural circumstances. The Countryside Agency[2] (2002) produced a rural-proofing checklist containing 15 questions that the government and its agencies should consider when developing new policies. While most of these questions are concerned with the provision and delivery of key services, infrastructure, business and the environment, two focus on rural disadvantage. The first asks about the impacts of policy on low-paid workers and part-time/seasonal forms of employment in rural areas, while the second question addresses the impacts of policy aimed at tackling poverty and social exclusion in rural areas, asking:

> How will it target rural disadvantage, which is not usually concentrated in neighbourhoods? Do the indicators to be used for identifying need measure deprivation issues that are particular rural features (e.g. access to services, access to job opportunities, low earnings and housing affordability)? (Countryside Agency, 2002, p 3)

While this commitment to 'rural-proofing' should have ensured that the rural dimensions of welfare policies are considered by the government, there has been little evaluation of the proofing process. Furthermore, 'rural-proofing' does not oblige government departments and agencies to assess the *actual* impacts of these policies on rural areas. Indeed, in its report on the state of the countryside, the Cabinet Office (2000) was able to offer very little evidence on the rural impacts of the government's flagship welfare policies. In fact, all that it provided were data on the New Deal for unemployed young people, stating that the scheme had been marginally more successful in rural areas, with 45% of rural participants securing work compared with 43% in urban areas. No evidence was provided on the rural impacts – actual or likely – of the national minimum wage or the new Working Tax Credit systems. While it can be argued that the government's welfare reform programme was still in its infancy in 2000, little evidence on the impacts of its policies in rural areas has emerged over the following eight years. As an illustration, the recent comprehensive review of evidence on disadvantage in rural England, undertaken by the Commission for Rural Communities (CRC)[3] (2006a) was unable to provide any statistical data on the performances of the government's flagship welfare and anti-poverty initiatives in rural areas.

What the CRC has done is raise important questions about the likely rural impacts of government welfare policies. In a recently published document, the CRC (2006b) highlights some of the dimensions of disadvantage in rural areas that require further consideration by the government in the design and implementation of welfare policies. In particular, it suggests that the welfare-to-work programme may represent a blunter policy instrument in rural areas since:

> rural employment disadvantage is not just about unemployment – the focus of most policy – but is more often about job insecurity, poor quality work or lack of training, where some face repeated periods of worklessness. (CRC, 2006b, p 1)

In addition, the Commission calls on the government to give more careful attention to the assessment of welfare initiatives to ensure that "policies to tackle disadvantage are not measured by over-simplistic targets that can be achieved by concentrating on urban areas alone, where the target group are easier to reach and the numbers are greatest" (CRC, 2006b, p 2).

The CRC identifies a series of priority actions for tackling rural disadvantage in more effective ways. These actions mainly focus on meeting the needs of individuals but also include area-based approaches to dealing with rural disadvantage, changing perceptions of rurality, disadvantage and rural disadvantage, and raising rural concerns within the government (see Table 11.1). Disappointingly, the CRC provides little detail on these priority actions in terms of how and by whom policy should be developed, stating that its aim is to initiate a debate on how they should be achieved. Nevertheless, some of the identified priority action areas are worthy of further discussion.

The first relates to the take-up of state benefits and tax credits. The CRC is concerned that cultures of self-sufficiency and difficulties associated with accessing welfare advice services may reduce the level of benefit take-up in rural areas, arguing that additional efforts are needed to raise awareness of people's entitlement to in-work and out-of-work benefits in the countryside. Second, it proposes that research is urgently required to examine the impacts of the national minimum wage in rural areas and its relations with the agricultural wages in order to examine the "extent to which potentially vulnerable workers in rural areas (such as migrant workers) and those in small rural workplaces are benefiting" (CRC, 2006b, p 13).

Third, it calls on the government to do more to ensure that the New Deal programmes include those who work intermittently or seasonally, particularly in the tourism and agricultural sectors, and who may not identify themselves as unemployed during their out-of-work periods. A fourth priority identified by the CRC is the provision of assistance to people with long-term illnesses and disabilities into work in rural areas:

> People with disabilities and long-term health problems living in rural areas face particular barriers, due to limited employment opportunities and the lack of transport and childcare. They are also less likely to have benefited from existing initiatives targeted at helping such people back into work.... One way forward is that the implementation of measures such as the rollout of Pathways to Work, included in the Welfare Reform Green Paper, should be designed carefully to ensure that they meet rural needs. (CRC, 2006b, p 14)

Fifth, the CRC uses limited evidence that low-income parents in rural areas have benefited less from the expansion of free nursery education than the national average to propose that "childcare needs to be provided sufficiently locally and flexibly to meet the needs of rural areas and this could be recognised more in the implementation of the childcare strategy" (CRC, 2006b, pp 14-15).

Table 11.1: CRC's priority actions for tackling disadvantage in rural areas

	Tackling financial poverty	
Individual level	1. Ensuring people take up benefits they are entitled to	
	2. Ensuring employees benefit from the National Minimum Wage	
	3. Ensuring support for unemployed people is tailored to the needs of intermittent or seasonal workers	
	4. Assisting people with long-term illnesses and disabilities into work	
	5. Ensuring people's skills and training needs are met	
	6. Supporting access to childcare	
	7. Improving financial inclusion	
	Tackling access poverty	
	8. Reducing travel costs	
	9. Providing alternative transport for people without cars	
	10. Ensuring that ICT benefits all groups	
	Tackling network poverty	
	11. Retaining local meeting and service places	
	12. Promoting informal social support	
	13. Increasing the 'disadvantaged voice' locally	
Place	14. Improving the quality of employment	
	15. Increasing the supply of affordable housing	
	16. Increasing transport provision and accessibility	
Perceptions	17. Challenging the myth of the rural idyll	
	18. Tackling the stigma of rural disadvantage	
Processes	19. Reflecting rurality in resource allocations	
	20. Consideration of rural disadvantage in all stages of policy	
	21. Ensuring that rural disadvantage is reflected in national priorities and PSA targets	
	22. Targeting of people not places	
	23. Set minimum standards for policy delivery	

Source: CRC (2006b)

Evaluating the impacts of welfare reform in rural areas

Recent years have witnessed the publication of new evidence on the changing scales of poverty and social exclusion in the UK. The government has produced a series of annual reports on trends regarding poverty and social exclusion based on a large number of indicators since the late 1990s. In the 2006 report (DWP, 2006b), the government highlights that the national situation regarding poverty and social exclusion continues to improve, with 40 of the 59 indicators included in its analysis showing a positive trend since the baseline (mostly 1997), including the proportions of working-age adults living in low-income households, children in workless and low-income households, and older people on low incomes. A further nine indicators exhibit a broadly constant trend since the late 1990s, while the data are shown to be moving in the wrong direction for seven indicators, which include infant mortality rates, life expectancy at birth, obesity amongst children, and employment disadvantage for the lowest qualified group.[4]

An alternative evaluation of poverty and social exclusion trends, produced by the New Policy Institute (NPI, 2006), highlights that 19 of 50 indicators analysed have improved, 16 have remained steady and four have worsened since 1998.[5] Other studies have also highlighted impressive reductions in unemployment levels and benefit receipt rates, as well as the positive impacts of the national minimum wage and Working Tax Credit on the situations of different groups of low-income workers (see Finn, 2005). The only benefit group that has increased in size since New Labour came into office has been Incapacity Benefit recipients and the government has recently announced that it intends to develop policy to reduce by one million the number of people on this benefit (DWP, 2006b).

While these analyses provide a useful indication of the national impacts of New Labour's welfare and anti-poverty programme, they do not permit an assessment of changing trends relating to poverty and the impacts of welfare reform in different spatial contexts. The remaining parts of this section begin to undertake this type of spatial analysis by setting out initial findings from an ongoing work on changing levels of low income and benefit receipt, and participation rates for the New Deals in rural England.

Spatial analyses of government survey data indicate that levels of low income in rural England have fallen slightly since the late 1990s. A study of poverty and social exclusion in rural England by Harrop and Palmer (2002) revealed that 21% of people in remote rural areas and 17% of those in accessible rural areas were in low-income households in 2000/01. A recent analysis – covering the period 2002/03 to 2004/05 – shows that these rates have fallen to 19% and 16%, respectively. For both types of area the level of low income remains below that recorded for urban areas (23% for the latest period) (NPI, 2006).

Reductions in the number of people claiming Jobseeker's Allowance (JSA) and Income Support in rural England have also occurred since the late 1990s. In 2006, 107,000 fewer people were in receipt of JSA in rural England than in 1999, representing a reduction of 37.8%, and the number of Income Support recipients fell by 434,000 or 51.0% across this period. These reductions in welfare caseloads are higher than those recorded for urban areas, where the number of JSA and Income Support recipients fell by 27.0% and 42.6% respectively between 1999 and 2006. Looking at the different categories of local authority area,[6] it is apparent that reductions in Income Support and JSA recipients have been largest in the 'most rural' (rural 80) areas and smallest in the 'major urban' areas.

An analysis of recent changes in earnings levels highlights different trends. While the average income for employees in rural England increased by 6.7% between 2004 and 2006,[7] this level of increase was slightly lower than that recorded by urban areas (7.0%). Of the six categories of local authority area, it was the 'most rural' areas that recorded the lowest level of earnings growth, at 6.1%. Rural areas are also characterised by lower levels of earnings, with the rural average standing at £402 per week in 2006 compared with £471 in urban areas. In fact, 11 of the 20 districts with lowest average income levels in England in 2006 were classified as rural. Earnings levels are lowest in the areas recording the smallest growth rate for earnings between 2004 and 2006, that is, the 'most rural' areas. Here the average income from work in 2006 was £382 per week, three quarters of the figure recorded by those working in 'major urban' areas.

Finally, the recent release of local data on the New Deals allows for an assessment, albeit limited, of their impacts in rural areas. Starting with the first of the New Deals – the New Deal for Young People – these data reveal that 248,000 unemployed young people in rural England had participated in this scheme by August 2006, with rural participants comprising one quarter of the national total. A further 197,000 unemployed lone parents in rural areas had started on the New Deal for Lone Parents by mid-2006, making up 31% of all participants in England. The New Deal for unemployed persons aged 25 years or over had involved 108,000 people living in rural areas (20% of the national total) and 73,000 people had participated in the New Deal for the older unemployed by August 2006, representing 16% of the English total.

It is possible to analyse the impacts of two of these New Deals – for unemployed young people and for the '25 and over' unemployed group[8] – in greater depth. This analysis confirms earlier findings from the Cabinet Office (2000) in showing that the New Deals have been slightly more successful in rural areas. For example, of the young people participating in the first of these New Deals, 47% of those in rural areas moved into employment on leaving the scheme compared with 42% of urban participants. A further 3% of young people in rural areas were in employment supported by benefits and 21% had moved off benefits but had unknown destinations. Across the six types of local authority area, the New Deal for Young People has been most successful in the 'most rural' districts, where 53% of leavers secured employment, and least successful in 'major urban' districts (40% having gained employment on leaving the scheme). A similar picture emerges in respect of the New Deal for unemployed people aged 25 years and over, with 35% of rural participants moving into employment on completion of the scheme, compared with 29% of leavers in urban areas.

Conclusion

New Labour's anti-poverty and welfare reform programmes have played an important role in reducing levels of poverty and social exclusion in the UK since the late 1990s. While the government has been criticised for its reluctance to address inequalities surrounding the distribution of income and wealth, its emphasis on paid employment as the main/sole route out of poverty, the restrictive nature of some of its reforms and its shift from citizenship to consumerism (Page, 2005), the NPI (2006, p 11) states that recent indicators show "just how important it was that government took up the cause of poverty and social exclusion after 1997 because little or no progress since then would have been achieved without it".

The government's approach to tackling poverty has largely been focused at the national level, with reforms to the tax and benefit system, the introduction of the national minimum wage and the implementation of the various New Deals impacting on unemployed and low-income groups in all parts of the UK. Other initiatives have been concerned with addressing the coexistence of different dimensions of social exclusion in particular metropolitan spaces. What is also clear, though, is that New Labour has recognised the presence of poverty in rural areas, as well as some of its distinctive features. While the prompts for this recognition of the rural dimensions of poverty include the (unexpectedly) large number of Labour MPs with rural constituencies in 1997, the campaigns of the Countryside Alliance to save hunting and the actions of the Countryside Agency to promote issues of rural disadvantage, it is clear that the New Labour government has sought not only to highlight how its national policies are benefiting poor and disadvantaged groups of the rural population but to develop initiatives to tackle rural forms of disadvantage. Among these initiatives have been the establishment in 2006 of the Commission for Rural Communities, which was given a specific remit to address disadvantage in rural England; the introduction of rural-proofing of new government domestic policy; the funding of a six-year rural social exclusion programme (see Milbourne, 2006); and the establishment of the Affordable Rural Housing Commission to examine problems associated with accessing housing in rural areas, which reported in 2006 (Affordable Rural Housing Commission, 2006).

Beyond highlighting these actions, it is difficult to assess the impacts that New Labour's policies have had on poverty and social exclusion in rural England. This difficulty arises for two main reasons: first, the government has been reluctant to provide sub-national data on the performance of its anti-poverty and welfare policies; and, second, there has been little independent research undertaken on the rural impacts of these policies. The spatial analyses of available data presented in this chapter would appear to indicate that New Labour's programme of reforms is impacting positively in rural areas. Levels of earnings have increased slightly and the number of people on JSA and Income Support has fallen dramatically over recent years. Furthermore, the New Deals for unemployed young people and the '25 and over' unemployed group seem to have performed better in rural areas, if the proportion of participants moving from welfare to work is used as a measure of their success.

While supportive of the government's welfare reform programme, the CRC has called for national policies to be made more sensitive to the needs of rural areas. Research evidence does point to some distinctive aspects of rural poverty and disadvantage. Among the working-age population, levels of unemployment are lower than in urban areas while low-paid and low-quality employment are more significant; older people constitute a much larger proportion of the poor population; and childcare facilities and public transport services tend to be less accessible (and less affordable) in rural areas. It is likely that these features of rural disadvantage will present obstacles to the successful implementation of welfare-to-work in rural areas.

A body of research evidence on the rural impacts of welfare restructuring is emerging in the US, where a similar programme of welfare reform was initiated in the mid-1990s (see Weber et al, 2002; Pickering et al, 2006; Tickamyer, 2006). This also highlights significant reductions in rural welfare caseloads since the introduction of welfare reform. However, poverty amongst working households in rural areas has been shown to have not declined (RPRI, 1999). In addition, while the living standards of those who have made the transition from welfare to work may have improved, it has been suggested that the longer-term impacts of welfare reform are dependent on a set of structural responses to poverty, linked to economic development and transport provision, to enable people to move beyond low-skilled and low-paid local employment.

The US welfare reform programme has also been associated with the devolution of certain elements of welfare provision to individual states. This has allowed for the development of flexible packages of welfare assistance that are better able to meet the specific needs of disadvantaged groups in particular rural places (Findeis et al, 2001). However, Duncan (1999) argues that there are dangers associated with devolved systems of welfare provision, most notably that they may become subverted by local elites who remain unsympathetic to the anti-poverty agenda. While welfare devolution of this kind has not been a feature of New Labour's welfare programme to date, the recent Green Paper on welfare reform (DWP, 2006a) proposes the development of more flexible localised systems to deal with problems in the city. It may only be a matter of time before these new systems of local welfare assistance are rolled out to other areas of the country.

Compared with the situation in the US, relatively little is known about the impacts of New Labour's anti-poverty and welfare reform programme on specific groups of the poor and disadvantaged population, or in different types of locality in rural England. For a government committed to evidence-based policy development and the process of rural-proofing, this evidence gap is surprising. A programme of research, involving the government, the CRC and academic researchers, is urgently needed to provide a comprehensive assessment of the rural impacts of welfare reform in England. Such a programme should also consider the connections (and collisions) between national and local systems of welfare provision in rural areas, given that key elements of national welfare policy continue to be delivered by local (state and non-state) agencies, and that a significant number of local initiatives to deal with poverty and social exclusion in different rural places have been developed over recent years (see Milbourne, 2004).

Notes

[1] The research, based on a survey of 3,000 households in 12 areas of rural England, showed an average level of poverty that was not dissimilar to that revealed by the McLaughlin study ten years earlier (McLaughlin, 1986). In addition, the poverty rate in nine of these 12 areas was in excess of 20% of surveyed households.

[2] The Rural Development Commission merged with the Countryside Commission to become the Countryside Agency in 1999.

[3] The Commission for Rural Communities was established by the government in 2006 to address the rural dimensions of disadvantage in England.

[4] There are insufficient data available to determine a trend for three indicators.

[5] The NPI also used a 'mixed' category. Data for some of the indicators used are not available.

[6] Local authority areas fall into one of the following categories: major urban; large urban; other urban; significant rural; rural 50; rural 80. The last of these categories is the most rural in character.

[7] Local earnings data are not available for previous years. These data relate to income levels for place of work.

[8] Local destination data for the other two New Deals were not available in 2007.

References

Affordable Rural Housing Commission (2006) *Final report*, London: Affordable Rural Housing Commission.

Alcock, P. (2005) 'From social security to social exclusion', *Benefits*, vol 13, no 2, pp 83-8.

Cabinet Office (2000) *Sharing the nation's prosperity: Economic, social and environmental conditions in the countryside*, London: The Stationery Office.

Clarke, J., Langan, M. and Williams, F. (2001) 'Remaking welfare: the British welfare regime in the 1980s and 1990s', in A. Cochrane, J. Clarke and S. Gewirtz (eds) *Comparing welfare states*, London: Sage, pp 71-112.

Cloke, P., Milbourne, P. and Thomas, C. (1994) *Lifestyles in rural England*, London: Rural Development Commission.

CRC (Commission for Rural Communities) (2006a) *Rural disadvantage: Reviewing the evidence*, London: CRC.

CRC (2006b) *Rural disadvantage: priorities for action*, London: CRC.

Countryside Agency (2002) *Rural-proofing – Policy makers' checklist,* Cheltenham: Countryside Agency.

Deacon, A. (2002) *Perspectives on welfare*, Milton Keynes: Open University Press.

DETR (Department of the Environment, Transport and the Regions) (1999) *Rural England: Summary of responses*. (Available at www.wildlife-countryside.detr.org. uk/consult/ruraleng/response/rural08.htm, accessed 25 November 1999)

DETR/MAFF (Department of the Environment, Transport and the Regions/ Ministry of Agriculture, Fisheries and Food) (2000) *Our countryside: The future – a fair deal for rural England* (the Rural White Paper), Cm 4909, London: The Stationery Office.

DoE/MAFF (Department of the Environment/Ministry of Agriculture, Fisheries and Food) (1995) *Rural England: A nation committed to a living countryside*, London: HMSO.

Duncan, C. (1999) *Worlds apart: Why poverty persists in rural America*, New Haven, CT: Yale University Press.

DWP (Department for Works and Pensions) (2006a) *A new deal for welfare reform: Empowering people to work*, Cm 6730, London: The Stationery Office. (Also available at www.dwp.gov.uk/welfarereform/empowering_people_to_work. asp)

DWP (2006b) *Opportunity for all*, Eighth Annual Report, Cm 6915-I, London: The Stationery Office. (Also available at www.dwp.gov.uk/ofa/reports/2006/)

Findeis, J., Henry, M., Hirschi, T., Lewis, W., Ortega-Sanchez, I., Peine, E. and Zimmerman, J. (2001) *Welfare reform in rural America: A review of current research*, Columbia, MO: Rural Policy Research Institute.

Finn, D. (2005) 'Welfare to work: New Labour's "employment first" welfare state', *Benefits*, vol 13, no 2, pp 93-7.

Giddens, A. (2000) *The third way and its critics*, Cambridge: Polity Press.

Glover, C. (2003) '"New Labour", welfare reform and the reserve army of labour', *Capital and Class*, Spring 2003, Issue 79, pp 17-23.

Harrop, A. and Palmer, G. (2002) *Indicators of poverty and social exclusion in England: 2002*, London: New Policy Institute.

Hutton, J. (2006) 'Foreword', in *A new deal for welfare reform: Empowering people to work*, Cm 6730, London: The Stationery Office. (Also available at www.dwp. gov.uk/welfarereform/empowering_people_to_work.asp)

Levitas, R. (1998) *The inclusive society*, London: Macmillan.

Lister, R. (1999) 'From equality to social inclusion: New Labour and the welfare state', *Critical Social Policy*, vol 18, no 2, pp 215-25.

Lund, B. (2002) *Understanding state welfare*, London: Sage.

McLaughlin, B. (1986) 'The rhetoric and reality of rural deprivation', *Journal of Rural Studies*, vol 2, no 4, pp 291–307.

Milbourne, P. (2004) *Rural poverty: Marginalisation and exclusion in Britain and the United States*, London: Routledge.

Milbourne, P. (2006) 'Poverty, social exclusion and welfare in rural Britain', in J. Midgeley (ed) *A new rural agenda*, London: IPPR, pp 76-93.

NPI (New Policy Institute) (2006) *Monitoring poverty and social exclusion in the UK 2006*, York: Joseph Rowntree Foundation.

Page, R.M. (2005) 'New Labour's social justice: as good as it gets?', *Benefits*, vol 13, no 2, pp 119-22.

Peck, J. (1999) 'New Labourers? Making a new deal for the "workless class"', *Environment and Planning A*, vol 17, pp 345-72

Pickering, K., Harvey, M., Summers, G. and Mushinski, D. (2006) *Welfare reform in persistent rural poverty*, University Park, PA: Pennsylvania State University Press.

Powell, M. (2000) 'New Labour and the third way in the British welfare state: a new and distinctive approach?', *Critical Social Policy*, vol 20, no 1, pp 39-60.

RGLMP (Rural Group of Labour MPs) (2000) *A manifesto for rural Britain*, London: RGLMP.

Rodger, J. (2000) *From a welfare state to a welfare society*, Basingstoke: Macmillan.

RPRI (Rural Poverty Research Institute) (1999) *Rural America and welfare reform: an overview assessment*, Columbia, MO: RPRI.

Shaw, J.M. (1979) *Rural deprivation and planning*, Norwich: GeoBooks.

Tickamyer, A. (2006) 'Rural poverty', in Cloke, P., Marsden, T. and Mooney, P. (eds) *The handbook of rural studies*, London: Sage, pp 411-26.

Walker, A. (ed) (1978) *Rural poverty: Poverty, deprivation and planning in rural areas*, London: CPAG.

Weber, B., Duncan, G. and Whitener, L. (2002) *Rural dimensions of welfare reform*, Kalamazoo, MI: W.E. Upjohn Institute for Employment Research.

TWELVE

Policing policy and policy policing: directions in rural policing under New Labour

Richard Yarwood

Introduction

In 2002 the annual 'State of the Countryside' report (Countryside Agency, 2002) contained, for the first time, a chapter dedicated to rural crime. Its inclusion suggested that policy makers and practitioners were taking greater interest in crime and policing in the countryside than had hitherto been the case in the 1990s (Yarwood and Edwards, 1995; Dingwall and Moody, 1999; Yarwood and Gardener, 2000). Certainly, the introduction of a number of initiatives between 2000 and 2006 implied that Labour gave greater priority to rural policing than the previous Conservative administration. However, while rural policing was made more visible in the policy arena, it is questionable whether the visibility of policing on the ground changed significantly. Further, more recent change in national policing policy suggests that the attention given to rural places may have been short-lived.

The provision of rural policing reflects broader changes in the pattern of service provision and the performance of governance in rural Britain, namely that greater responsibility has been placed on local communities to work in partnership with other agencies to deliver local services (Woods, 2006). Consequently, policing raises wider questions about the changing nature of decision making and governance in rural communities and the extent to which police partnerships represent a new form of governance (Woods and Goodwin, 2003; Goodwin, 2006). This chapter examines policing policy under New Labour and argues that government policy has been propelled by moral panic and rural protest rather than forming a coherent part of the national policing plan.

When examining these issues it is important to realise that ideas such as community, criminality and rurality are socially constructed and contested, with important consequences for rural policing (Yarwood and Gardner, 2000; Yarwood, 2001). In this context, one of the most significant changes in law under New Labour has been the 2004 Hunting Act that criminalised hunting with hounds. A consequence of the Act has been that some groups who had previously campaigned for a greater police presence in the countryside now resent coming under greater scrutiny from the police. Given that Labour's rural policing policy has taken a community-based approach, the Act has raised questions about whose vision of rurality and rural community is being policed and what, if any, are the consequences of contests over these ideas.

This chapter starts to explore some of these issues. It is structured into two main sections. The first examines some of the contexts that have driven changes to Labour's policing policies. The second section examines rural policing under New Labour, identifying three main phases of policy development that have had different implications for the policing of rural communities.

Contexts

The countryside was, and is, fortunate enough to experience lower than average rates of reported crime. Consequently, between 1960 and 2000, rural crime and policing received little attention from policy makers, academics or the police themselves (Yarwood, 2001). Rural areas were particularly vulnerable to the restructuring of police forces according to 'market-led', neoliberal principles of service efficiency enshrined in the 1960 Police Act (Lupton, 1999; Yarwood, 2007a, 2007b). Driven by the demands of efficiency, scarce resources were targeted on crime hot spots in urban locations. Policing constabularies became larger, with resources clustered in central areas to maximise the efficiency of emergency responses (O'Conner, 2005). Police stations and houses were closed in rural settlements and their officers regrouped into urban locations that provided a central base from which to respond reactively to emergency calls. By 1991 only 2% of parishes in rural England had a permanently staffed police station (Rural Development Commission, 1992). Following these changes, the police became more accountable to central government than their local communities (Smith, 1986). This strategy reflected a view that policing should be reactive rather than proactive in nature.

For superintendent turned sociologist Malcolm Young, this was a logical approach. He argued that rural areas had been over-policed in the past due to the unrealistically high expectations of rural residents, who viewed the rural police officer as "a badge of an unreconstituted vision of a world which has the squire, the village post office, the pub and the doctor as its pivotal places and persons" (Young, 1993, p 140). Consequently he saw little merit in the following situation:

> At one time we recorded nil burglaries on the whole of the Bromsgrove subdivision ... yet had a CID establishment of one detective inspector, four detective sergeants and thirteen detective constables. In Newcastle West subdivision, my ex-partner had recorded 400 burglaries in the same period on a subdivision not remotely staffed by a commensurate number of detectives. (Young, 1993, p 139)

Yet, as the 1990s progressed, the media noted that crime in rural areas appeared to be rising more quickly than in the cities. While recognising the low visibility of the police and their remoteness from many rural communities, the Conservative government's Rural White Paper emphasised that the solution to these problems lay with active, rural citizens taking greater responsibility for policing:

> It is particularly important for those who live in rural areas to act as the eyes and ears of the police. (DoE/MAFF, 1995, p 95)

The paper advised rural residents to fit window locks and improve their personal security. When a lack of police became a concern for rural residents, they were expected to be good, 'active citizens' by volunteering for service in Neighbourhood and Street Watch Schemes or as Neighbourhood Special Constables. Although the social and spatial uptake of these schemes was sporadic in rural areas, they had the potential to improve police–public relations and feelings of security without unduly placing demands on police time or resources (Yarwood and Edwards, 1995).

While this approach appealed to a particular type of rural citizen (Woods, 2006), the 1990s also witnessed challenges to hegemonic visions of rural law and order through a growth in neo-nomadic groups, the sabotaging of hunts and loud, outdoor 'raves'. The government's response was to pass legislation that outlawed these activities and aimed to exclude these lifestyles from rural areas (Sibley, 1994, 2003; Young, 1999, 2002). In some areas 'Traveller Watch' schemes used active citizens to maintain surveillance on these 'deviant other' groups and to inform the police of their movements. Such policing was, therefore, exclusive rather than inclusive, emphasising a need to consider critically how the term 'community' is deployed by policy makers and practitioners. This is particularly pertinent given New Labour's emphasis on community and their changes in legislation that were seen, by some, to challenge long-established meanings of rural community.

New Labour and rural policing

The continuation phase (1997 to 2000)

The 1997 election of Labour to power initially saw the continuation of many of the trends established by the Conservative government. The neoliberal approach to policing was maintained with the police required to devise annual plans that detailed crime control targets, objectives and expenditure (McLaughlin, 2001). In turn, these led to the publication of 'league tables' of police performance that allowed the government to monitor and direct, from a distance, police operations. In keeping with neoliberal policing regimes in many countries, gaps in policing provision were still expected to be filled by active citizenship (Crawford, 1997, 2003; Goris and Walters, 1999; Hughes et al, 2002; Yarwood, 2007a, 2007b). Significantly, the emphasis was on communities, rather than individuals, to work in closer, more formal partnership with statutory agencies (DETR/MAFF, 2000; Dean and Doran, 2002):

> local communities can identify problem areas, contribute to joint solutions with the police and provide vital intelligence through initiatives such as neighbourhood watch. (DETR/MAFF, 2000, p 41)

These policies point to a form of governmentality characterised by two key strands:

1. A strategy of 'responsibilisation' that views local communities as the cause of and solution to the problems facing rural places (Lockie et al, 2006). The state aims to encourage, enable and support community-based groups to contribute to the policing of their own localities (Rose, 1996).
2. The development of performance targets, local policing strategies and their support with targeted, conditional funding suggesting that, rather than a 'hollowing out' of the state or a shift from government to governance in decision making, the government was directing policing 'at a distance' or 'through community' (Garland, 2001; Woods and Goodwin, 2003). They are forms of 'technology' through which the government can ensure that policing is conducted in particular ways (Foucault, 1991).

These principles have reflected New Labour's general approach to public service delivery. They have continued to guide rural policing, despite some superficial and reactive changes in their implementation, as the following sections reveal.

Rurality refocused (2000 to 2006)

Barely had the strains of *Things can only get better* faded when things got an awful lot worse in terms of rural policing. In 1999 Tony Martin was convicted of murder for shooting dead one of two burglars of his isolated Norfolk farm house and sentenced to life imprisonment. Martin argued that he had little choice but to defend himself against repeated attacks to his property given that the police were too far away to respond effectively to emergency calls for help. Martin's case attracted intense media scrutiny and public interest, raising questions about the legal position of self-defence and the provision of policing in rural places. Martin's stance was treated sympathetically in many quarters. On his release from prison (following an appeal that reduced his crime to manslaughter) he signed a publishing deal with the *Daily Mirror* to tell his story and, following a 2004 poll of listeners to BBC Radio 4's *Today*, MP Stephen Pound sought to introduce a Private Member's Bill to allow homeowners to use 'any means' to defend their homes.

At the same time, the introduction of anti-hunting legislation prompted opposition to the Labour government from the Countryside Alliance (CA), a vocal and well-organised pressure group formed in 1997 with a mission to campaign for "the countryside, country sports and a rural way of life" (Countryside Alliance, 2004, p 2). Although primarily concerned with defending hunting with hounds, the CA exploited the issues raised in the Martin case to criticise the government for its neglect of rural services, including policing (Countryside Alliance, 2004). Further weight was given to these arguments when research revealed that many dominantly rural police forces were underfunded in comparison with their more urban counterparts (ORH, 1999). The foot and mouth outbreak of 2001 also helped to bring rural areas and their problems to the forefront of public and media attention.

The Martin case and a vociferous rural lobby prompted the government to take action on the issue of rural crime. Consequently a range of initiatives, supported by new funding streams and governmental structures, were introduced with the aim of improving the visibility of policing in rural areas.

Between 2001 and 2006 the government introduced the Rural Policing Fund (RPF) to improve the visibility and accessibility of the police in the countryside in the 31 most rural (Aust and Simmons, 2002) forces in England and Wales. It had a budget of £30 million per year that remained constant and was not increased with inflation and was made available to individual forces provided that "that they [could] demonstrate real improvements in the policing of rural areas" (DETR/MAFF, 2000, p 43).

This money was used by police constabularies in three main ways. First, many forces used these monies to fund additional officers in rural areas, measuring their success against crime reduction figures or improvements in public satisfaction. These officers frequently had a community-based remit and acted as 'beat managers'. Beat managers are regular, uniformed police officers that have special responsibility for policing specific localities in a holistic manner. Their task is:

> the identification of casual factors within their beat area and through multi-agency working, to bring about lasting quality of life changes within the community. This will result in reducing the fear of crime and achieving a reduction in the demand upon the Police Service. (Baker et al, 2001, p 9)

There is evidence (Yarwood, 2005) that beat managers and their proactive working methods had some success in improving the visibility of the police in rural areas and meeting public expectations of the service. However, the geographical distribution of beat managers varied considerably, both between and within constabularies, and so not all rural areas enjoyed the benefits of these officers. Further, their relationship with the public could be compromised if they were only in post for a short period (West Mercia Constabulary, 2006).

Second, and linked to this community-based approach, forces developed a number of innovations to improve their visibility. These included mobile police stations and tele-information technology, such as telephone or email warnings of crime, in selected areas (Yarwood and Cozens, 2004).

Third, many forces aimed to develop forms of partnership working. In some cases this extended the Neighbourhood Watch idea into 'Farm Watch' or Rural Watch schemes. Other, more innovative, approaches developed local-scale partnerships between the police and public. West Mercia Police, for example, pioneered a Rural Safety Initiative (RSI) (Yarwood and Cozens, 2004). The RSI was a parish-based partnership between the police, represented via a beat manager, and the local public, represented by a committee of volunteers that included at least one member of the parish council. The operation of RSIs was guided by crime and safety audits based on public consultation exercises. In turn, these were based on previous initiatives aimed at 'designing-out' crime from schools or businesses and consequently they placed strong emphasis on making the environment of participating villages safer. However, these initiatives not only attempted to take account of the physical rural environment, but also how rurality and locality were imagined by the public. The following principles were followed by RSIs:

- maintaining the rural image;
- enabling the sustainability of rural communities;
- recognising the legitimate fears of those associated with the rural community and working to allay them;
- adopting a logical approach which allows the difference between perceived and actual problems to be identified;
- recognising the importance of cost-effectiveness;
- understanding that any process must embrace the principle that every community's individual issues are site specific (Small, 2001).

West Mercia's RSI was piloted in four parishes, selected by senior police officers. Thereafter four schemes were established when they were requested by the public. This meant that the geographical coverage of the RSI reflected micro-level political engagement (Woods and Goodwin, 2003) between police and community rather than a response to crime or fear of crime 'hot spots'. Like Neighbourhood Watch, its geography reflected the willingness of communities to engage with the police in this initiative as well as the personal initiative, skill and permanency of local beat managers. While there was some interest in RSI (it was adopted by some other constabularies with large rural areas), it was superseded, much to the annoyance of the officers who pioneered it, by the introduction of local policing teams in 2006.

Its fate perhaps reflected many of the initiatives funded by the RPF.[1] While many forces introduced new methods of rural policing, they were characterised by a rather piecemeal approach. Few forces seemed keen to adapt rural policing strategies and to incorporate these initiatives in coherent, structured plans for rural policing in their constabulary (Yarwood and Cozens, 2004).

Gloucestershire Constabulary was one of the few forces that developed a specifically rural strategy (Gloucestershire Constabulary, 2003). This was based on ten initiatives that applied to rural areas. Some of these relied on technological solutions, such as introducing mobile police stations and a 'watchword' telephone system to alert Neighbourhood Watch coordinators of issues, but the majority focused on the development of partnership working on a range of scales. At the strategic level the police aimed to work with statutory organisations, notably Gloucestershire Rural Community Council, to improve visibility through a series of coordinated community initiatives. At a local level, ten beat managers sought to work more proactively with local communities, encouraging them to take greater responsibility for rural policing. While this approach reflected broader government thinking on the delivery of policing, the delivery and longevity of this kind of local-level partnership working in the rural areas of Gloucestershire appeared to be the exception rather than the rule. This is despite legislation introduced to compel partnership working in policing.

The 1998 Crime and Disorder Act obliged local authorities and the police to work in partnership to reduce crime and improve community safety. The resultant 'Crime and Disorder Reduction Partnerships' (CDRPs) are required to conduct a crime and safety audit every three years and to use evidence from this survey to plan, monitor and evaluate strategies to deal with locally identified issues. The execution of these audits was guided by the Home Office, but a degree of autonomy was granted for partnerships to address local conditions, including rurality, as they saw fit. Consequently some partnerships chose to examine rural crime and policing in some detail. Cornwall's six CDRPs, for example, collaborated to evaluate their rural residents' experiences, perceptions and opinions of crime, safety and policing (Mawby, 2004).

Parish and community councils, the lowest tier of government in the UK, had a duty under the 1998 Crime and Disorder Act to consider "the crime and disorder implications of all their activities, and to do all they reasonably can to prevent crime and disorder" (Dean and Doran, 2002a, p 9) and had a right to be consulted in the development of district- or county-wide strategies. In keeping with Labour's 'responsibilisation' approach to governance and its vision for more empowered, responsible parish councils (DETR/MAFF, 2000), parish councils were viewed as being in a strong position to represent local, rural viewpoints in strategy formation. This led to four new obligations for parish councils:

1. to consider the impact of all their functions and decisions on crime and disorder in their local area, under Section 17 of the Crime and Disorder Act 1998;
2. to review how they exercise their powers and deliver their services, in order to comply with Section 17;

3. to be fully involved in their local Crime and Disorder Reduction Partnership (led by the district authority and police force);
4. to pay for crime and disorder reduction by using their precept for funds, Parish Plan Grants and payments from developers under the Town and Country Planning Act, Section 106. (Dean and Doran, 2002b)

This is part of a discourse that views local communities, rather than wider social structures, as the cause of and solution to the problems facing rural places (Lockie et al, 2006). Labour's policing policy reveals that, far from withdrawing from service provision, central government is adopting new ways to encourage, persuade, enable and support community-based groups to contribute to the policing of their own localities (Rose, 1996). Rural communities are obliged to address their own problems by following directorates and guidance issued by central government, a situation described as governance through community by some commentators (Rose and Miller, 1992; Rose, 1996; Higgins and Lockie, 2002; Lockie et al, 2006; Woods, 2006). Community is "a means of government: its ties, bonds, forces and affiliations are to be celebrated, encouraged, nurtured, shaped and instrumentalized in the hope of producing consequences desirable for all and for each" (Rose, 1996, p 335). Far from being autonomous, the local crime partnerships are subject to surveillance and scrutiny by government agencies (Garland, 2001; Higgins and Lockie, 2002). Thus, the RPF relied on setting and achieving performance targets to secure continued funding. Other commentators have also noted that while Crime and Disorder Reduction Partnerships were initially allowed to adopt a 'what works works' approach (Home Office, 1998), they have become more regulated over time with less scope for autonomous action (Phillips, 2002).

However, only 59 of the CDRPs introduced by the 1998 Crime and Disorder Act (or 16% of all those in England and Wales) operate in rural areas (Aust and Simmons, 2002). Despite the requirements for parish councils to be fully involved in their local CDRP, a survey of parish councillors in West Mercia revealed that the majority of parish councils (84%) had had no direct involvement with their local safety partnership (Yarwood, 2005). Furthermore, empirical evidence suggests that while the police and local authorities make efforts to consult, and even welcome the involvement of, voluntary actors, the burden of auditing and planning crime and disorder falls largely on their shoulders (Phillips, 2002). Consequently, they undertake the lion's share of work in CDRPs and community participation is limited. Despite policy efforts to broaden responsibility, policing remains the liability of the state and the police.

Rurality to locality (2006 onwards)

More recently, less policy emphasis has been given to specifically rural policing and, instead, locality has been emphasised. The 2004 Policing White Paper, *Building communities, beating crime*, makes virtually no mention of rural policing other than an acknowledgement that local forces and authorities should recognise 'the difference between policing urban and largely rural areas' (Home Office, 2004a, p 105). This has had two implications for rural policing, at the strategic and local levels respectively.

First, the government's abortive plans to reform police authorities raised questions about rural priorities. In 2005, following suggestions in the 2004 White Paper, there were controversial proposals to merge 43 forces into as few as 12 to tackle better the threats of terrorism, Internet crime, organised crime and civil disasters (O'Conner, 2005). These plans had particular implications for predominantly rural forces. For example, there were suggestions to merge the five forces in the South West of England into one regional force and to merge the four Welsh forces into one national authority. These plans were opposed by many police authorities, who argued that less emphasis would be given to local policing to the detriment of rural residents. Only two rural forces, Cumbria and Lancashire, favoured merging with each other but failed to come to a decision on the detail of these changes. In light of these difficulties and sustained opposition from the police, not to mention rural advocates and pressure groups, the plans for merged police forces were abandoned in July 2006 (BBC, 2006).

Second, less priority has been given to rural areas in the development of local policing practices. Following the publication of the White Paper, the National Policing Plan for 2005-08 outlined that police forces are expected to develop neighbourhood policing teams staffed by police officers, including special constables and community support officers, neighbourhood wardens and, to a lesser extent, volunteers. In short, they resemble CDRPs that operate at very local levels.

These policies have started to make an impact at the local level. For example, West Mercia police's Rural Safety Initiative, discussed earlier, was replaced after a short life with Local Policing Teams (LPTs), known as PACTS (Partners and Communities Together), which were tasked with providing local policing demanded in the policing White Paper. LPTs are led by a Local Police Officer (LPO) who is supported by dedicated community support officers, neighbourhood wardens and special constables. LPTs aim to work in partnership with local people and other statutory agencies to provide "an effective, problem-solving approach to the priorities identified by local communities" (West Mercia Constabulary, 2006, p 3). LPOs are required to undertake specialised training for this role that focuses on community-based engagement and working.

Unlike the RSI, every part of the constabulary is covered by an LPT and LPO. However, LPT policy makes no specific mention of rural communities and policing, although it follows the National Policing Plan's stipulation for local policing to recognise differences between urban and rural communities. Inevitably, though, LPOs in rural areas will have much larger areas to cover than their colleagues in urban places and LPOs may not, therefore, be that local to some rural communities! Some problems are starting to emerge: one serving officer has suggested that in his constabulary not all local authorities are willing to engage in the process and so geographical gaps are emerging in the provision of LPTs, especially in rural places (personal communication). Given the lack of specific rural policies in the National Policing Plan, this situation is likely to be repeated in other constabularies.

Furthermore, in 2006 the RPF, introduced by Labour in 2000, was merged with three other funding streams with the aim of giving local police authorities more flexibility and control on the use of these monies. The government emphasised that this was not the abolition of the RPF and that levels of funding for rurality would be maintained (*Hansard*, 2006); yet, given the continued performance culture in policing, there must be a temptation for police forces to spend this money in high-crime areas or in places where it will yield visible, achievable results. Inevitably these will be urban places. Consequently, there is a danger that the emphasis given to specifically rural policing may decline with these policies. As the Martin case fades from public memory, it has been replaced by other moral panics, such as a perceived increase in illegal migration, and real and perceived threats from terrorism in the minds of the media and public, that have refocused the government's and the police's priorities.

If the introduction of policing initiatives between 2000 and 2006 reflected a government under pressure from a rural lobby, the quiet relegation of the rural from the policing agenda may also reflect a decline in the influence of the rural lobby. While the Conservative administration passed a number of laws aimed at excluding particular lifestyles or activities deemed to be at odds with elite visions of country life (Halfacree, 1996; Young, 2002; Sibley, 2003), Labour criminalised hunting with hounds. This struck at the identity and lifestyles of many rural residents, prompting widespread and well-organised protest (Woods, 2003, 2004). The police have been required to enforce the ban on hunting, which has led to complaints from the Countryside Alliance that rural areas were being over-policed, or at least policed in the wrong way: "it is especially frustrating for rural communities to see their police allocating time to offences [i.e hunting with hounds] which are nowhere prioritised in the National Policing Plan whilst serious crimes ... go increasingly unaddressed" (Countryside Alliance, 2004, p 45). More significantly, if the pressure groups such as the Countryside Alliance are less keen on a heavily policed countryside, perhaps this has allowed the government to reduce policy emphasis on rural areas and to focus on what it sees as more pressing concerns of terrorism and immigration. The focus on locality appears to be leading to the policy spotlight moving away from rurality once again.

Conclusions

During New Labour's time in office, debates about rural policing have revolved less around whether rural areas are being policed but have focused on what offences, or version of rurality, are being policed. These have been particularly pertinent given the application of Labour's ubiquitous partnership approach to service provision, including rural policing. There has been debate over whether partnership working favours traditional views of rurality, such as one that equates rurality with farming (Herbert–Cheshire, 2000), or whether they offer an opportunity for new elites to influence rural politics (Woods, 2006). With regards to rural policing, this chapter has demonstrated that the pendulum has swung towards and then away from local elites during the past ten years.

In turn, this raises questions about the power of local elites to influence policy and, in turn, the nature of rural society. While Sibley (2003) has maintained that legislation has continued to reflect an elite discourse of power and rurality, Young (2002) asserts that, although elite crime concerns are loud, they amount to little more than an old-fashioned rhetoric that has insufficient power to influence contemporary rural society. The introduction of the 2004 Hunting Act and the quiet relegation of rural policing from the policy agenda suggests that Young's opinion holds greater sway, at least for the moment.

Changing policing policy suggests that despite the rhetoric of partnership working and responding to local need (Yarwood and Cozens, 2004), policing is driven more by central government than the whim of local elites. This may, of course, be no bad thing as the police should be concerned with rural policing rather than policing the rural (Yarwood and Gardner, 2000). In terms of governance, however, the practice of rural policing continues to represent government at a distance rather than the development of autonomous decision making.

While the public, professors and policy makers postulate about policing policy, it is the police themselves who are called to deal with crime and the fear of crime on a daily basis. The rural police officer's lot is not a happy one: he or she has to cover diverse beats and even more diverse communities, all the while following performance targets and bureaucratic procedures that are driven by a fluid policy arena. Barely have rural initiatives been developed, than they are scrapped and replaced by Local Policing Teams. As both Fyfe (1991) and Herbert (1996) have suggested, it is perhaps time to focus a little more on the lives and work of police officers themselves. There is a need to research the ways that policing is practised 'on the ground' in different rural spaces. This should be sensitive to the individual and collective roles of police officers within the changing legal and social structures of the countryside and how it is governed (Yarwood, 2007b). While all research should, of course, be critical, there is scope for some humanity and an understanding that the task they face is difficult, frequently unappreciated and increasingly driven by procedures and demands that complicate rather than clarify how to police the rural.

Note

[1] The Commission for Rural Communities is currently conducting research to evaluate the effectiveness of the RPF that should present a clearer evaluation of its effectiveness.

References

Aust, R. and Simmons, J. (2002) *Rural crime: England and Wales*, London: Home Office.

Baker, J., Williams, D. and Herrington, D. (2001) *Best value review of territorial policing*, Worcester: West Mercia Constabulary.

BBC (2006) 'Axed police mergers cost millions'. (Available at http://news.bbc.co.uk/1/hi/uk/5334230.stm)

Crawford, A. (1997) *The local governance of crime: Appeals to community and partnerships*, London: Clarendon Press.

Crawford, A. (2003) 'The pattern of policing in the UK: policing beyond the police', in T. Newburn (ed), *Handbook of policing*, Cullompton: Willan, pp 136-69.

Countryside Agency (2002) *State of the countryside*, London: Countryside Agency.

Countryside Alliance (2004) *Rural policy handbook*, London; Countryside Alliance.

Dean, M. and Doran, S. (2002a) *Section 17 of the Crime and Disorder Act 1998: A practical guide for parish and town councils*, London: NACRO/Countryside Agency.

Dean, M. and Doran, S. (2002b) *Partnerships: Section 17: A guide for parish and town councils*. (Available at www.crimereduction.gov.uk/legislation20.htm)

DETR/MAFF (Department of the Environment, Transport and the Regions/Ministry of Agriculture, Fisheries and Food) (2000) *Our countryside: The future – a fair deal for rural England*, (the Rural White Paper), Cm 4909, London: The Stationery Office.

DoE/MAFF (Department of the Environment/Ministry of Agriculture, Fisheries and Food) (1995) *Rural England: A nation committed to a living countryside*, London: HMSO.

Dingwall, G. and Moody, S. (eds) (1999) *Crime and conflict in the countryside*, Cardiff: University of Wales Press.

Foucault, M. (1991) 'Governmentality', in G. Burchell, C. Gordon and P. Miller (eds), *The Foucault effect: Studies in governmentality*, Hemel Hempstead: Harvester-Wheatsheaf, pp 87-104.

Fyfe, N. (1991) 'The police, space and society: the geography of policing', *Progress in Human Geography*, vol 15, pp 249-67.

Garland, D. (2001) *The culture of control: Crime and social order in contemporary society*, Chicago: University of Chicago Press.

O'Conner, D. (2005) *Closing the gap. A review of the fitness for purpose of the current structure of policing in England and Wales*, London: Her Majesty's Inspector of Constabulary.

Phillips, C. (2002) 'From voluntary to statutory status: reflecting on the experience of three partnerships established under the Crime and Disorder Act 1998', in G. Hughes, E. McLaughlin and J. Muncie (eds), *Crime prevention and community safety: New directions*, London: Sage, pp 163-182.

Rose, N. (1996) 'The death of the social? Re-figuring the territory of government', *Economy and Society*, vol 25, pp 327-56.

Rose, N. and Miller, P. (1992) 'Political power beyond the state: problematics of government', *British Journal of Sociology*, vol 43, pp 173-205.

Rural Development Commission (1992) *1991 survey of rural services*, London: Rural Development Commission.

Sibley, D. (1994) 'The sin of transgression', *Area*, vol 26, pp 300-3.

Sibley, D. (2003) 'Psychogeographies of rural space and practices of exclusion', in P. Cloke (ed), *Country visions*, Harlow: Pearson, pp 218-31.

Small, I. (2001), *Rural Safety Initiative*, Worcester: West Mercia Constabulary.

Smith, S. (1986) 'Police accountability and local democracy', *Area*, vol 13, pp 293-98.

West Mercia Constabulary (2006) *Local Policing Team guidance*, Worcester: West Mercia Police.

Woods, M. (2003) 'Deconstructing the rural protest: the emergence of a new social movement', *Journal of Rural Studies*, vol 19, pp 309-25.

Woods, M. (2004) 'Politics and protest in the contemporary countryside', in L. Holloway and M. Kneafsey (eds), *Geographies of rural cultures and societies*, Aldershot: Ashgate, pp 103-25.

Woods, M. (2006) 'Political articulation: the modalities of new critical politics of rural citizenship', in P. Cloke, T. Marsden, and P. Mooney (eds), *Handbook of rural studies*, London: Sage, pp 457-71.

Woods, M. and Goodwin, M. (2003) 'Applying the rural: governance and policy in rural areas', in P. Cloke (ed), *Country visions*, Harlow: Pearson, pp 245-62.

Yarwood, R. (2001) 'Crime and policing in the British countryside: some agendas for contemporary geographical research', *Sociologia Ruralis*, vol 41, pp 201-19.

Yarwood, R. (2005) 'Crime concern and policing the countryside: evidence from parish councillors in West Mercia Constabulary, England', *Policing and Society*, vol 15, pp 63-82.

Yarwood, R. (2007a) 'Getting just deserts? Policing, governance and rurality in Western Australia', *Geoforum*, vol 38, pp 339-52.

Yarwood, R. (2007b) 'The geographies of policing', *Progress in Human Geography*, vol 31, pp 447-66.

Yarwood, R. and Cozens, C. (2004) 'Constable countryside? Police perspectives on rural Britain', in L. Holloway and M. Kneafsey (eds), *Geographies of rural cultures and societies*, Aldershot: Ashgate, pp 145-72.

Yarwood, R. and Edwards, W. (1995) 'Voluntary action in rural areas: the case of Neighbourhood Watch', *Journal of Rural Studies*, vol 11, pp 447-60.

Yarwood, R. and Gardner, G. (2000) 'Fear of crime, culture and the countryside', *Area*, vol 32, pp 403-11.

Young, J. (1999) *The exclusive society: Social exclusion, crime and difference in late modernity*, London: Sage.

Young, J. (2002) 'Crime and social exclusion', in M. Maguire, R. Morgan and R. Reiner (eds), *The Oxford handbook of criminology* (3rd edn), Oxford: Oxford University Press, pp 459-86.

Young, M. (1993) *In the sticks: Cultural identity in a rural police force*, Oxford: Clarendon Press.

- It is recognised that substantial investments by both the government and employers are being made in improving skills but the commitment needs to be more ambitious if Britain is to compete in the global economy.

A key theme of the Leitch Review of Skills has been the governance mechanisms and institutional frameworks put in place over the past decade across employment and training policy sectors. It has been questioned whether there are too many agencies, partnerships and actors involved in these initiatives. Before assumptions are made for Leitch (HM Treasury, 2006), we need to know more about what is happening on the ground and explore whether local stakeholders are clear about the various policy roles and responsibilities, and perhaps more importantly whether these measures are working. The mantra of the Leitch report *World class skills* is that there is a 'shared responsibility' with 'three levels in concert' – government, the employer and the individual (Skills for Business, 2007). It is in this context that the Department for Innovation, Universities and Skills (DIUS) has responded to Leitch by creating the UK Commission for Employment and Skills to take stock of how we have arrived here, to examine these 'three levels in concert', and to offer solutions so that a 'skills revolution' (DIUS, 2007) can happen across the whole of the UK – North, South, East, West, with cities and rural territories performing to their best.

This chapter explores this legacy and challenge by focusing on, and learning from, the New Deal – a key aspect of employment, training and welfare reform since 1997 and a major contributing factor to the fall in unemployment over the past decade. Since 1998, the New Deal has required participation in a series of 'options' (across work, employment and training) in return for welfare benefits. Priority over time has increasingly been given to immediate placement in the labour market, termed 'work first', so as to embed the work ethic at the earliest opportunity and, more importantly, to instil a lifelong philosophy of employability (see Peck, 2001). The New Deal, like any public policy, is delivered through local 'action frameworks' and has had significant implications for employment and training in rural Britain. While the aims, intentions, discourses and languages of the policy are created at the point of central development, a key aim of the chapter is to uncover how things have been practically practised in New Deal rural delivery. With a focus on rural Wales, and with concerns framed by partnership formation and the links between rurality and delivery, the authors have drawn on semi-structured interviews to tell the story in the words of the actors involved. Names and places have been made anonymous to provide confidentiality. The questions are posed by 'S'/'SW' – Suzie Watkin, as part of research in this field undertaken between 2003 and 2007.

Governing the New Deal: partnership frameworks

As outlined by Theodore and Peck (1999) there are various means of locally implementing the New Deal. A key aspect of New Labour's approach to economic and social development has been not to prescribe a national top-down solution but to allow localities some element of 'choice', according to the specificities of local circumstances. In short, for this government, national problems require local solutions and geography matters (DfEE, 1997). In some territories the New Deal is delivered through a 'consortium' model that incorporates a range of agencies from the public, private and voluntary sectors. The partners in our case study are the Jobcentre (now referred to as Jobcentre Plus), a private training organisation, a voluntary sector support organisation, the careers service and another voluntary organisation that provides New Deal mentors. At first sight, there is a glaring lack of representation from employers, who are a key part of delivering the work experience element of the New Deal. Each 'partner' has a different role. The Jobcentre, mainly through the New Deal Personal Advisers (NDPAs), manages each client as they 'progress' through the system, and acts as a sort of institutional 'bridge' between the client and the other partners, bringing them in as they see fit. The training company holds the contract to deliver New Deal training, including the Gateway to Work course, which is a two-week confidence and skill building and jobsearch course at the start of the programme. The voluntary organisation has the role of finding work experience placements for clients. The careers service and mentoring scheme are referred to on an ad hoc basis when particular customers are felt to benefit from their input.

In policy rhetoric, and at first sight, the consortium framework appears to make sense. The partners work together on a range of adult-based learning so they know each other and their institutional structures well. Also, and crucially, it is couched in the terms of 'partnership' and accountability. The New Deal is not just delivered by a faceless jobcentre, but by a range of partners with local knowledge and specific experience of training, of supporting the voluntary sector, or of working with young people.

On closer scrutiny though, the consortium model poses a few difficulties in rural practice. The first, and most major, issue in terms of rural partnerships is a general lack of choice: these partners might be around the table because they are most suitable to deliver the work, but they might also be there because there is simply no one else to do it. The training company may be the only organisation in the county equipped with the offices and officers to deliver the training elements of the New Deal. The voluntary organisation may be the sole organisation of its kind in the area. Interviewees made these points clear:

> D: [Our training company] took it cos nobody else wanted it – no, I didn't say that.
> S: Is that true?
> R: Can't possibly be true, can it?

and repeatedly [sic] tells lies to avoid going to work […] she should be
signed off for absenteeism […] what happened … bugger all.
It really helps if your mother is the Manager of Corporate Services
…
Please don't repeat this with my name attached.
Steer a steady course and keep a careful watch.

So, is this a true consortium gathered in the interests of the young people it works
for? Or, is it merely upholding values whereby benefit recipients are seen to be
working for their benefits, all the better if in a charity shop or tidying up a park,
as opposed to being encouraged to look for a satisfying occupation where they
are less likely to return to benefits?

Funding for clients also heavily dictates what is done, in an expression of the
'marketisation' of public policy. It seems incongruous that on the one hand the
group works in partnership to deliver the programme, yet on the other hand some
of the partners benefit financially from 'keeping the client for themselves'. The
Jobcentre pays out 'on profile' in advance of the expected number of attendees,
and 'claws back' any underspend. One organisation receives cash for placing
clients on voluntary placement, while another is paid for delivering training or
employer-based work experience.

The mentoring scheme also relies on a stretched voluntary service, with the
mentoring organiser attempting to cover a range of groups, including young
offenders, with limited volunteer support, time and skills:

> SU: You know the habits of a lifetime are not going to be turned around
> by a few energetic enthusiastic sessions with an advisor – "Oh yes,
> that's a good idea, I really do fancy work" – when they've been doing
> fine thanks dealing drugs or you know, robbing houses or whatever
> it is a lot of them have been doing. So again we've had this thing
> – the mentoring system, where they had an adult with them but that
> hasn't worked very well, by the time it's taken to get someone who
> fits whatever it is you're looking for, weeks might've passed and then,
> how many hours a week can they offer? It sounds very good on paper,
> but in practice it's really not worked at all in the way that we, it was
> hoped it would, or that it's supposed to on paper.
> SW: But then I guess that they might have the right sort of skills that
> people would need from a mentor?
> SU: Well, that's questionable really cos some of them, most of them […]
> they were very good people to volunteer their time, but they didn't
> have any skills really. They had very little, if any, training whatsoever.
> Some of them were deeply troubled people themselves, because some
> of them were clients that I've seen myself, and so I know that they
> were perhaps not the best people to be offering, you know, fancying
> that they were going to be a counsellor without any of the background

and intelligence in a nutshell to be able to do it properly. So I was quite dubious about some of the people that I realised were mentors, and I would question what help they could have really given. Having said that there were one or two that were absolutely brilliant and really did contribute something considerable, but they were in the minority. Definitely the minority. (Sheila, careers service)

The voluntary services also feel put upon in terms of their capacity to deal with some of the clients, particularly those with deep-seated problems:

R: We shouldn't get those people but we do get them, time after time.
M: We get angry people, upset people, people with alcohol problems, and you just can't foist that onto a placement. And a lot of these, the voluntary organisations, they're understaffed, underfunded, they're nice people, cos that's the nature of their, you know, they don't like to cause a fuss, they don't like to be bombastic, they're nice – that's why they're in the job, and you're putting them in a really difficult situation. (Rose and Margaret, voluntary organisation)

SW: It must put pressure on the placement providers as well.
SU: But it does, it's not fair, it's not fair, it's not fair. And a lot of the people who go there have got enormous problems and need an awful lot of support, and you know, well, they've got a place to run, for God's sake so you know, hugely under-resourced really and questionable as to whether the resources that have been used on it could have been better spent and I think they could have. (Sheila, careers service)

There are issues around capacity across the partnership, in terms of placement provision, staff time, financial resources etc. The lived experiences of the New Deal clearly did not live up to the promises and claims made in initial policy statements (see Blair, 1997; DfEE, 1997):

SU: There was this huge hullabaloo with balloons and God knows what, and we were all just looking at each other in, you know, amazement and concern thinking "Here we go again, a fantastic front and what have we got? We've got no training in place, we've got nowhere we can send these kids to, you know, what placements are available with local employers? Is there anything in it for them? Have they been brought on board?" And in short it was a shambles, a complete and utter shambles. And any of the work that's been done has been done by the people on the ground trying to pull it together. Because it was just, it seemed that all they wanted were wonderful success stories and spectacular results to front this policy and, as ever, it

fairly creative things, like say dry stone walling or something like that but they can't get into it. We've talked a lot this afternoon about how cliquey places were, if you knew somebody they'd look after their son or daughter or whatever, and even the people born and bred round here said that was the case, and a lot of the people from outside just don't get into the community. Families need to be here for a long time. (Roy, a Gateway Course tutor)

Michael highlights further problems of the 'rural gaze', whereby the reputation of a young person's family can have ill-effects on their prospects, compared with 'strangers' in the community:

M: ... and then this local knowledge, people knowing everybody else's bloody business really, isn't it? And what's frustrating sometimes is an employer will take somebody on who moves into the area and he knows nothing about them and they could be a murderer couldn't they? But they'll take them on because they don't know them, but Joe Bloggs who lives round the corner, his family have been there all their lives, who they know that's a bit dodgy, they won't even touch. That is frustrating but that's how it is, and it's sometimes hard to break that.
S: So it's difficult even with the training and work experience to overcome that for people?
M: Yeah, yeah, I think it's difficult to shift that prejudice, it's not impossible but it is difficult. (Michael, an NDPA)

So it seems that only a small minority who have long-standing and untarnished family backgrounds are able to take advantage of rural networks – again excluding people with multiple barriers to work and training, including publicly reported crime:

W: It can work two ways; it makes it easier to approach some people because it's a closely knit sort of, people are known; to the converse people are known and it's "Oh no, thank you very much". Like headlines in the local paper: "God, that bloke's starting with us on Monday", you know. The prejudices are in place before they step through the door. (William, an NDPA)

If you are a young person living on benefit, then access to your own transport is pretty much impossible, and public transport is very often inadequate and expensive, just for getting to signing-on days, let alone travelling to regular work (see also Haughton et al, 2000; Jones and Gray, 2001). In many rural places it can be unbelievably difficult to travel a few miles down the road, with buses running once a day, or even once a week, and which rarely fit with conventional working hours. Some New Deal providers have begun to offer driving lessons as incentives to complete other parts of the training, but this still relies on access to a vehicle. Other ways of overcoming transport barriers include the reimbursement of travel costs for New Deal interviews, which Personal Advisers try to arrange with people's signing-on days to cut down their travel. Also people may be given help with rail travel:

> M: Well, the rurality is the biggest problem here [...] transport to start with. OK, we reimburse all travel costs to interviews here anyway so they're never out of pocket from coming to New Deal interviews. We try and call them in on a day that they're signing [...] so as much as possible I'll try and see them the same time [...] same with the Gateway to Work courses. They were reimbursed at the end of each day, so from coming to see us they shouldn't be any worse off at all. We do have rail passes for them, half price, so they can travel for the period that they're on New Deal. (Monica, an NDPA)

In one interview Carol, a Personal Adviser, talked about a situation where a rural regeneration charity had bought some mopeds with the intention of loaning them out to young people for employment access, but, apparently because of the range of partners working in the areas, no one seemed to be aware of who had responsibility for the resource and what paperwork was needed, and so the mopeds ended up unused and just gathering dust.

So transport, or rather that lack of it, is a big problem for rural young adults. The Gateway Course tutor suggested that distance is very relevant to earnings, especially in the sort of low-paid jobs that New Deal clients tend to enter into the cost of private or public transport can make it difficult to justify coming off benefits when they might lose up to two days' pay just to get to work. This also impacts on many other rural difficulties, such as the limited types of jobs available:

> C: The transport's the biggie, cos we've got people up in the hills and things like that.
> S: I guess you've got a pretty wide catchment area here?
> C: Yes, and we haven't got a lot of factories or anything in this area, so if you've got people that haven't got a lot of skills, cos we have a fair few vacancies, but they're looking for particular skills, so I mean the New Deal can help to bring people up to certain skills, but I do feel that we're lacking in, some people don't want to go any further, do they? They just want a job that they can do and we haven't got that always. (Carol, an NDPA)

Sheila interrogates this further and seems to suggest that people actively shape their own transport restrictions in order to avoid work:

severing links with the few employers who become involved, as well as a fear of losing interested employers due to a lack of suitable clients:

> M: The intention was that we would have employers on board, sign them up to New Deal, which is ideal isn't it? Brilliant. If you get all these employers interested [...] wanting to go and then [...] every week they can start a new employee, but in this area we've just never been able to do that because the numbers coming on to New Deal are low and also they're not always wanting to do the kind of work that the employers are offering anyway, so we could sign up an employer to New Deal but it doesn't mean to say that we can give them an employee [...] not for maybe a year, and by that time the person you've dealt with had moved away, the personnel manager, whoever they are, so as I say I don't think it's worked in that respect. (Michael, an NDPA)

So, for Michael, an effect of rurality is a sustained difficulty in matching employers and clients, especially within a valid timescale, and this is exacerbated by the small size of the majority of employers, meaning they do not have the time to provide 'input', as Anne terms it:

> A: They're such limited employers that you're constantly using the same one. I just wonder at what point employers will hold their hands up and say "No more!" because from 15-year-old work experience kids going from school, then skill build, every programme, you're out there asking an employer to support a learner with initially there's no benefit to them because they're certainly not an asset because you've got to put so much input into them. And where you've just got so many one-man bands [...] the difference between say putting a learner in Boots the chemist where you've got a supervisor and staff and a manager and all of that, than putting somebody into Jones the newsagents where they've got one person and another part-time person, these are the differences. Where you've got several staff you can, and they've got the structure and the facilities there, but because in our rural areas so much of it is one-man bands or two-women bands or whatever. (Anne, training company)

However, rurality also brings some benefits, surprisingly perhaps *because* of the close local networks of people:

> S: But at the same time those sort of tight local networks, do they kind of help in any way, maybe you get to know employers better and the things that they're looking for.

M: Yeah you do. I think most of the employers in this area as well are quite small, in relative terms very small. I mean there's no large employers so you do tend to find that the employers are hands on. I mean they're not managers, they're people who do the jobs, and some of them are more understanding for that reason. They just want people there who can do the job. At the same time they're not the best payers. It's a really weird situation where you've got low unemployment but employers are not prepared or not able, I don't know which it is, or whatever it is, you don't get employers paying a lot of money. (Michael, an NDPA)

The loss of meaningful training options on the New Deal compounds the issue of a lack of employers, and, perversely, highlights the lack of skilled workers in the labour market, leaving a residual "lower spectrum":

SU: I think it was a great mistake, I suppose there was a political reason for doing it, I don't know what, money or something I expect, usually is. Just for watering it down to what it now is to move people into jobs as quickly as possible. And – I don't know that in this area that it's working, because I mean if we had an ideal situation where there were employers keen to take on young people and there were vacancies and – you just needed work experience with an employer to knock them into shape and give them some idea of what work was like or to start to shape them, then fine, [but] *there aren't those large companies waiting to take on a new generation of young people. Jobs in this part of the world are few and far between, they're dotted all over the place and without any kind of structure to help them get there because of course transport is a huge thing and you're talking about that lower spectrum of the market: they haven't got transport....* Offering them a few weeks' work experience, well they've done that, that's what's not worked for them in the past, there's not a proper structured training provision, if there were some skills that were being offered and they could train to do something – plumbing or electrical work or painting and decorating, those sorts of things... it's funding, it all comes down to funding, it seems to me a cynical political exercise like so much of these things, to say "Look what we're doing", but when you absolutely examine it, or look at it closely in any way you realise that it ain't gonna work except for a very few people. (Sheila, careers service; emphasis added)

Finally, the rural providers do not enjoy the economies of scale that they imagine their urban counterparts benefit from:

A: It's just easier to manage if you only have one centre, we have to have six centre managers and six clerical assistants, and all the

References

Blair, T. (1997) Speech at the Aylesbury Estate, June, London: Prime Minister's Office.

DfEE (Department for Education and Employment) (1997) *Design of the New Deal for 18-24 year olds*, London: DfEE.

DIUS (Department for Innovation, Universities and Skills) (2007) *World class skills: Implementing the Leitch Review of Skills in England*, London: DIUS.

DIUS/DWP (Department for Innovation, Universities and Skills/Department for Work and Pensions) (2007) *Opportunity, employment and progression: Making skills work*, London: DIUS/DWP.

DWP (Department for Work and Pensions) (2007) *In work, better off: Next steps to full employment*, London: DWP.

Green, A. and Hardill, I. (2003) *Rural labour markets, skills and training*, London: Defra (Department for Environment, Food and Rural Affairs).

Green, A. and White, R. (2007) *Attachment to place, social networks, mobility and prospects of young people*, York: Joseph Rowntree Foundation.

Haughton, G., Jones, M., Peck, J., Tickell, A. and While, A. (2000) 'Labour market policy as flexible welfare: prototype Employment Zones and the new workfarism', *Regional Studies,* vol 34, 669-80.

HM Treasury (2005) *Skills in the UK: The long-term challenge*, Leitch Review of Skills, Interim Report, London: HM Treasury.

HM Treasury (2006) *Prosperity for all in the global economy – world class skills*, Leitch Review of Skills, Final Report, London: HM Treasury.

HM Treasury/DTI (Department for Trade and Industry)/ODPM (Office of the Deputy Prime Minister) (2006) *Devolving decision making: 3 – meeting the regional economic challenge: the importance of cities to regional growth*, London: The Stationery Office.

Huggins, R. (2001) 'The skills economy and its development: examples and lessons from a rural region', *Policy Studies*, vol 22, pp 19-34.

Jessop, B. (2002) *The future of the capitalist state*, Cambridge: Polity.

Jones, M. (1999) *New institutional spaces: Training and enterprise councils and the remaking of economic governance*, London: Routledge.

Jones, M. and Gray, A. (2001) 'Social capital, or local workfarism? Reflections on Employment Zones', *Local Economy*, vol 16, pp 178-86.

Lindsay, C., McCrackem, M. and McQuaid, R. (2003) 'Unemployment duration and employability in remote rural labour markets', *Journal of Rural Studies*, vol 19, pp 187-200.

Mead, L. (ed) (1997) *The new paternalism: Supervisory approaches to poverty*, Washington, DC: Brookings Institute Press.

Monk, S., Hodge, I. and Dunn, J. (2000) 'Supporting rural labour markets', *Local Economy*, vol 15, pp 302-11.

Peck, J. (1996) *Work-place: The social regulation of labor markets*, New York: Guilford.

Peck, J. (2001) *Workfare states*, New York: Guilford.

PIU (Performance and Innovation Unit of the Cabinet Office) (1999) *Rural economies*, London: The Stationery Office. (Also available at www.cabinetoffice. gov.uk/strategy/work_areas/rural_economies.aspx)

Shucksmith, M. (2000) *Exclusive countryside? Social inclusion and regeneration in rural areas*, York: Joseph Rowntree Foundation.

Skills for Business (2007) *The Leitch Review, summary: A roadmap directing UK towards world class skills by 2020. A concise summary interpretation*, Wath-upon-Deame: Sector Skills Development Agency.

Theodore, N. and Peck, J. (1999) 'Welfare-to-work: national problems, local solutions?', *Critical Social Policy*, vol 61, pp 485–510.

do this the author has focused on treatment of the institutions which take the lead in their governance: the National Park Authorities (NPAs). The first section provides a brief introduction to the system, highlighting some key points about the nature of NPAs. The main section then considers the policy and institutional changes that have impacted on the work of NPAs since 1997. It begins with broader shifts that have affected the environment in which NPAs operate before moving on to the 2002 Review of English National Park Authorities. In the final section consideration is given to what the changes of the last decade could mean for the future governance of National Parks.

The National Park system

The English and Welsh National Parks were established through the Attlee government's 1949 National Parks and Access to the Countryside Act for the purposes of environmental conservation and the promotion, understanding and enjoyment of the countryside.[4] These twin purposes endured largely unchanged until the 1995 Environment Act reformed their wording and added an explicit duty to take into account the social and economic well-being of Park communities. During the 1950s seven Parks were designated in England and three in Wales. The Broads was effectively added to the National Park family in the 1970s, although at this stage it was not formally a National Park (Lowe et al, 1986).

National Parks were created in an era of acute interest in the future of rural land use. They were designed to provide symbolic protection and access by a Labour government keen to legislate on a cause which was passionately supported by several leading Labour Party figures of the time. However, as MacEwen and MacEwen (1982) extensively document, the 1949 legislation never seriously interfered with the rights of landowners or the national policy imperative to maximise agricultural production set out in the 1947 Agriculture Act. To ensure that National Park creation represented no threat to agricultural productivism the NPAs were initially boards or committees of local government. The membership of these bodies then ensured that local economic interests prevailed. Gradually the NPAs became more powerful, emerging as staffed institutions with growing degrees of autonomy from parent local authorities by the 1970s. At the same time the dominance of agricultural productivism was gradually being eroded, a process which gathered momentum in the 1980s. The combination of changing governance arrangements and shifts in policy allowed NPAs to pursue their purposes more effectively, although significant challenges to the conservation and recreation ethic remain to this day.

Contemporary NPAs are unusual types of organisations – ones which defy easy categorisation. The NPAs have, since 1997, been free-standing local authorities, possessing some of the functions of a conventional local authority, most notably with regard to planning. But NPAs also have many of the characteristics of non-departmental public bodies – they carry out functions on behalf of populations who do not live within their boundaries and they have responsibilities for the delivery of certain 'national' policies. As a consequence they sit simultaneously in both local and central government structures. Reflecting this duality they are governed by a membership that is drawn from the conventional local authorities in the Park area together with Secretary of State appointees selected on the basis of possessing specific knowledge or expertise relevant to Park management or being a parish councillor within the Park.

The NPAs are minor players in rural governance, with the English NPAs having a collective budget for 2006/07 of £43.12 million (Council for National Parks, 2006). NPAs have some of the powers of a conventional local authority, especially with regard to development control, forward planning and access to the countryside. They are also rich in 'human capital',[5] allowing them to work on a discretionary basis in order to further the National Park purposes. However, they have no direct powers to shape land management within their boundaries. The result has been the creation of institutions with extensive information-gathering abilities and a capacity to 'steer' the management of their territories through the use of external monies and the provision of advice.

The legislation governing Scottish National Parks was conceived in a very different era to the 1949 legislation. The 2000 National Parks (Scotland) Act states that north of the border National Parks have four aims: to conserve and enhance the natural and cultural heritage; to promote the sustainable use of natural resources; to promote understanding and enjoyment; and to promote the sustainable economic and social development of the Park communities. The Authorities established in Scotland also differ from their English and Welsh counterparts in their structure. There are still 'national' appointees and local authority representatives but they are joined by directly elected members who represent Park residents.

Devolution has been highly significant to the governance of the UK's National Parks but its effects have been uneven across the NPAs. In addition to enabling the establishment of the Scottish Parks devolution has resulted in the development of three distinct National Park systems within the UK. In Scotland the NPAs are accountable to the Scottish ministers and Parliament – the UK government has no involvement. Likewise, in Wales the NPAs look to the Assembly and the Assembly Government and experience little Whitehall interference. In England the NPAs are still responsible to central government and have therefore been the least affected by constitutional change (although they have experienced minor repercussions from the regionalisation process). These three systems are increasingly autonomous, with the result that in 2006 the national representative body for the NPAs was reorganised. The Association of National Park Authorities (ANPA) still exists to promote awareness of, and learning between, all 14 Parks in the UK, but there are now separate structures that deal with policy and strategy matters in England, Wales and Scotland.

It is important to bear in mind that Defra's responsibilities for National Parks effectively only apply in England. This is in stark contrast to the more complex governance of agriculture and land management policy. The Scottish and Welsh

the time of writing, yet to take full effect. Although, as noted above, the NPAs felt some minor repercussions as a result of the creation of the Regional Development Agencies in 1999 (Thompson, 2005), these are likely to be insignificant compared to the impacts of the creation of Natural England.

The institutional reform process that culminated in the formation of Natural England began in 2003, when Lord Haskins was asked to review rural delivery in England. His report (Defra, 2003) subsequently spawned the 2004 Rural Strategy (Defra, 2004a). This set out plans for far-reaching reforms with the twin aims of achieving greater bureaucratic simplicity and more devolution in decision making.[7] The major reform of the Rural Strategy was the creation of Natural England through the merging of English Nature, parts of the Countryside Agency and Defra's Rural Development Service. The agency is charged with delivering land management policy (including the implementation of the agri-environment schemes) and is the government's statutory advisor on landscape and environmental conservation. The 2006 Natural Environment and Rural Communities Act cites the purposes of Natural England as:

a) promoting nature conservation and protecting biodiversity,
b) conserving and enhancing the landscape,
c) securing the provision and improvement of facilities for the study, understanding and enjoyment of the natural environment,
d) promoting access to the countryside and open spaces and encouraging open-air recreation, and
e) contributing in other ways to social and economic well-being through management of the natural environment.

There is a clear similarity between the purposes of National Parks and the remit of Natural England. The likeness in these remits raises a series of questions on what will differentiate Natural England from the NPAs. Clearly Natural England will be a much bigger institution than any individual NPA and will possess a far wider geographical remit. However, the wording of the 2006 legislation forming Natural England means that its purposes will be virtually the same as those of the Authorities. It could therefore be argued that the objectives that Natural England will pursue will be to make the National Park purposes in some sense 'ubiquitous' to the countryside as a whole. This is not to argue that all rural space is now effectively a National Park but that throughout England emphasis is now being given to environmental and social objectives alongside the continued pursuit of economic competitiveness for agriculture and other land-based industries. Differences in policy between rural areas will arise as a result of the differential emphasis placed on these three objectives, but the goal of pursuing all three concurrently through the language of sustainable development is now central to English rural policy.

The analysis so far has considered how the National Parks have fared as a by-product of policy: the recent institutional and policy reforms[8] already discussed have taken place at the European and national levels to effect change in policy and practice throughout these territories, not just in the National Parks. Indeed, the consequences of these changes for the Parks were a peripheral concern for their exponents and architects. The analysis now turns to consider the treatment of the Parks when they have been the explicit focus of governmental attention, by concentrating on the Review of English National Park Authorities.

The Review of English National Park Authorities

The Review of English National Park Authorities (henceforth referred to as the Review) was carried out by Defra in 2001/02. It focused on governance, accountability and remit, examining the working practices and internal structures of the NPAs to ensure that five years after they had become free-standing in local government there were no serious problems with their operation. Unlike the Edwards Review of 1992 it was not an independent review carried out 'outside' government (although an external advisory panel was convened). The 2002 Review was never intended to be a comprehensive examination of the principle and practice of National Parks, it was always explicitly designed as a check that the NPAs were doing their job as defined by the existing legislation (Defra, 2002a).

Following its launch in July 2002 the findings were put out to public consultation and stakeholder and public comment was invited. The final stage of the Review was the production of a 54-point Action Plan published in April 2003. The major message to come out of the 2002 Review is that only incremental and minor changes are required to the governance of National Parks. In stark contrast to New Labour's proclamations on the need to reform both local government and the civil service in the cause of 'modernisation', the NPAs are constructed as broadly fit for purpose. The minor recommendations included capping membership of the authorities at 25, slightly increasing the number of members who are appointed by the Secretary of State, and consideration of the introduction of independently appointed chairs.

Of greater significance for the governance of National Parks was the headline recommendation of the Review that a 'common vision' for English National Parks should be developed by Defra. As argued elsewhere (Thompson, 2005), this signalled the growing influence of central government in articulating the agenda of National Parks, positioning Defra as the definer of this vision and the individual NPAs as family members collectively working towards its realisation. Authorities are increasingly constructed by both the Association of National Park Authorities (ANPA, 2002) and by Defra as exemplars of sustainable rural development, the lessons from which have resonance for the management of the countryside as a whole. It would seem, on first appearances, that National Parks are 'coming in from the cold' and starting to play a role in mainstream rural policy in an era where Defra is seeking to articulate a vision for a 'sustainable' rural England.

But this vision of the National Parks as exemplars of sustainable rural development seems to be a way of incorporating the NPAs into policy discourse

the Parks. However, the size of the actual investment leaves the impression that the Fund is a tokenistic attempt to link the traditional National Park purposes with a more recent sustainable development agenda. The tokenism looks half-hearted. Defra has been enthusiastic in terms of linking National Parks into a national rural agenda but it remains indifferent when it comes to backing up this enthusiasm with substantial investment.

So far this chapter has highlighted some of the major changes and reforms that have affected National Parks and has argued that many of the most important developments have been European and national, with the implications for National Parks being at best a minor consideration. It has also demonstrated that where initiatives have been specific to National Parks New Labour has been quick to endorse the Park concept and integrate them into its mainstream agendas, but slow to consider the longer-term implications for their governance and to back this enthusiasm up with substantial investment. The next section considers what the longer-term consequences of New Labour's treatment of the Parks might be.

Where next for the National Parks?

Explaining New Labour's record on the rural environment necessitates understanding the shifting nature of rural policy. This is because, just as in the 1940s, the rural environment is effectively governed through the policy framework for agriculture. Unlike the 1940s, however, the 'environment' is on the ascendant in public policy terms. Conservation can no longer be pushed to the geographical periphery, to be effectively contained by a protected area system, but now figures in policies for all farmed landscapes. The resultant investment in the rural environment through agri-environment schemes has had tangible effects on land management in the Parks. But this has happened across the countryside, aside from anything that could be described as a National Parks policy. Instead National Parks policy has been swept up into a bigger national and European agenda that revolves around the notion of sustainable rural development.

Analysis of the 2002 Review and the responses made to it by the NPAs and the wider National Parks movement reveals something of a 'coalition' around the notion that the National Parks should be examples of 'sustainable rural development'. Increasingly the way in which the NPAs portray themselves and the way in which Defra constructs their role are congruent – both emphasising the need to balance environmental, social and economic objectives in ways which do not fundamentally degrade the environment. There would therefore seem to be agreement about the place of National Parks in English rural policy. But while on the surface this congruence of vision may lead to the assumption that the future is rosy, a more critical analysis of New Labour's treatment of National Parks reveals problems with the current coalition that look set to become future challenges.

The first challenge concerns the very definition of 'sustainable rural development'. Developed out of both global debates on the management of the environment and more parochial national concerns about the future of rural communities, the notion of sustainable rural development seeks to bring together a series of sometimes competing but always complex demands, imperatives and anxieties. Recent work undertaken by the author for Northumberland National Park Authority on the practice of running its SDF highlighted how difficult it is to simultaneously achieve the traditional purposes of conservation and recreation while also minding the social and economic health of the Park and contributing to the government's numerous objectives for, and indicators of, sustainable development. Sustainable rural development in practice is both a contestable concept and a highly ambitious one. The result is that there is still much work to be done on what it means to be an agent of sustainable rural development in a National Park and how the NPAs' limited resources can be marshalled to achieve it.

The idea of the National Parks neatly slotting into a mainstream Defra agenda in which they play an important role as exemplars of sustainable rural development is also problematic. It has already been highlighted why National Parks may not be very good examples and why the NPAs themselves might doubt the wisdom of promoting this construction. The notion that the National Parks have a central place in New Labour's policy for a sustainable countryside evades some deeper questions about how they fit into the reformed policies and institutional arrangements. If all the countryside is of economic, social and environment value then how can we justify having special governance arrangements (and special promotion arrangements) for the National Parks? If Natural England exists to promote sustainable rural development in England as a whole, why do we still need NPAs to do this job in defined areas? How does this sit with the principle of simplification argued by Haskins (Defra, 2003) to be of vital importance to making sense of New Labour's rural policies?

It might seem that the questions raised about the relevance of the NPAs in the 21st century add up to a case for ditching the NPAs. However, this would be premature. There is a strong justification for the survival of NPAs that rests on their constitution and approach. Unlike the host of quangos now central to the governance of rural areas (such as Natural England) NPAs have some democratic credentials. Part of their membership is elected, albeit only indirectly in England and Wales, while through the ministerial appointments system they maintain the advantages of access to specialist expertise associated with the agency model. Furthermore, Scotland now provides a model of direct democratic accountability. Ultimately this could be an important positive differentiating factor as concern about the effectiveness, responsiveness and legitimacy of rural governance arrangements grows (Woods, 2006). Furthermore, many Parks across the UK are now putting community engagement at the heart of their work, a process facilitated by their 'localness' as institutions. It is more difficult to imagine a national quango successfully working intensively in individual communities in the way that NPAs are increasingly able to. In an era when 'endogenous' approaches to rural development are being encouraged in European rural policy NPAs seem to be in tune with this approach. The authorities can claim a distinctive role in bringing together environmental and socioeconomic imperatives at a local level to achieve forms of management appropriate to local circumstances, a process bolstered by local representation on their membership.

The NPA model, which for the time being at least will operate alongside Natural England, will form a reference point through which to evaluate how the new agency is suited to achieving its objectives. If the actual work of NPAs can only be of limited use in the wider countryside because of the particularities of their geography, their governance arrangements could offer an institutional model that could be more widely emulated.

Conclusions

Both the 'popular' and New Labour imaginary of National Parks paints them as places apart, spaces unlike the rest of rural and urban UK that require special measures for their protection. Over the last 50 years this has legitimised the evolution of a special set of governing arrangements which have resulted in the modern NPAs. But the idea that the National Parks are distinctive 'places apart' has been eroded not by change within but by the gradual reformulation of governmental objectives for the countryside as a whole. Concepts of the value and appropriate utilisation of land have undergone some profound shifts over the last two decades so that the policies and institutions that we might associate with environmental governance are not confined to protected areas but are found in the full diversity of the UK's landscapes. New Labour's policies for National Parks have yet to catch up with this new reality. The result is the need for some profound thinking about the function of a National Park and the role of an NPA if both are to avoid becoming an anachronism – left behind by a government unwilling to turn its enthusiasm for a concept into a progressive policy that more fully articulates what the existence of National Parks (and NPAs) brings to rural governance in the 21st century.

Notes

[1] Dispute over the designation of the South Downs means that in June 2008 the Park still has not been designated.

[2] Indeed there are significant differences in their treatment in England, Wales and Scotland.

[3] In January 2006 it was announced that National Park budgets would be frozen for the next two years representing a budget cut in real terms. Following press coverage (BBC, 2006) and non-governmental organisation criticism the government announced an extra £3.1 million of additional funding for 2007–09 (Council for National Parks, 2006).

[4] The purposes of the English and Welsh National Parks (as stated in section 61 of the 1995 Environment Act) are (1) to conserve and enhance the natural beauty, wildlife and cultural heritage of the Parks and (2) to promote opportunities for the understanding and enjoyment of the special qualities of the Parks by the public.

[5] The largest Authority – the Peak District – employs around 220 full- and part-time staff.

[6] The contradictions between agricultural and National Park policy are best illustrated in MacEwen and MacEwen (1982) and MacEwen (1991). These document the case of Exmoor and the threat to its iconic moorland in the late 1970s. Malcolm MacEwen, as the leading protagonists in the affair, gives a richly detailed account of the conflict and its broader consequences.

[7] As stated in the introduction, National Parks are not prominent in the Rural Strategy. They are mentioned three times in the text, including a rather vague reference to NPAs needing to work in partnership with the new integrated agency (Natural England).

[8] Of course other policy reforms apart from changes to the CAP have also affected the Parks – the introduction of access legislation and EU environmental directives come immediately to mind – but space demands brevity, and reform of the CAP remains the major determinant of land management, at least in England.

References

ANPA (Association of National Park Authorities) (2002) *Approaching a model of sustainable rural development*, Cardiff: ANPA.

BBC (1999) 'Two National Parks for the Millennium'. (Available at www.bbc.co.uk/1/hi/uk/460884.stm, accessed 18/07/06)

BBC (2006) 'Lakes info centres axed in cuts'. (Available at http://news.bbc.co.uk/1/hi/england/cumbria/4249909.stm, accessed 09/08/06)

Centre for European Protected Area Research (2004) *Evaluation of the National Parks Sustainable Development Fund*, Main Report, March 2004, London: CEPAR. (Available at www.defra.gov.uk/wildlife-countryside/issues/landscap/authorities/pdf/sdf-report.pdf)

Council for National Parks (2006) 'Knight comes to rescue on National Park funding'. (Available at www.cnp.org.uk/press_release_06_04_06.htm, accessed 21/07/06)

Defra (Department for Environment, Food and Rural Affairs) (2002a) *Review of English National Park Authorities*, July 2002, London: Defra. (Also available at www.defra.gov.uk/wildlife-countryside/issues/landscap/authorities/pdf/enpa-review.pdf)

Defra (2002b) *New £1 million fund for sustainable development projects in National Parks*, Defra Press Notice, 2 July 2000. (Available from the archive on the Government News Network website at www.gnn.gov.uk)

Defra (2003) *Rural delivery review: A report on the delivery of government policies in rural England* (the Haskins Report), London: The Stationery Office.

Defra (2004) *Rural strategy*, London Defra. (Also available at www.defra.gov. uk/rural/pdfs/strategy/rural_strategy_2004.pdf)

Defra (2004) *Delivering the essentials of life: Defra's five year strategy*, Cm 6411, December, London: The Stationery Office. (Also available at www.defra.gov. uk/corporate/5year-strategy/5year-strategy.pdf)

Defra (2006) 'Environmental Stewardship: latest news', (Available at www.defra. gov.uk/erdp/schemes/es/default.htm, accessed 23/08/06)

Lowe, P., Cox, G., MacEwen, M., O'Riordan, T. and Winter, M. (1986) *Countryside conflicts: The politics of farming, forestry and conservation*, Aldershot: Gower Publishing Company.

MacEwen, M. (1991) *The greening of a Red*, London: Pluto Press.

MacEwen, A. and MacEwen, M. (1982) *National Parks: Conservation or cosmetics*, London: Allen and Unwin.

Miliband, D. (2006) Evidence presented to Environment, Food and Rural Affairs Select Committee on the UK Government Vision for the Common Agricultural Policy, UK Parliament. (Available at www.parliament.uk/parliamentary_ committees/environment_food_and_rural_affairs/efra_uk_government_s_ vision_of_cap.cfm

Murdoch, J., Lowe. P., Ward, N and Marsden, T. (2003) *The differentiated countryside*, London: Routledge.

Northumberland NPA (2000) *Farming in Northumberland National Park: Findings of the 1999–2000 farm survey*, Hexham: Northumberland National Park.

North York Moors NPA (2006) 'Sustainable Development Fund'. (Available at www.moors.uk.net/content.php?nID=361, accessed 09/08/06)

Thompson N. (2005) 'Inter-institutional relations in the governance of England's National Parks: a governmentality perspective', *Journal of Rural Studies*, vol 21, no 3, pp 323-34.

Woods. M. (2006) 'Rural politics and governance', in J. Midgley (ed) *A new rural agenda*, Newcastle: IPPR North, pp 140-68.

Part Four
Conclusion

FIFTEEN

Beyond New Labour's countryside

Michael Woods

Introduction

In a review of the impact on the British countryside of the policies of Margaret Thatcher's Conservative government, Cloke (1992) observed that "the Thatcher era has ushered in new 'structured coherences' in some rural localities" (p 292). The restructuring of state relations, Cloke noted, had limited the ability of government agencies to intervene in rural planning and development; the deregulation of planning and the privatisation of utility companies had created new opportunities for investment and the exploitation of rural resources; and the privileging of middle-class interests had helped to generate new markets for countryside commodities. Collectively, these processes had produced a new marketplace rural economy, while also intensifying conflicts between the interests of production and consumption in the countryside.

The countryside during the Blair era has been a far more turbulent place than it was during the Thatcher years, with rural issues occupying a more central position in political debate and discourse. Yet, the ideological imprint of New Labour on rural Britain is far less discernible than that of Thatcherism.

As the contributions to this volume have described, the New Labour administration will be associated with a number of historic Acts which have recast the legislative and administrative framework through which rural Britain is governed. It introduced three historic pieces of legislation pertaining to the countryside – the 2000 Countryside and Rights of Way Act, the 2004 Hunting Act, and, in Scotland, the 2003 Land Reform Act – all of which mark the culmination of long-term struggles by the political Left and represent symbolic defeats for the traditional rural establishment (see Chapters 6 and 8). However, the number of people in the countryside directly affected by these three items of legislation constitutes only a very small minority of the total rural population.

Beyond these measures, however, it may be questioned whether it is possible to identify a distinctive and coherent New Labour legacy in the British countryside. To some extent this reflects the vagaries of New Labour's political philosophy, with the ideological device of the 'third way' interlaced with pragmatism. Nonetheless, as detailed in Chapter 1, during the first Blair administration Labour set out at length a vision for the countryside that implied a new approach. Yet, the chapters in this volume demonstrate that the translation of this vision into practice has been, at best, inconsistent. In some cases, genuine achievements in policy reform have been compromised by failures in policy implementation – as Alan Greer describes for the Single Payment Scheme in Chapter 9. In other cases, political pragmatism has intervened leading to compromises or the abandonment of more radical proposals (see, for instance, Neil Ward's discussion of the fate of the ideas floated in the 1999 *Rural economies* report in Chapter 2; or the case of the Hunting Act examined in Chapter 6).

In many respects, Labour's rural policy has represented a broad continuation of the neoliberal approach initiated under Thatcherism and refined in the Rural White Papers of the Major government. Its encouragement of community-led solutions, active citizenship and partnership working, for example, is a development of the 'governing through communities' strategy of governmentality identified in the Rural White Papers by Murdoch (1997), as Graham Gardner discusses in Chapter 10. In other areas, such as agricultural policy and planning for housing development, New Labour's attempts to resolve problems inherited from the Major administration have arguably been only partially successful (see Chapters 7 and 9). More positively, Mark Shucksmith in Chapter 4 and Paul Milbourne in Chapter 11 both report a reduction in levels of poverty and social exclusion in rural communities under New Labour, suggesting at least some degree of success for the 'third way' agenda of combining free-market principles and social justice.

As such, it is difficult to discern a distinctive and consistent New Labour ideological agenda reshaping rural Britain in the same way that Thatcherism impacted on rural economic and social relations. Rather, the contributions to this book have mapped out and described a far more complex and dynamic set of initiatives, struggles and compromises that have characterised New Labour's rural policy. This concluding chapter draws together the evidence from the preceding chapters to assess the overall impact of New Labour's rural policy and to consider its long-term significance for the British countryside.

The social and economic impact of Labour's rural policy

The technocratic tendency of New Labour's approach to rural policy has produced at least one notable legacy in the generation of a wealth of statistical data and evidence relating to the social, economic and environmental characteristics of rural areas. This has resulted not only from the exercise of describing the rural as part of the political construction of the countryside (see Chapter 1), but also from the later work of the Rural Evidence Research Centre and the annual publication of State of the Countryside reports by the Countryside Agency and the Commission for Rural Communities. The accumulation of these data has been intended to both inform the development of policy and to allow policy delivery to be measured and monitored. Thus, the 2000 Rural White Paper outlined 15 headline indicators designed to "track progress towards the Rural White Paper vision" (Defra, 2004, p 91) (Table 15.1). As such, in theory, assessing the social and economic impact of Labour's rural policy should be relatively straightforward.

Table 15.1: Headline rural indicators identified in the 2000 Rural White Paper, and progress made

1. Equitable access to services
Indicator: Geographical availability of key services in rural areas: % of households within x km of food shops, post offices, cashpoints, child nurseries, primary schools, GP surgeries (services used later modified)
Trend: **Mostly Negative.** % of rural households within threshold distance has decreased for all key services except cashpoints, supermarkets and GP surgeries (CRC, 2007)

2. Tackling poverty and social exclusion
Indicator: % of people in rural wards in low-income bands.
Trend: **Negative.** Households on low incomes in sparse rural areas increased from 26% to 30% between 2004 and 2006 (CRS, 2006)

3. Better education for all
Indicator: Qualifications of young people in rural areas (Key Stages 2, 3 and 4 results)
Trend: **Positive.** Increase in pupils achieving 5 or more A*–C GCSE grades, 2002–05 (Countryside Agency, 2004; CRC, 2007)

4. An affordable home
Indicator: Proportion of rural population disadvantaged in access to housing (ratio of income to house prices or mortgage costs used, but adjusted between SOTC reports)
Trend: **Negative.** Affordability ratio for both median house prices and lower quartile significantly worsened in 2001–06; % of rural population spending >50% of income on mortgage payments increased, 2002–03 (Countryside Agency, 2004; CRC, 2007)

5. Better rural transport
Indicator: Proportion of households in rural areas within about 10 minutes walk of an at least hourly bus service (measure later increased to 13 minutes)
Trend: **Positive.** Increase from 35% to 48% for communities <3,000 population, 1996–2002 (Countryside Agency, 2004); increase from 40% to 49% for villages, hamlets and isolated dwellings, 2002–05 (CRC, 2007)

6. Safer communities
Indicator: Recorded crime levels and fear of crime in rural areas.
Trend: **Mostly Positive.** Decrease in reported crimes for most categories, 2001–05, and slight decreases in fear of crime, 2001–05 (CRC, 2006)

7. High, stable levels of employment
Indicator: Employment activity rates in rural areas, unemployment rates in rural areas.
Trend: **Positive.** Steady fall in unemployment rates, 1997–2005; stable level of economic activity, 1997–2005 (CRC, 2006)

8. Prosperous market towns
Indicator: Proportions of market towns that are thriving, stable or declining (based on service provision, business activity and employment)
Trend: Indicator abandoned due to methodological problems (Countryside Agency, 2004)

Table 15.1 *(continued)*

9. Thriving rural economies

Indicator: Business health: new business start-ups and turnover of businesses in rural areas

Trend: **Positive**. 7% increase in new VAT registrations, 1995–2004; significant increases in business turnover (CRC, 2007)

10. A new future for farming

Indicator: Total income from farming and off-farm income; agricultural employment.

Trend: **Mixed**. Overall trend of slight increases in farm income for most, but not all, farm types; slight increase in number of farms with income over £40k pa; sharp decrease in full-time agricultural employment (CRC, 2006)

11. Protecting and enhancing the countryside

Indicator: Change in countryside quality including biodiversity, tranquillity, heritage, and landscape character

Trend: **Mixed**. 20% of landscapes described as showing signs of neglect and loss of character, 1999–2003, compared with 10% showing enhancement. Described as arresting previous trend of decline (CRC, 2006)

12. Restoring and maintaining wildlife diversity

Indicator: Populations of farmland birds; condition of Sites of Special Scientific Interest (SSSIs)

Trend: **Mostly positive**. Slight increase in populations of 'farmland generalist' bird species, but slight decrease in populations of 'farmland specialist' bird species (CRC, 2007); increase in number of SSSIs in 'favourable' or 'recovering' condition, 2003–05 (Countryside Agency, 2004; CRC, 2006)

13. Protection of natural resources

Indicator: Rivers of good or fair quality; air quality (low level ozone) in rural areas

Trend: **Mixed**. Fluctuating lengths of river with nitrate pollution, 1995–2005; fluctuating number of days with moderate or worse air pollution, 1997–2005 (CRC, 2006, 2007)

14. Increase enjoyment of the countryside

Indicator: Numbers of people using the countryside and types of visit; kind of transport; and level and type of spend

Trend: **Mixed**. Slight decrease in total number of visits to countryside from 1.3 billion in 1996 to 1.125 billion in 2002–03; ncrease in average spend from £7.30 in 1998 to £8.60 in 2002–03 (Countryside Agency, 2004)

15. Community involvement and activity

Indicator: Community vibrancy: % of parishes in four categories (vibrant, active, barely active, sleeping) assessed on numbers of meeting places, voluntary and cultural activities, contested parish elections

Trend: Indicator abandoned due to methodological problems (Countryside Agency, 2004)

Sources: Rural White Paper (2000); State of the Countryside Reports (Countryside Agency 2004; CRC, 2006, 2007).

However, in practice, the usefulness of the various available data has proved to be uneven and problematic. For instance, the *Review of the Rural White Paper* in 2004 noted that there were a number of problems and limitations with several of the Rural White Paper indicators. In some cases, the indicators were made up of a number of different data sources and it was difficult to establish what the composite indicator showed; in others, appropriate data sources had not been identified. Data were also collated for different spatial units and through different techniques. Problems also arose from issues of confidentiality and data sharing, and in the correlation of data with policy outcomes (Defra, 2004). Further problems of consistency and comparability have been generated by changes in the variables measured, and by the change in the base territory of 'rural England' following the adoption of a new rural definition in 2004.

Thus, the precise quantitative measurement and evaluation of policy outcomes is not always possible (as Paul Milbourne has discussed in more detail with respect to social exclusion in Chapter 11). Nonetheless, the State of the Countryside reports have attempted to track progress against the headline indicators in broad terms, and it is similarly possible to draw some broad conclusions about the impact of New Labour's rural policy from the available data.

As Table 15.1 shows, reliable and comparable data are available for 13 of the 15 headline indicators. The other two indicators, relating to 'prosperous market towns' and 'community vibrancy' involved the development of new classifications of communities-based composite data that in both cases ran into methodological difficulties and were accordingly abandoned (see also Edwards and Woods, 2004).

Broadly positive trends can be identified for six of the indicators, relating to education, public transport, crime rates, employment, business start-ups and biodiversity. In several of these cases, however, the improvements recorded shadow national trends, rather than necessarily reflecting the outcomes of specifically rural policies. Pupil attainment at Key Stages 2 and 3 and in GCSE examinations has increased in rural areas, but only in line with the national trend (CRC, 2007). The reported incidence rate of burglary fell by 15% in areas of village, hamlets and isolated dwellings between 2001/02 and 2004/05, but it fell by 25% in urban areas (CRC, 2006), suggesting little about the impact of new approaches to rural policing as discussed by Richard Yarwood in Chapter 12. The curvature of the decreasing unemployment rate in rural areas has closely tracked that in urban areas (CRC, 2006). Business start-ups have increased in rural areas, but they have also increased in urban areas, and there are significant variations between regions and districts (CRC, 2006, 2007).

Similarly, the *Review of the Rural White Paper* acknowledged that the overall increase in the populations of farmland and woodland birds – as with other indicators of biodiversity – was likely to be affected as much by seasonal weather variations as by the impact of any government policies in the short time horizon concerned (Defra, 2004). Hence, arguably only one indicator shows a clear rural policy impact. The proportion of households in areas of village, hamlet and isolated dwellings within 13 minutes' walk of at least an hourly bus service increased from 39.7% to 49.2% between 2002 and 2005; while the corresponding figure for urban areas fell from 95.7% to 95.0% (CRC, 2007).

By contrast, the three indicators showing broadly negative trends were all areas that had been identified as priorities for rural policy early in the New Labour administration. Access to services in rural areas has deteriorated overall, with the proportion of rural households within two kilometres of post offices, primary schools and public houses, and within four kilometres of banks, GP surgeries, petrol stations and secondary schools, all decreasing between 2000 and 2007 (CRC, 2007). Of the services monitored, only access to supermarkets and cashpoints had increased. The impact of efforts to tackle poverty and social exclusion has also been questionable. Mark Shucksmith (Chapter 4) and Paul Milbourne (Chapter 11) both report reductions in rural poverty under New Labour, but note the limitations of available data. The State of the Countryside Reports have presented only limited data on this indicator, but the 2006 report indicated that 35,000 additional rural households had fallen into the low-income band since 2004, an increase of around 4% (CRC, 2006). Both mean and median household incomes for all rural households, however, increased between 2004 and 2007 – but at a slower rate than for urban households (CRC, 2007).

The most dramatic change has been with respect to housing affordability. The formula used to calculate this measure has been changed between State of the Countryside reports, but even taking this adjustment into account the pattern is stark. In 2001, average mortgage costs in rural areas were 3.9 times average income. By 2003, the ratio had increased to 4.5 (Countryside Agency, 2004). In 2006, a slightly different measure showed that average house prices in rural areas were 8.1 times average income (CRC, 2007). The ratio between lower quartile incomes and lower quartile house prices was 8.5 (CRC, 2007). Annual completions of affordable housing units in rural areas have increased under New Labour, from 1,215 in 2000/01 to 2,255 in 2006/07 (CRC, 2007), yet this is a tiny proportion of the total rural housing stock and does little to compensate for the failure to address the larger issue of rural housing supply, as documented by Nick Gallent in Chapter 7.

For the remaining four headline indicators the patterns are mixed. Net farm incomes, having slumped in the late 1990s, increased marginally overall between 2001 and 2005, but the recovery was greater for dairy and cereal farms than for livestock farms (CRC, 2006). The proportion of farms with net incomes above £40,000 doubled from 8% in 1999/2000 to 16% in 2004/05; yet a quarter of farms still recorded a negative income in 2004/05 (CRC, 2006). The rural tourism sector has also experienced variable fortunes. Total visits to the countryside in 2002/03 were around 14% lower than in 1998, possibly as a lingering effect of the foot and mouth disease (FMD) crisis, which cost the tourism industry up to £3 billion (Anderson, 2002), although average visitor spend had increased (Countryside Agency, 2004). Elsewhere, analysis in the 2006 State of the Countryside Report suggested that rural landscapes were twice as likely to have experienced neglect or loss of character between 1999 and 2003 than to have showed enhancement, although it also noted that this marked a halt in the rate of decline recorded in previous studies (CRC, 2006). Finally, levels of air and river pollution have fluctuated over the period of the New Labour government, although as with biodiversity indicators, these are more likely to have been influenced by climatic conditions than government policies (CRC, 2006, 2007).

Thus, in spite of the proliferation of rural indicators and datasets, finding evidence for an objective analysis of the social and economic impact of Labour's rural policy is less than straightforward. The diversity and dynamism of the contemporary countryside is not adequately reducible to a series of statistical tables. There are complex regional and local differences, and annual variations. Moreover, the patterns and trends observed are not necessarily the product of rural policies, or, indeed, of any government policy. More specific evaluations of particular policy instruments and schemes have highlighted successes such as the Vital Villages programme to support community initiatives, and various agri-environmental schemes. Yet these initiatives have tended to have limited lives, and in several cases, including Vital Villages, have fallen victim to spending cuts and institutional reforms. At the same time, government macro-economic policies have created the climate in which the rural housing affordability gap has widened, income polarisation has increased, and the export competitiveness of British agriculture has been squeezed. Rural-proofing has failed to protect rural communities from the excesses of these policies, or from the impact of reforms such as the post office rationalisation programme.

Getting beyond the figures to the actual experience of residents in New Labour's countryside is even more challenging. Suzie Watkin and Martin Jones provided a glimpse in Chapter 13 as they discussed New Deal participants in mid-Wales, demonstrating that while overall employment rates may have increased, the individual circumstances of many unemployed young people in rural communities have not necessarily improved. More broadly, one can agree with Paul Milbourne's conclusion in Chapter 11 that while there is evidence for New Labour's policies making a difference overall in areas such as poverty and social exclusion, it is less certain that these improvements have actually been experienced across the board by people living in rural areas.

The political impact of Labour's rural policy

If the social and economic impact of New Labour's rural policy is ambiguous, the political impact is arguably more clear-cut. As discussed in Chapter 1, the impetus for the development of a distinctive New Labour rural policy came as much from political motives as from any assessment of need in rural areas. Throughout the first term of the Blair government, repeated predictions were made that Labour would experience a rural backlash in the 2001 general election as voters expressed discontent over the crisis in farming, the threat to ban hunting, and the scale of proposed rural housing development. Press coverage of the Rural White Paper in

November 2000 was accompanied by assertions that it would not be enough to "change the widespread perception in rural communities that the Government not only does not understand them, but does not really like them" (*Daily Telegraph* editorial, 29 November 2000), or to "assuage a tide of rural dissatisfaction which could well rob Labour next May of some of the rural seats which, rather to its surprise, it captured in 1997" (*Guardian* editorial, 29 November 2000) (Woods, 2002).

An earlier article in the *Guardian*, reporting on a visit by Deputy Prime Minister John Prescott to rural areas, had suggested that Prescott was "likely to find that tub-thumping on the village green or in the market place will not be enough to satisfy restless country folk or nervous (rural) Labour MPs" (Hetherington, 1998, p 15). On the day of the 1998 Countryside March, *The Sunday Telegraph* highlighted the electoral vulnerability of Labour MPs in rural marginal seats including Norfolk North West, Selby, Monmouth, and Lancaster and Wyre (Neale and Wastell, 1998). From a different direction, Friends of the Earth had warned in January 1998 that plans for greenfield development would cost Labour MPs seats in Wellingborough, Northampton South, Lancaster and Wyre, Keighley, and the Forest of Dean (Woods, 2002).

Opinion poll analysis, however, suggested that Labour's support in rural constituencies was more solid than these predictions imagined. The most detailed analysis, conducted by MORI in the wake of the September 2000 fuel protests, showed that support for Labour in the 86 most rural constituencies had increased from 26% at the 1997 general election, to 42% in August 2000 and was still at 33% in October following the fuel crisis. As such, it was noted, "there is precious little evidence that the fuel crisis, supposedly a key issue for rural voters, swung votes from Labour to Conservative" (Mortimore, 2000). Had an election been held in October 2000, MORI concluded, Labour would have gained six rural seats from the Conservatives.

The apparent contradiction between these assessments reflects the sophistication of Labour's rural political strategy. The moves to articulate a New Labour vision for the countryside may have been read as a defensive reaction to the threat posed by the Countryside Alliance and farm protests, but in seeking to shift the rural political debate onto the territory of social issues such as health and education, it in fact represented an approach not of recapturing disillusioned hunting supporters, but rather of shoring up Labour support in the majority rural population that cared little for hunting or farming. This approach was championed by a number of rural Labour MPs, drawing on their own constituency experience. As Peter Bradley, MP for the Wrekin, explained to *The Observer* in June 2000, "one of the reasons I think we may surprise a lot of people is because Labour MPs in rural seats have penetrated those parts of their constituencies that Conservatives never knew existed" (Hinsliff, 2000, p 11).

The success of the strategy was apparent in the 2001 general election result. The swing from Labour to Conservative in rural constituencies was little different from the national swing (Table 15.2). Only in the seats that had been at the centre of the FMD epidemic did Labour Party support fall by significantly more than the national average, but as several of these were safe Labour seats with large majorities in northern England, the slip was comfortably absorbed without any of the seats being lost. Indeed, arguably in only one constituency lost by Labour in the 2001 election were rural issues a significant factor – Carmarthen East and Dinefwr (Woods, 2002).

Table 15.2: Labour vote in selected rural constituencies at the 2001 general election

Constituency type (number of seats)	Labour vote 2001	Change 1997–2001	Swing Lab–Con	Labour seats 2001	Change on 1997
Hunt kennels in seat (159)	30.5%	-1.6	+2.1	48	-3
Three or more hunt kennels in seat (34)	23.3%	-2.4	+3.1	6	-1
Top 20 farming seats (20)	21.4%	-2.3	+2.8	2	-1
One or more cases of FMD in seat (93)	36.2%	-2.5	+2.5	46	=
20 or more cases of FMD in seat (19)	30.6%	-3.3	+3.7	7	=
High car ownership and low population density (60)	25.5%	-1.8	+2.9	5	-2
Partially rural seats on ACORN classification (76)	25.5%	-1.2	+2.3	15	=
All GB constituencies (641)*	42.0%	-2.2	+1.8	412	-6

* Excluding Northern Ireland

Source: Woods (2002)

The avoidance of a rural meltdown for Labour in 2001 may have contributed to a retreat in the prominence afforded to rural policy by the party during its second term. Equally, it may have emboldened the government's attitude on controversial issues such as the hunting ban. Either way, the electoral outcome in 2005 was similar to 2001 – a swing from Labour to Conservative in rural constituencies that was broadly in line with the national swing (Table 15.3). The difference in 2005, however, was in the approach of the countryside lobby. In 2001, it had incorrectly presumed that the tide of rural discontent apparently manifest in the Countryside Rally and Countryside March would be matched by switching allegiances in the polling booth. What it had failed to realise was that only 7% of participants in the Countryside March had voted Labour in 1997 (Woods, 2005).

In 2005, the countryside lobby adopted a new strategy of targeting anti-hunting MPs in marginal constituencies. A new organisation, Vote-OK, was established in

Table 15.3: Labour vote in selected rural constituencies at the 2005 general election

Constituency type (number of seats)	Labour vote 2005	Change 2001–05	Swing Lab–Con	Labour seats 2005	Change on 2001
Hunt kennels in seat (159)	26.3%	-4.2	+2.4	40	-8
Three or more hunt kennels in seat (34)	20.4%	-2.9	+2.1	2	-4
Top 20 farming seats (20)	20.2%	-1.2	+0.7	2	=
Partially rural seats on ACORN classification (60) (England and Wales only)	22.1%	-3.6	+1.8	5	-5
All GB constituencies (628)*	36.2%	-5.8	+3.2	356	-56

*Excluding Northern Ireland

Source: Woods (2006)

January 2005 to coordinate on-the-ground campaigning support for pro-hunting candidates in 130 marginal seats with anti-hunting incumbents. Vote-OK claims to have directed 7,500 pro-hunting activists to help in the target constituencies, and to have contributed to the defeat of 29 sitting MPs. These included both Labour and Liberal Democrat MPs, in both rural and urban seats, but they did include several rural Labour MPs, including the former chair of the Rural Group of Labour MPs, Peter Bradley, in the Wrekin.

A rural third way?

If the short-term impacts of New Labour's rural policy are inconclusive, what of the longer-term legacy? The prospectus for a distinctive New Labour rural policy articulated through documents such as the *Rural economies* report (PIU, 1999), *Manifesto for rural Britain* (RGLMP, 2000) and the Rural White Paper (DETR/MAFF, 2000) early in the administration included ambitions not only to address immediate problems but also to achieve longer-term change. In order to assess how far these ambitions have been advanced, three key elements can be distilled from these documents for closer consideration: the motif of modernisation; the strategy of 'governing through communities'; and the 'third way' splicing of free-market and social justice principles.

As Neil Ward demonstrated in Chapter 2, the mantra of modernisation formed a unifying rhetorical device within New Labour discourse at the time of its election in 1997, including in its approach to rural policy. The motif of modernisation helped to position New Labour as radical and forward-looking, yet lost clarity through repetition and broad application. With respect to rural policy, modernisation was applied with, and can be read with, a number of different reasons. In its broadest sense it implied the need to update the political construction of the countryside to reflect the character of the modern rural economy and society, challenging the primacy of agriculture (see Chapter 1). In an associated application, modernisation was used to present opponents as defenders of outdated tradition in debates over controversial issues such as the hunting ban (Chapter 6) and the right to roam (Chapter 8).

More specifically, the cause of modernisation has been attached to the drive for agricultural policy reform and to new approaches to welfare. In the latter context, modernisation, as Ward notes in Chapter 2, refers to a new emphasis on creating social conditions to maximise individual liberty. This has been followed through in programmes such as the New Deal, examined by Suzie Watkin and Martin Jones in Chapter 13 (see also Chapter 11).

The most significant application of 'modernisation' in rural policy, however, has been to promote the modernisation of the policy process itself. This has encompassed a number of different elements, as Ward describes in Chapter 2, including 'joined-up' governance, evidence-based policy making, partnership working and the introduction of management theory perspectives. Several chapters have provided evidence of the application of these devices across different aspects of rural policy, including in agricultural policy reform (Greer, Chapter 9) and planning policy (Gallent, Chapter 7), and attempts at evidence-based policy making with respect to hunting (Chapter 6). Graham Gardner in Chapter 10 notes the positioning of the Quality Parish and Town Council scheme as a 'modernisation' of rural community governance, while Nicola Thompson in Chapter 14 discusses the Review of English National Park Authorities, designed to produce a 'modernisation' of National Park governance. In particular, the task of 'modernising rural policy delivery' was given to Christopher Haskins after the FMD outbreak in 2001 and expressly involved the application of business principles to rural governance. In doing so, however, it revealed the contradictions of the modernisation approach, with one dimension of modernisation resulting in the dismantling of institutions that championed other aspects of the modernisation agenda.

The modernisation of the rural policy process is closely related to a second key element of New Labour's approach – the development of the 'governing through communities' mode of governmentality (Rose, 1996a, 1996b). Murdoch (1997) argued that the 1995 Rural White Paper for England represented a shift in rural policy to the 'governing though communities' strategy, replacing national planning with a conception of rural England as a patchwork of self-resilient communities, and state intervention with the facilitation of community action. As Graham Gardner discusses in Chapter 10, New Labour has not only continued the approach, but developed it.

Indeed, New Labour can be argued to have modified the strategy of 'governing through communities' in three respects. First, compared with the Conservative's Rural White Paper, more emphasis has been placed on collective as opposed to individual action. This has been put into practice through initiatives such as the

Quality Parish and Town Council scheme (discussed by Gardner in Chapter 10), as well as efforts to engage local communities with responsibility for addressing issues such as crime (see Yarwood, Chapter 12), economic regeneration and affordable housing. Second, Labour has also refined the principle that responsibilities can be assigned to communities of interest as well as to geographical communities. Thus, for example, the 2000 Countryside and Rights of Way Act has been implemented through consultation with 'access partnerships' which, while geographically focused, have engaged communities of landowners and communities of walkers (see Parker, Chapter 8). Third, when reference is made to the role of individual citizens within these communities, New Labour evokes both the rights and the responsibilities of the citizen. Community empowerment, for example, is premised on an expectation of citizen participation (see Gardner, Chapter 10). Good citizenship is engendered through structures that encourage self-governance, including the intention that the Single Payment Scheme will promote the adoption of sustainable practices by farmers (see Greer, Chapter 9).

The modernisation agenda and the strategy of governing through communities are both expressions of the 'third way', New Labour's attempt to construct an ideological vision that escapes from the dichotomy of free-market liberalism arrayed against state-centred social democracy. The 'rural third way' has meant rejecting the Labour Party's historical commitment to national planning in rural policy, while also balancing the market-oriented economic focus of Conservative rural policy with a concern for social justice. Thus, significant progress has been made in highlighting and tackling problems of rural poverty and social exclusion, as well as issues concerned with rural housing, transport and service provision; yet these priorities have been addressed through solutions founded on market principles, from welfare-to-work schemes to community land trusts. At the same time, New Labour's failure to adequately resolve the problem of rural housing supply reflects at least in part its reluctance to dilute the principle of a market-led housing system and adopt more prescriptive planning measures; while its interventions in EU agricultural policy debates are consistent with the goal of liberalising agricultural trade. Abandoned proposals, such as pay-as-you-enter National Parks, floated in the 1999 *Rural economies* report, similarly hinted at the application of market solutions to environmental challenges.

However, the novelty of the 'rural third way' under New Labour can be overstated. The necessity of balancing the diverse strands of rural Conservatism noted in Chapter 1 meant that rural policy was never fully exposed to free-market principles under the Thatcher and Major governments. Indeed, the Rural White Papers for England and Scotland in 1995 (less so the Welsh Paper) might be argued to have pre-empted the 'third way' by tempering enthusiasm for marketisation with a recognition of the need for some degree of regulation to uphold social and environmental goals.

The institutional legacy

If the evidence for the long-term bearing of New Labour's policies on the social and economic formations of the British countryside is mixed, there is at least one aspect in which New Labour can be considered to have had a substantial and distinctive impact on the way in which rural Britain is governed. Mark Goodwin, in Chapter 3, argued that New Labour has transformed the institutional landscape of rural policy in England, in the process rendering the rural 'thinkable' in new ways. Changes have been made at all levels of rural governance, from government departments down to parish councils, through a vast intermediate array of agencies and authorities, partnerships and forums. However, the consistency of these reforms may be questioned, with some earlier developments being subsequently reversed later in the Blair administration.

For example, the two institutional reforms that most faithfully reflected the tone and tenor of New Labour's rural discourse were the establishment of the Countryside Agency in 1999, and the formation of the Department for Environment, Food and Rural Affairs (Defra), in 2001. Yet, in both cases, the initial aspirations were not sustained. The Countryside Agency was created by the combining of functions from the Countryside Commission and the Rural Development Commission, but was intended to be more than the sum of the parts of these predecessors. Over seven years, the Countryside Agency played a key role in constructing New Labour's countryside in several ways. First, it provided a focus for integrated rural policy making and delivery, bringing together responsibilities for social and economic development, conservation and recreation in rural areas. Second, it was explicitly charged with championing and articulating rural issues within government, forming to some extent a quasi-governmental counterbalance to the representations of groups such as the Countryside Alliance. Third, it contributed significantly to the statistical re-description of the countryside and the development of evidence-based policy making through research studies, statistical tracking and the production of annual 'State of the Countryside' reports. Fourth, the Countryside Agency placed an emphasis on social policy that had been absent in its predecessors, highlighting issues of rural poverty and social exclusion and access to housing and transport, in line with New Labour's efforts to shift the discursive terrain of rural politics. Fifth, it supported the practical application of a 'governing through communities' mode of governmentality (see Chapter 10) by providing funding for community initiatives through schemes such as Vital Villages.

However, while the work of the Countryside Agency was widely lauded within the rural development community, this view was not shared by Lord Haskins. As Neil Ward observes in Chapter 2, Haskins demonstrated an antipathy towards much of Labour's wider rural policy agenda, and this was evident in his critique of the Countryside Agency. The Haskins Report questioned the value of the agency, arguing that its role as rural champion and in integrating rural policy development had been superseded by the creation of Defra. It presented the agency as obscuring the division of responsibilities in rural policy delivery by blurring mainstream delivery and demonstration and pilot projects; and criticised the agency as overly centralised. This last point was illustrated by a critique of the Vital Villages programme, with Haskins querying "the value to the taxpayer of assigning a national agency to distribute grants that, for the most part, have a low average value" (Haskins, 2003, p 47).

On Haskins' recommendation, the Countryside Agency was dismembered and its functions transferred to Defra, the Regional Development Agencies, a new integrated land-management agency, Natural England, and the Commission for Rural Communities (CRC). Significantly, the CRC, which assumed the Countryside Agency's advocacy and watchdog roles and its responsibilities for social disadvantage, was not part of Haskins' plan. It was only the intervention of senior Defra civil servants in persuading Secretary of State Margaret Beckett of the value of these functions that made the case for the CRC and avoided the complete emasculation of the Countryside Agency's social policy remit that had once been central to New Labour's rural policy rhetoric.

The story of Defra has also been beset by problems. The idea of an integrated rural affairs department was floated in the early stages of the development of New Labour's rural policy, and the Rural Group of Labour MPs' Manifesto for Rural Britain included a proposal for a Cabinet-ranking Minister for Rural Affairs (RGLMP, 2000). However, the idea was dropped from the 2000 Rural White Paper and only resurrected when MAFF's handling of the FMD crisis in 2001 exposed its insularity. Defra was hence created through the merger of MAFF with the rural and environmental functions of the previous Department of the Environment, Transport and the Regions (DETR) immediately after the 2001 general election.

The formation of Defra was described at the time by Environment Minister Michael Meacher as "an inspired seizure of the best opportunity for reform in decades" (Meacher, 2001). The aspiration was that the new department would facilitate an integrated approach to the rural economy, and to agricultural and environmental concerns, as well as giving rural policy equal prominence with urban policy. In practice, the continuing segmentation of sections has constrained integration, and an imbalance of personnel and resources has seen rural concerns – and particularly the work of the rural communities division – heavily overshadowed by environmental concerns. The rural agenda of Defra also suffered in the Haskins Report, which, as Ward notes in Chapter 2, seemed determined to clip Defra's wings. Furthermore, the need to recoup financial losses associated with the mismanagement of the Rural Payments Agency led to spending cuts across Defra, including on rural programmes. Collectively, these factors significantly compromised Defra's ability to deliver on its promise.

More broadly the reforms introduced by the Haskins review substantially altered the institutional architecture of rural policy delivery in England across all scales (see Chapter 3). However, whether it represented a fundamentally new approach, or simply a reshuffling of existing pieces, is debatable. The confusion of organisations and relations that Haskins rightly sought to simplify had intensified under Labour, but its origins pre-dated 1997. The concepts of partnership working, active citizenship and community engagement were all championed by New Labour as elements in its 'third way', yet they had already been present in rural policy for two decades (Edwards, 1998). Moreover, in rural policy perhaps more than urban policy, the evolution of delivery structures was informed by the conditions attached to EU programmes (see Chapter 4), and reflected a broader trend in neoliberal rural governance evident not only in Europe but across advanced liberal states (Cheshire, 2006; Cheshire et al, 2007).

As such, the most significant and enduring institutional legacy of New Labour for rural policy is likely to prove to be the rescaling of rural governance that has accompanied its programmes of devolution and regionalisation. The establishment of the Scottish Parliament, Northern Ireland Assembly and National Assembly for Wales, each with extensive rural policy responsibilities, were truly historic events. Already, clear differences have emerged in the political construction of rural society in England, Scotland and Wales (see Chapter 1), and divergence in rural policy between the four nations. In England, the strengthening of the regional tier of governance has also created the potential for differentiation between regions in the formulation and implementation of rural policy. Together devolution and regionalisation have marked a final break with the principle of national planning that was one of the major legacies of the 1945 Labour government to rural policy, and the capacity of any future government at Westminster to shape rural policy for Britain as a whole will be severely constrained.

The politicisation of the countryside

There is one further legacy that New Labour will leave for the British countryside, albeit unintentionally. Since 1997 there has been an unprecedented political mobilisation of rural residents in Britain, organised around a number of different issues, but significantly including opposition to several of Labour's rural policies. Emblematic of this mobilisation has been the rise of the Countryside Alliance. Formally constituted in 1998 with the merger of the British Field Sports Society (BFSS) and two smaller groups, the Countryside Movement and the Country Business Group, the Countryside Alliance had within a few years recruited 100,000 members, the majority of whom had never previously belonged to a political organisation. There have been mass membership rural organisations before – the National Farmers' Union (NFU) boasted over 200,000 members at its peak in the 1950s – but the new rural movement has also been characterised by large-scale active participation by supporters in protests and demonstrations.

The Countryside Rally in 1997 attracted 120,000 participants; 250,000 people took part in the 1998 Countryside March; and 408,000 in the Liberty and Livelihood March in 2002. Over 100,000 people are claimed to have attended Countryside Alliance regional rallies during the winter of 1999/2000, and 15,000 to have joined the 'March on the Mound' in Edinburgh in December 2001

(Clayton, 2004). Although many individuals will have participated in several of these demonstrations, it can be surmised that the Countryside Alliance has engaged well in excess of half a million people in demonstrations and protests over the last decade, the majority having no previous experience of protest activity (Woods et al, 2008).

The blockades and protests mounted by farmers in the winter of 1997/98 were similarly largely unprecedented in modern British agricultural politics. The original picket at Holyhead involved around 400 farmers, with generally between 200 and 500 individuals active at other sites (Woods, 2005). More importantly, the blockades set a precedent, with over 100 protests by farmers mounted between 1996 and March 2000 (Reed, 2004). The period since 1997 has also witnessed a proliferation in the number of local campaigns opposing wind-farm developments; school, hospital and post office closures; new supermarkets; and housing developments – intensifying a trend of local rural conflicts dating back to the 1980s (Woods, 2003).

The scale of these political mobilisations is clearly at odds with the traditional image of the countryside as a conservative, restrained, even 'apolitical', society (Woods, 2005). Remnants of the traditional restraint were evident in elements of the rural protests – the voluntary cessation of the fuel blockades in September 2000, for instance – yet there is throughout a strand of increasing militancy, with pickets and marches being replaced by direct action (Woods, 2005). In turn, established lobby groups such as the NFU have been forced to adopt more radical positions, and organisations such as the National Trust have been drawn more fully into campaigning on rural issues.

Many of these protests and demonstrations may, of course, have happened without a Labour government. To a large extent they are a manifestation of a 'politics of the rural' produced by social and economic restructuring in which the meaning and regulation of the rural is the heart of the conflict (Woods, 2003). Yet, it is unlikely that rural protests would have attained the scale that they did without the provocation of the proposed hunting ban, or the organising myth of defending the countryside against an uncaring 'urban' Labour government. Furthermore, it is the scale of the mobilisations that is significant in determining their impact for rural society. First, there is now a large number of individuals in rural communities who have acquired new political skills and capacities, in campaign organisation, lobbying and communication. Second, there is now a vast array of examples of rural campaigns and protests on diverse issues that can be copied and learned from by other individuals developing new campaigns. Third, there has been an attitudinal shift, with many rural residents overcoming an inherent wariness of protests and demonstrations and developing a willingness to fight.

Thus, ironically, the mobilisation of rural protests since 1997 has helped to create a cohort of empowered rural citizens with the skills and capacities needed for the success of Labour's 'governing through communities' strategy. Making this transition, however, will require bridging the gap between territorial politics and identity politics that has become increasingly apparent in New Labour's countryside, and that points to the political limitations of Labour's rural strategy. New Labour perceived the governance of the countryside to be a territorial problem. It therefore invested considerable efforts in describing and defining the territory of the rural, attempting to 'fix' the rural spatially as an object of governance. This allowed it to make statements about the interests and needs of the rural population that challenged the assertions of the Countryside Alliance and other opponents, and to develop policies aimed at addressing these majority needs. Furthermore, having highlighted the geographical diversity of the countryside, its programmes of devolution, regionalisation and institutional reform have permitted greater territorial differentiation and targeting of rural policy.

However, many of the participants in the rural protests were motivated by a sense of rural identity that is founded less on territorial residence than on adherence to a traditional rural way of life. Although this identity is rooted in place – whether the local village or the more amorphous 'place' of the 'countryside' – it does not have a precise and discrete territorial expression. Thus, as the Countryside Alliance described its own understanding of rural identity:

> The Countryside Alliance believes the countryside is best defined by
> its inhabitants. Families involved in traditional, conservation-minded
> farming and allied trades are part of the true rural population. So too are
> people who participate in country sports, and support an identifiable
> rural culture and rural system of values. This includes many recent
> settlers from towns, as well as many who, by circumstance, are forced
> to live in towns and cities for at least part of their lives. (Countryside
> Alliance, 1998)

The 'countryside' described here is a minority world within the territorial rural delimited by the government's new classification of rural and urban areas, and the individuals adhering to the cultural characteristics outlined are a minority within the territorial rural population. They may care about health and transport and access to services, but they have been mobilised politically in order to defend a 'rural identity' that is framed by agriculture and hunting. As such, they perceive themselves to be the 'victims' of Labour's rural policies, becoming increasingly isolated and embittered as their interests have effectively been marginalised.

Cloke (1992) identified the 'rural disadvantaged' as the 'real victims' of rural policy in the Thatcher era. The winners and losers in New Labour's countryside are perhaps more varied. There are previously marginalised or neglected rural social groups who have benefited both materially and politically – including families living in poverty and ethnic minorities. Yet, there are also many 'disadvantaged' rural residents whose situation has not improved – from participants on ill-suited New Deal programmes to low-income households struggling to afford local property prices. The supermarket companies have flourished under New Labour, with consequences for rural areas both from their advance into smaller and smaller towns and from their influence over farm-gate prices, while new investment opportunities have arisen from the expansion of renewable energy schemes. Those able to sell land for development have also gained from escalating land prices. Yet, there are also village shops and petrol stations that have been forced out of business; tourism businesses that could not weather the impact of the FMD restrictions; farms hit by falling prices; and factories that have closed with manufacturing relocated abroad. Many rural residents will consider the quality of rural life to have improved, with greater access to the open countryside, an enhanced communications infrastructure and a proliferation of community initiatives; yet, for others, rural life has been fundamentally damaged by the ban on traditional hunting. Thus, the greatest impact of New Labour's rural policy is to be found not in the relative performance of rural areas against urban areas, but in the widening of economic, cultural and political differences in the countryside itself.

References

Anderson, I. (2002) *Foot and mouth disease 2001: Lessons to be learned inquiry report*, Report by Dr Iain Anderson to the Prime Minister and the Secretary of State for Environment, Food and Rural Affairs, HC 888, London: The Stationery Office. (Also available at http://archive.cabinetoffice.gov.uk/fmd/fmd_report/index.htm)

Cheshire, L. (2006) *Governing rural development: Discourses and practices of self-help in Australian rural policy*, Aldershot: Ashgate.

Cheshire, L., Higgins, V. and Lawrence, G. (eds) (2007) *Rural governance: International perspectives*, London: Routledge.

Clayton, M. (2004) *Endangered species: foxhunting – the history, the passion and the fight for survival*, Shrewsbury: Swan Hill.

Cloke, P. (1992) 'The countryside', in P. Cloke (ed) *Policy and change in Thatcher's Britain*, Oxford: Pergamon, pp 269-96.

Countryside Agency (2004) *State of the countryside report, 2004*, Cheltenham: Countryside Agency.

Countryside Alliance (1998) *What we stand for*, published online at www.countryside-alliance.org.uk

CRC (Commission for Rural Communities) (2006) *State of the countryside report, 2006*, Cheltenham: CRC.

CRC (2007) *State of the countryside report, 2007*, Cheltenham: CRC.

Defra (Department for Environment, Food and Rural Affairs) (2004) *Review of the Rural White Paper*, London: Defra.

DETR/MAFF (Department of the Environment, Transport and the Regions/Ministry of Agriculture, Fisheries and Food) (2000) *Our countryside: The future – a fair deal for rural England* (the Rural White Paper), Cm 4909, London: The Stationery Office.

Edwards, B. (1998) 'Charting the discourse of community action: perspectives from practice in rural Wales', *Journal of Rural Studies*, vol 14, pp 63-78.

Edwards, B. and Woods, M. (2004) 'Mobilising the local: community, participation and governance', in L. Holloway and M. Kneafsey (eds) *Geographies of rural cultures and societies*, Aldershot: Ashgate, pp 173-96.

Haskins, C. (2003) *Rural delivery review: A report on the delivery of government policies in rural England*, London: Defra. (Also available at www.defra.gov.uk/rural/pdfs/ ruraldelivery/haskins_full_report.pdf)

Heatherington, P. (1998) 'The shires revolt', *The Guardian*, 2 August, p 15.

Hinsliff, G. (2000) 'Hunt lobby scents blood at election', *The Observer*, 18 June, p 11.

Meacher, M. (2001) 'Gummer is wrong', Letter published in *Guardian*, 9 July, p 15.

Mortimore, R. (2000) 'Rural voters', Mori poll digest commentary column, 20 October, available at www.mori.com

Murdoch, J. (1997) 'The shifting territory of government: some insights from the Rural White Paper', *Area*, vol 29, no 2, pp 109-18.

Neale, G. and Wastell, D. (1998) 'We want our own MPs, say the marchers', *The Sunday Telegraph*, 1 March, p 1.

PIU (Performance and Innovation Unit of the Cabinet Office) (1999) *Rural economies*, London: The Stationery Office. (Also available at www.cabinetoffice. gov.uk/strategy/work_areas/rural_economies.aspx)

Reed, M. (2004) 'The mobilisation of rural identities and the failure of the rural protest movement in the UK, 1996-2001', *Space and Polity*, vol 8, pp 25-42.

Rose, N. (1996a) 'Governing "advanced" liberal democracies', in A. Barry, T. Osbourne and N. Rose (eds) *Foucault and political reason*, London: UCL Press, pp 37-64.

Rose, N. (1996b) 'The death of the social? Re-figuring the territory of government', *Economy and Society*, vol 25, pp 327-65.

RGLMP (Rural Group of Labour MPs) (2000) *A manifesto for rural Britain*, London: RGLMP.

Woods, M. (2002) 'Was there a rural rebellion? Labour and the countryside vote in the 2001 general election', in L. Bennie, C. Rallings, J. Tonge and P. Webb (eds) *British parties and elections review: Volume 12 – The 2001 general election*, London: Frank Cass, pp 206-28.

Woods, M. (2003) 'Deconstructing rural protest: the emergence of a new social movement', *Journal of Rural Studies*, vol 19, pp 309-25.

Woods, M. (2005) *Contesting rurality: Politics in the British countryside*, Aldershot: Ashgate.

Woods, M. (2006) 'Rural politics and governance', in J. Midgley (ed) *A new rural agenda*, Newcastle: IPPR North, pp 140-68.

Woods, M., Watkin, S., Anderson, J. and Guilbert, S. (2008) *Survey of Countryside Alliance members*, Grassroots Rural Protest Project Working Paper, Aberystwyth: Aberystwyth University.

Index

Note: Page numbers in *italic* refer to tables and boxes.